HOLDING SPACE

HOLDING SPACE

AMINATA CAIRO, PH. D.

A storytelling approach to
trampling diversity and inclusion

AMSTERDAM

This book is dedicated to my students and all those young people who blessed my path.

I hear you. I see you. I feel you.

This is for you.

ACKNOWLEDGEMENT

To all my relations, thank you for the inspiration and guidance to write this book. This is for all of us. A special thank you to those who listened to me often at the weirdest hours and gave me feedback and sometimes asked for more, Winnie, Steven, Lester, Rolando, Rosalba, and especially Samir. Thank you Nasim for always letting me know if this was understandable even for a younger audience. Thank you Essien for the inspiration. Thank you Laura Rumbley for your editing skills. Thank you for my artistic family. Thank you Mommy and Maymouna for the singing. Thank you Tripp for the music. Thank you Gordon and Gerben for the compositions. Thank you Jason for the art. Thank you Gordon and Donna for everything business.

PREFACE
WI KON DYA

It was 17 January 2017, when I sat down in a large theater waiting for Aminata Cairo's inauguration as the new lector on Diversity and Inclusion at the Hague University of Applied Sciences. I had attended many lectures and other presentations, in settings like this before, however this time something was going to be different. It would be the first time that I was invited to be in an academic space, a learning environment as my full and whole self unapologetically.

At the beginning of her lecture, a group of seasoned Afro-Surinamese performers descended down from the staircase while inviting us to join in singing the sentence 'Wi kon dya', which in the language of my mother 'Sranang tongo' means: we came or come here. Now this sentence is central to the experience of any person who has set their mind to learning in an institutional setting, but especially for those who have taken generational leaps and crossed oceans to do so. Now before I get ahead of myself let me start at the beginning, in Surinamese culture upon meeting someone new we ask: who is your mother, who is father? In this way we can position the person in the bigger scheme of things and often find a relative, acquaintance or friend in common. So, let me start there, my name is Daphina Misiedjan my mother is Wilma Morsen and my father the late Martin Misiedjan. They moved from Suriname, a former Dutch colony, to the Netherlands in the 1970s to pursue higher education. Before retiring, my mother worked in hospitals as a microbiologist and as an infection prevention and control specialist within the field of dentistry. My dad studied medicine but after some detours winded up in government policy. In addition, he has left a wonderful legacy as the initiator of foundations which to this day (almost 20 years after his passing) still support children from marginalized communities in their education.

With these two as parents it is maybe no surprise that I ended up teaching myself. However, the road to where I stand now was not self-evident in a society that underestimates and disadvantages black and brown people. Similar to Aminata, if it was not for those who broke boundaries, pushed ceilings and gave me a hand I would not have made it here. And unsurprisingly many of them were educators. Educators who held space. This included, the Latin teacher, Mr. Arends who gave me a leadership position in high school and Ms. Wijngaarde who pushed me in personal leadership.

Making it to this stage, can have different effects on different people. What Dr. Cairo, points to in this book is that making it into academe does not mean it is all that you are and all that you have accomplished. Aligning your identity with that of the university as an institute is only part of it. Aligning yourself and tapping into all you are connected to is what the true work, the love-work is all about. And once you accomplish that, you can hold the space for somebody else with responsibility and honour.

So therefore, coming together with so many other people in that theater in January 2017 using my voice which sometimes still struggles with my mother tongue in a place that was not made for me, helped me realize that despite all of that I am still here - Mi kon dya. And now it is my pleasure to invite you to delve into this book as you delve into your own educational journey and know you are not alone. Wi kon dya.

Daphina Misiedjan
Assistant Professor
International Institute of Social Studies

PREFACE

This book is a tough read. At least so when you expect a normal book. A normal book typically starts with some acknowledgements – thank you's that the author needs to get out of the way before she or he can get to business: the actual book. Holding Space doesn't work like that. In a way, acknowledgement is all this book has to offer. A deep acknowledgement that we – each of us – are part of something bigger. Something that is around is, that precedes us and that will outlive us. As far as Aminata Cairo is concerned, we are more than just connected to the 'something bigger'; we are born into it, we live, love and work because of it. That's why we need to acknowledge and honor it, she says. In saying so, and – more importantly – in consistently doing so in this book, Aminata goes against the popular belief that at end of the day, it is all about what you as an individual have accomplished. It is not that simple, Aminata holds.

So, this book isn't simple. Sure, it is eloquently written, with powerful examples and without the obfuscating academic jargon. But the lessons to be learned don't come easy. To Aminata, there is no straightforward, checklist-like method to holding space. Holding Space inspires you to take out the machete and clear the space unapologetically. But it also asks you to be kind, to postpone judgement and to forgive. It summons you to speak out and it begs to you to be quiet. Be brave yet be humble. In an easy read, the lessons to be learned would be offered as tips and tricks that align smoothly. Reading Holding Space on the other hand, is hard work. As a reader you need to acknowledge the elusiveness of the "love-work" that holding space is. To appreciate that there is difference between digesting slow-cooked advice and consuming superficial takeaways.

To me, Holding Space is principally about rethinking the nature of relationship between the Dominant and the Other. Aminata Cairo proposes a non-rigid, non-static understanding of this relationship. She points out that while a dominant position may appear comfortable, it is also an inherently precarious and fragile state. Relationships are not set in stone, she asserts, and goes as far as to claim that "anybody can be in the dominant position at any given time." As I understand it, the dynamic dominant-other model offered in this book is an invitation to read each situation with an open mind, to study the power dynamics and to then see what needs to be done.

Now admittedly, this reading may very well be informed by the experience of Aminata holding space for me.

After the murder of George Floyd by the Minneapolis police in May 2020 I too was wondering what to do. I took to the internet for help and found a Dutch website called withuiswerk.nl ('whitehomework.nl'), inspired by the 'anti-racism resources for white people', and with an equally straightforward message: educate yourself, white people. Being a white, male, heterosexual, able-bodied, tenured university professor I pretty much tick all the privilege boxes. Browsing withuiswerk.nl I figured the first step in figuring out what to do would be to start examining these privileges. In detail, and to the point where – I guessed – things could get pretty uncomfortable. For various reasons I thought it would make sense to open things up to others and start a 'homework club', the members of which would help each other engage in critical self-study using the prescribed resources from withuishuiswerk.nl. While opening things up to others, I intuitively (and paradoxically, perhaps) opted for an exclusive club. This was to be a club for people like me, ready to do some digging into the privileges we enjoy. I figured that while the focus would be on racism, we'd probably touch upon sexism as well. So, in terms of critical self-examination, teaming up with white males only would be a good starting point.

I take some pride in being politically naïf, but I decided to check with Aminata anyway: 'what do you think?' She replied: 'you'll get criticized for it, but it is a great idea, go for it'.

And so, I started recruiting members. 'Wanted: white males', on our university intranet, on our narrowcasting channels, but also through LinkedIn. White males interested in joining the club started contacting me. But they weren't the only ones reaching out to me. I got e-mails from colleagues, asking for clarification. News got to me that there was 'unrest'. Questions were asked, concerns were raised. By the university participation counsel, by the university supervisory board even. Before I knew it, I was on the phone with our press officer, discussing scenario's on how to control the situation.

It was pretty intense, and I quickly went from being that authority whose voice goes without saying to being that person who had deviated from 'official' inclusion policy that says everybody should feel welcome everywhere and all the time. I got frustrated, upset even, with not being able to properly voice my story. While nobody seemed to question my good intentions, the exclusive nature of the homework club was a 'hard sell', its 'optics' weren't great, and the existence of an all-white, all-male club could be used to their advantage by people who were already questioning the inclusiveness of the institute. This wasn't good.

In a way, I guess, the experience was valuable for me. After all, the whole idea behind the homework club was to go where it would get uncomfortable. You want to get a small taste of what is like of not being able to get through – well, there you have it.

But Aminata wasn't smirking with Schadenfreude. She made it clear that she wasn't happy at all with the kind of diversity and inclusion rhetoric that promotes feelings of entitlement: I should have access to your story. That too is a dominant tendency, Aminata made it clear, and as such, the controversy around the homework club demanded the love-work of holding space.

As the story unfolded and needed to be contained, Aminata stood with me. Kind-hearted but unapologetically. A black woman clearing the space for a white male. Because that's what the situation demanded in Aminata's eyes.

Holding Space – Is it a novel, Aminata asks, an academic text, or both? Who cares, does it matter? Must it matter? Can it just be an informative journey? I hope you read on and find out.

I urge you to do so.

Jacco van Uden
Professor of Change Management
The Hague University of Applied Sciences

CONTENTS

INTRODUCTION

Every story starts somewhere, has to have something to draw you in. If the story is told well, it will hook you, lock you in and mesmerize you. Some of my favorite writers have some strong opening sentences like "You better not never tell nobody but God." from <u>The Color Purple</u> by Alice Walker, or "Ships at a distance have every man's wish on board." from <u>Their Eyes Were Watching God</u> by Zora Neale Hurston, or "What you looking at me for?" in <u>I know Why the Caged Bird Sings</u> by Maya Angelou. Or you could get more dramatic, like "It was inevitable: the scent of bitter almonds always reminded him of the fate of unrequited love." in <u>Love in the Time of Cholera</u> by Gabriel García Márquez. But these are from novels, literary highlights. What I am about to share with you is not a literary highlight by any means. Nor is it an academic text, even though I want to address an issue that is based in academia and hope to reach people in academia as well as those outside of its walls. You will be drawn into a story nonetheless and every story deserves a good start. To kick off this story, then, I have written an introduction to help you orient yourself in this journey of text. Is it a novel, an academic text, or both? Who cares? Does it matter? Must it matter? Can it just be an informative journey? I hope you read on and find out.

KRI KRA, KRI KRA

Introduction — Ch. 1

My name is Aminata Cairo and I am a mother, daughter, sister, dancer, psychologist, anthropologist, of Surinamese descent, of former Dutch and current American nationality, a former lector of inclusive education, the first black lector in the Netherlands, and a Lyman T. Johnson Scholar. I start with this introduction, as it is the story I bring to the table.

I am a storyteller, or so I have been told. One night at an event organized by students, after my speech and during the break before the next part of the program, I stood near the person who was going to present after me. Unaware of my presence, he spoke freely. "She is nice, but she is a story-teller, my presentation has content." It stung a little, I must admit, but I thought, "Well, that's interesting." Apparently, this person believed that stories had little true informative value. It was especially interesting to me, since he came from a northern African culture known for its storytelling and poetry. I wondered if he was aware of this fact, and if so why he chose not to value it. I didn't confront him; he was entitled to his opinion. But I stored the experience.

Storytelling is not always appreciated or taken seriously. We tell stories to children or for entertainment. However, as a part of my heritage, storytelling is also a means to learn your place in the family and affirm your existence in the world as a whole. I come from a family of storytellers, from a culture where oral abilities are heralded as extremely valuable. I remember my late uncle, one of the greatest storytellers in Suriname. He would tell me how, as a child, he and his siblings would sneak out at night and crawl under the house to get within earshot of the adults. There was no television, so the adults would gather and tell stories in the shared courtyard. Here they would gather with relatives and neighbors and share stories, *tak' tori*. Some were pure for entertainment, others were a mixture of wise lessons and entertainment, the so-called *ondrofeni tori*. There might be critters underneath the house and being caught would result in corporal punishment for sure. Yet, the risk was worth it. The stories would never disappoint, and the later it would get, the looser and more risqué the stories would become. Those stories shaped him, and in turn they shaped me.

Those with traditions of storytelling believe that stories touch us and affect us on a deep level. Hence, the message of a story might not become clear to us until weeks, months or even years later. Stories can stir something deep within us and plant a seed for change that will sprout when the time is right.

One of my greatest sources of inspiration, Lewis Mehl-Madrona, blends his Native American heritage and teachings with his Western side. He uses stories as part of his healing methodology. He shared with me that the illnesses we experience are part of a larger storied experience, and that in order to facilitate healing we have to change the story. He told me that among the early Cherokee if various healing modalities offered no improvement to someone suffering from illness, they would remove them from their family and village and settle them into a whole new family in another village. They would receive a new name and identity, basically a new story, similar to our present-day witness protection program. By being totally cut off from their old story that inevitably linked them to their illness, they were forced to live a new story.

This illustrates not only how central our stories are to our well-being, but also that our stories are interwoven with those of others. Our lived stories are shaped by the inter-connectedness with other people's stories. When we get sick, our illness becomes part of the stories around us. People's stories affect us and ours affect theirs. And sometimes, in order to change, we have to radically disrupt our stories and create totally new ones.

This storytelling approach to change speaks to me and makes sense to me. We are each living a story, which we participate in as being valid. If we want to change that story, we just have to change it. But before we can change it, we have to understand the story and how it works. Subsequently, we have to understand the effort it requires to change and be brave enough to follow through. After all, some of the stories we participate in are, in fact, not valid at all, but have been around for so long that we have accepted them as normal and receive comfort from its normalcy.

My academic training has facilitated a narrative approach, as well. As a clinical psychologist, my clients entrusted me with their stories, and by joining with their stories – even for a short time – I was able to assist them in their journeys seeking to alter those stories. I then studied anthropology, which focuses explicitly on the process of unearthing people's stories and is the perfect vehicle to assist people in telling their own stories.

My lifetime of experience with and through stories has brought me to what I do today, which is to Hold Space. Specifically, I hold space for the stories that are normally overlooked, silenced, marginalized or dismissed. My ultimate goal is to normalize these spaces as part of the larger multi-storied mosaic. If the larger space is transformed by it, then that is beautiful. However, this is not what I set out to do, not anymore. Striving for that goal, celebrated in the ideas of "diversity" and "inclusion," merely leads to disappointment, I have found. Terms such as diversity and inclusion are misleading. Diversity and inclusion practices tend to misdirect people and focus on the visible presence or absence of marginalized stories in the larger, dominant space. These practices often fail to address how we relate in those spaces, and the inherent inequalities maintained within them. Unless we not only acknowledge but also change the way how we do stories in these spaces, nothing will really change and the space shaped by dominant stories will prevail. I no longer try to pursue change in the larger dominant sphere, but instead focus on the smaller spaces in front of me that I can influence.

Initially, throughout this book I will use the terms of diversity and inclusion as they are commonly used. However, as the story progresses, I will more and more remove myself from that terminology, as it reflects my own distancing from the concepts. Instead, I will increasingly make references to Holding Space. Because we need to hold spaces for people to stand and have their story heard without censorship, judgment, ridicule or silencing. We need to hold spaces where people are treated with dignity, humanity and respect. And that's what I intend to do, using stories. After all I am a storyteller, or so I have been told.

HOLDING SPACE

Introduction — Ch. 2

Holding space, taking up space, filling up the space, claiming space. What are you doing in this space? Occupying it, claiming it, filling it. You with your big butt, broad hips, brown skin, kinky hair, and different sounds. What are you doing here? Standing here, sitting here, laying here, occupying space. Breathe in, breathe out.

I hold the space and not just any space, but I claim and carve out a piece out of this larger space that is made up of dominant particles and is totally oblivious to the value of the space that I hold and bring. The space I occupy is different and therefore inherently suspect and questionable.

I hold the space, unapologetically. Me with my big butt, broad hips, brown skin, kinky hair, and different sounds. I, who have been overlooked, yet at the same time visible, hyper-visible. That visibility used, magnified, exoticized, ridiculed, admired or exploited.

My being in this space, claiming it, holding it, usurping it, is an act of rebellion. Because this space was never intended for me to be in it. I am here by grace, exception, tolerance, or forced normalcy. I do not belong and yet here I am. I do not fit, not in the way I look, think, speak, move, or express myself. I am an anomaly at worst, an entertaining curiosity at best, and yet here I am, demanding to be taken seriously.

I claim this space without explanation. I claim it because I breathe and choose to be here. All I have to do is be present. "My existence is my resistance," I heard an indigenous woman say once.

By holding the space, I am forcing you to see me, acknowledge me and take some responsibility for your feelings about your relationship with me. And I have to do nothing but be. Breathe in, breathe out.

And in being, claiming this space, I force you to acknowledge all those others who are connected to me and stand with me. Those seen and unseen. Those of the present and the past. Those who are yet to come. Those who are out there, not yet strong enough to claim their own.

While holding this space, I choose to take the position of neutral. That means I will not apologize, comment on or ease your discomfort. In taking the neutral position I allow you room to explore your own stance and position, the accompanying emotions, and allow you to do with them what you must.

My neutrality is a gift to you, a vote of confidence in your humanity, capability and the belief that you are not as fragile as you think you are.

My neutrality is an investment in myself, a vote of confidence that I can love from afar. That I can extend grace and compassion rather than cut someone off, wipe them out and erase them from my data bank. Because that I can do very well. I can drop somebody like a bad habit and keep moving, a trait I inherited from my ancestors.

My newfound neutrality, then, is a commitment to my own growth and belief that I can become a more humane human being.

And, thus, I hold space. I stand, sit, take shape as needed. And whenever you move throughout this space while ignoring me and mine, my belly will start to burn. My ancestors will whisper in my ear and push me in my back, forcing me to speak up and speak out, to utter sounds and roar. I take a deep breath, summon their strength and out it comes, disallowing you to ignore me, us, all of us. This space forces you to encounter me and those I am connected to and represent. This space offers both of us, all of us, room to grow, to encounter each other for real, to engage, to breathe, to become better, more humane and possibly transform the space, if we are brave enough to enter.

FROM THEORY
TO LIVED STORY

Introduction — Ch. 3

The journey of this book involves a story that is embedded in lived experience and all its implications. It is fed by academic theory and theorists, who deserve acknowledgement and praise for their contribution. I draw from Indigenous Knowledge, Afrocentrism, Blues Aesthetic, Holy Hip Hop, Decolonialism, as well as Black, Third World, and Caribbean feminist theories. I am ever so grateful to Linda Tuhiwai-Smith, Patricia Hill-Collins, Christina Zanfagna, Lewis Mehl-Madrona, Parin Dossa, Chandra Mohanty, Gyatry Spivak, Gloria Wekker, Lila Abu-Lughod, Audrey Lorde, Aiwa Ong, Gloria Anzaldua, George Sefa Dei, Patricia Mohammed, Naomi Adelson, Albert Murray, Joe Kincheloe, Shawn Wilson, Riyad Shahjahan, Rosalba Icaza and Rolando Vázquez.

These people's hard work has inspired, soothed and nurtured me. They have helped me to organize my thoughts in a certain way. They have helped shape the vision and path for this journey. Their work provided familiarity and resonated within me, where the standard canon did not. In doing, so they served as vital light posts along the way and for that I am extremely grateful.

In addition, the story is fed by the knowledge of elders, sages, relatives and strangers, whose wisdom and guidance have equally touched and shaped me. They might not have written books or articles, but their wisdom contributed significantly to lighting my path. My four mothers, father, aunties, uncles, friends—males as well as females and transgenders— my spiritual leaders, and those angels who passed through simply to deliver a message or bring enlightenment somehow. Their names are not listed so as to not exclude any of them, and there were some whose names I never learned.

And so, I pour libations to these sources of inspiration, as I have poured libations to my ancestors so many times before. The water flows into the earth, highlighting the connection of life essences while acknowledging and honoring their contributions. With each pour of the liquid, I give pause and reverence. I take a moment and give thanks. I give thanks not only to them, but to the larger forces that guided and inspired them. I give thanks because they heeded those forces. And no, most of them are not dead, but they do serve as soil beneath my work, nevertheless. My foothold in my story is stronger because of them.

But that's where they will be in this story, in the soil. I will not unearth and excavate, as it may inevitably draw you into rabbit holes of academic distraction. We will not get caught up in the unfurling of layer after layer of explorative theory, the discussion of which giving credence to academic legitimacy and worth. Instead, you will taste the presence of these theorists and sages as their cadences will echo and reverberate throughout my work. If you bend and put your hand to the soil, you will feel their pulse. If you still feel the need to uncover them, feel free to do some digging and excavating yourself. They are there and worth the effort.

This work will not get caught up in proving my right to be in academia. I have done that work long enough. This work is not meant as the next grand theoretical contribution. Instead, it supplements all the theory about diversity and inclusion with insights gleaned from lived experiences. In doing so I hope to provide a story about diversity and inclusion that is different from the standard approach. I hope to bring some resonance to others who, like me, searched for something different, something recognizable to connect with.

This story has a foothold in academia and the academic experience but expands beyond those boundaries. Ultimately, I am simply holding space for those of us who think, walk, and speak just a little differently. Not as a lesser than, but merely different. This is for those for whom action matters inside or outside academia. The story will speak for itself.

FOUNDATION

Ever since I was little, seven has been my favorite number. My favorite color was sky blue. My favorite color would change as I grew, but my favorite number never did. As I grew older, I learned that seven was a sacred number, a whole number. Seven apparently has been a special number in many religions, from the seventh heaven in Islam to the seven first steps of the Buddha and everything in between. There are seven days of the week, seven notes in the musical scale, and so on. My fascination with the number seven is not uncommon, I have come to find out. Whether it is a cultural phenomenon we have all learned to embrace does not really matter to me. What has mattered to me are the Native American teachings that taught me there are four directions, south, east, west, north.
In addition to these four directions, there is up (the sky), down (the earth), and within. I was told that when you can orient yourself in regard to those seven directions, then you know who you are and where you are in relation to your place in the world.
And, so, I must lay out a foundation on which to bring forth my stories. It makes sense that this foundation has seven pillars, seven stories that tell you who I am and where I am in relation to this world as I bring my story to you.

MA PO CLEARING THE SPACE

Foundation — Ch. 1

Out of the many ancestors that support my path, there is a specific one with whom I have an affinity. Her name was Paulina, but I only know her referred to as Ma Po. She raised four girls, fathered by three men, mostly by herself. She walked with a machete on her hip and took no s***t off anybody. When a man got fresh or otherwise trespassed her sensibilities, out the machete would come, and she would chase them off running. There would be no need to come back after that. It might explain why her children's fathers did not stick around.

She was my great-grandmother and my aunties have compared me to her on several occasions. I am not sure if that has to do with her toughness or her inability to live with a man. I suspect the latter, but I don't mind.

My favorite story about her is how she facilitated the birth of my mother. Ma Po was a rural midwife. She delivered hundreds of babies in the Saramacca district in Suriname among her fellow peasant family households. Eventually, a Dutch doctor came into the area. There was a decree that she had to be certified by him in order to become a legitimate midwife, although this was something she had been doing already for many years.

My grandmother was pregnant with my mother. When the time came to deliver, Ma Po was supposed to assist in the birth under supervision of the doctor so she could receive her certificate. So, off to the clinic they went. My grandmother was steadily in labor as Ma Po was making preparations for the birth, all under the watchful eye of the doctor. Suddenly the doctor excused himself, as he was called away.

His absence was long, however. In fact, his absence was so long that my great-grandmother delivered her granddaughter, took care of her daughter and had the baby laying in her mother's arms by the time the doctor returned. Because he didn't witness her actively delivering the baby, he did not certify her.

Ma Po packed up her daughter and granddaughter and went home. Not only did she never return to the clinic (my mother was the only one out of Ma Po's eight grandchildren that was not born at home), she picked up her midwife practice and continued delivering babies as if the encounter with the doctor had never happened. She did not need his legitimization, nor anybody else's for that matter. And if anybody wanted to argue that position, her machete would quickly set the offending party straight.

I think of Ma Po, with her hands on her hips and a machete always within reach. I think of her clearing the bush with that machete, opening the space for us. She cleared the way for my mother that day—and so, ultimately, for me—unapologetically. If I look at all like her, I hope it is in that way.

It is because of her that I do not call myself a feminist. She claimed space fearlessly, long before the term "feminist" was in vogue. In Suriname, she would be called a *kan kan uma*, or a *dya dya uma*, but I think she would not have cared about those labels either. She did not need a label, any kind of label, to define her. She is in my DNA.

To Ma Po, who cleared and held the space for me, *Gran tangi*. Thank you, and may I clear the path fearlessly for others, as you did for me.

Auntie and Ma Po — Source: Family Baarn collection

THE PATH BETWEEN MY MOTHER AND ME

Foundation — Ch. 2

The relationship between mothers and daughters can be tricky. The expectations mothers have for their daughters as surrogate, second, improved versions of themselves can prove to be a burden. And yet, there is something special between the one who gave me life and myself.

Born and raised in a loving but poor peasant family, my mother was sent at age nine or ten to live with a rich, white doctor's family. This was a fate similar to her sisters, who did not end up with rich white families but were placed in foster families, nonetheless. These arrangements were made supposedly so that these rural children could continue their schooling. In truth, they would not be sent to school, but were instead instant house servants. My aunt shared how the day she entered the household of her new 'family,' baby number nine was born. Her duties were clear, and schooling was not a part of the program.

My mother and her sisters do not speak much about that period of their lives. Their body language and tone of voice make it clear that the memories are painful, so one respectfully lets it rest. On rare occasions they might share something spontaneously. My mother shared how her tonsils were clipped without anesthesia because the doctor did not believe in wasting medicine on dark-skinned children.

She was envied by her siblings because she was sent to a wealthy family and periodically was sent home with gifts. She believes she earned her placement due to her lighter skin tone in comparison to the others. But, she assured me that the material goods never made up for not feeling loved.

She shared how it was her greatest wish to dance. She had to take her charges —the children of her host family—to dance class and had to wait outside and watch how they received what she so dearly desired. As a result, she put me in ballet class at age two and supported any dance endeavor I wanted to pursue. It is interesting how obstacles on one's path can become the markers you fight for on the path you lay out for someone else. Once I found out this part of her history as a teenager, I was ready to break with this white side of my family. Yet, she taught me about love and forgiveness, as she maintains a loving relationship with her charges.

Somehow (through means that will forever remain hidden) my mother, by then in her twenties, was able to enroll herself in a nursing program in the Netherlands with only a fourth-grade education. She told me that if she were to stay in Suriname she would not have been able to become more than a nanny or a cleaning lady, given her education, so she was determined to leave to pursue an opportunity by any means necessary. As she traveled by ship, she arrived three days late but was allowed to enter the nursing program in The Hague.

She enjoyed studying and did well. Some of the friendships she made with her fellow classmates would last the duration of her life. At the end of that first year when it was time for the final exams, she was told that she could not participate because she had missed the first three days of enrollment, and in fact had to redo the whole first year.

My mother did not hesitate and again – by means that will forever remain unknown – she arranged her own transfer to a nursing program in Amsterdam and unenrolled from the program in The Hague. She left and never looked back.

She was, after all, the granddaughter of Ma Po. My mother graduated on time and with honors. Her determination and strength are markers on my own path.

She married my father while finishing nursing school. Two years later she had me. She put me in swimming, judo, gymnastics, rhythmic gymnastics, and of course dance. All those things she did not get to do as a child she put in my path. Time and time again, she has shown me that she never allowed her limited start in education to be a limitation. She partook in pastry classes, gardening, community theater, line dancing, taught herself how to speak English, and as of today, at age 86, has been volunteering at a retirement home for over 25 years. Our paths have clashed at times because of her over-involvement in mine, but our paths are inextricably intertwined. And thus, as I carve this path, I walk not just with her but also *for* her and *because* of her.

Gran tangi, ma. Thank you for investing in my path as much as you did your own. May I carry the message that our paths are stronger when they are linked together.

Me and ma — Source: Family Cairo

Auntie, my second mother — Source: Maritha Kitaman

THE QUIET PATH OF MY SECOND MOTHER

She came when I was nine years old. I vaguely remember her from when I was younger and visited her in Suriname, but I clearly remember when she came and moved to the Netherlands when I was nine. My father was in the hospital once again, for up to seven months or so. Many years later I would find out that he was not expected to live, but he did manage to come out of the hospital, that time. My aunt left behind her job and house in Suriname to come to the Netherlands to help her sister with us, my brother and me.

She was everything I needed at that point in my life. She was my refuge, and she was calm and kind. Never feeling that I truly fit in in the Netherlands, she introduced me to Surinamese culture and community. She took me to the Surinamese community center where I learned African dance and where I was confronted with the many children who had just immigrated from Suriname. The year was 1975, the year of Surinamese independence and people left Suriname by the thousands, afraid of what would become of them without Dutch colonial security. After meeting those newly immigrated children at the community center, I was in a rush to learn *Sranan Tongo,* and calmly she would translate any item I would point at in the house.

My aunt worked as a social worker in those days, helping those new Surinamese arrivals get settled in pensions, which were accommodations specially designated to make sure they were contained from the traditional Dutch population. She did it with that same loving calmness and kindness with which she did everything. She hasn't stopped serving people since. Now, more than 40 years later, I know no other person who works as tirelessly as she does to help other people. I have never known her to be involved in fewer than five service and social organizations at any one time. Even now, in her late 80s, she still volunteers for various Surinamese organizations. She is always ready to be of assistance, always ready to go without being asked .

My aunt offered me a safe haven when I was teenager. I would go to her house almost every weekend. She would make popcorn on the stove in a little pot and we would play dominoes. I still make popcorn the exact same way. We could speak, or not. Often it would not be necessary, so we wouldn't. We would play in silence. Questions about Surinamese culture or traditions I would always discuss with her before I would with anybody else, and she would always listen and answer to the best of her abilities. She was proud of the fact that I cherished my Surinamese culture, but she would never express it in words. She would just smile.

Around her I could always just be, would never have to be more than what I was. My presence and abilities were never questioned. Whatever new adventure I would concoct would be greeted with "Oh that sounds wonderful, I am sure you will do fine." Even when she had questions and would ask me if I was sure, when I would respond that I was sure, she would smile and nod affirmingly. If I was sure then she was, too. Not only was she sure about my capabilities, she would be matter of fact about it, as if my capabilities were a given. There are no words to describe what it means to have someone believe in you so wholeheartedly, without question, without doubts, especially during your formative years as a teenager.

Some people have mistaken her calmness and kindness for weakness. They could not have been more wrong. Her ability to show up for people and to love unconditionally and relentlessly is a source of strength I have not seen in many people. And again, I am reminded of Ma Po. Here is yet another granddaughter who clears space unapologetically, but with a calmness and kindness as effective as any machete.

As I am writing this, my aunt, my second mother is in her 88th year and we are starting to notice some changes. She is starting to get confused or forgetful. She is starting to see people who are not present, at least not to us, and interacts with them. So, now it is my turn to hold the space for her and to extend calmness, kindness, and affirmation that she is fine. The other day, I asked her if the people she saw frightened her. She said they didn't, so I told her not to worry about it then, because I have found it is people's reactions to her behavior that upsets her. She is starting to eat less and drink less. She told me, people think this is about old age, but it is not. I know what she meant. She and I don't have to say some things to each other. And so, I went and bought some dominoes the other day and we played in silence like we used to.

Gran tangi, auntie. Thank you for paving my path with unconditional affirmation and kindness. May I carry the message that people deserve to have their humanity confirmed without fuss, just because they are.

Godmother Zambia Nkrumah — Source: Edward White

LOVE-WORKING THE SPACE

Foundation — Ch. 4

She loved to tell everybody how she came to embrace me as her child. At age 21 and a junior in college, I and another student received a scholarship to attend a Black Arts conference in Louisville, Kentucky. They had given us a college car and had paid for our hotel and the conference. We felt like stars. We were the youngest and greenest people at the conference. I soaked it all in. I got to meet the grand Ruby Dee and was instantly mesmerized by her performance. I never looked at her as a normal person again, this heralded creature.

After the first night, my companion and I found out, to our horror, that the college had reserved our hotel room for one night only, instead of two. As we stood in the lobby of the hotel trying to figure out what to do, two women dressed in beautiful African garb came near us. My companion was ready for us to leave. I was not ready to throw in the towel yet and was adamant about wanting to stay. Sure, we didn't have money for another night at the posh hotel, but where there's a will there's a way, right? For sure, there had to be a way to stay.

"What's wrong, suga'?" I turn to hear the sweetest Southern voice come out of one of the African women, a beautiful caramel colored woman – who later turned out was born and bred in Kentucky and not Nigeria or elsewhere on the continent. Her eyes are kind, and she repeats "What's wrong?". In great despair, I pour my heart out to this total stranger. My companion is rather quiet and probably horrified by my actions.

"Well don't you worry. You can just come home with me and spend the night at my house." I never hesitated for a moment. My companion had plenty of doubts, but somehow I was able to convince her and got her to join me on this adventure. Her fears were not substantiated. We had a ball. Even my companion relaxed. While my companion slept, this lady and I talked late into the night. In the morning, she made us breakfast. Well rested, fed and relaxed we returned to the conference for the second day with our newfound friend and benefactor.

When I left the conference, I said goodbye to our gracious host. She embraced me and told me I was welcome to come back any time. I knew she meant it. And so, I took her up on her offer. I did return, every subsequent school holiday. The Greyhound bus was my trusted steed. My companion, who was from the US, never returned to visit our benefactor. But for me, as an international student, her hospitality was a gift. She became my family and loved me as if I was her own.

She held space for me as a mother, sister, and friend. She introduced me into her family with a matter of factness that was unquestioned. That I belonged was a given. I watched how she did community work, tirelessly, relentlessly. I watched how she forged her own identity based on African roots, Christianity, Yoruba spiritual beliefs, African American cultural traditions, social justice, education, and the arts. She had taken on her first name from an African nation and her last name from the first Ghanaian president after independence. Zambia Nkrumah blended and forged them in a way that was uniquely hers.

I watched her ceaseless fighting and commitment to holding up her community. She didn't just hold the space, she worked it. Holding up people, let alone a community, is hard work. I attended Kwanzaa gatherings at her house that became so large they had to move to the community center.

I attended too many community events to recall, visited people's houses in support, and participated in all kinds of activities. She demonstrated motherly love to anyone who needed it. She collected godchildren left and right, making each one feel like they were her own. By the time 20 years had passed since our first encounter, she had at least 17 children who called her godmother and each one of us felt special.

She was there for every one of my four graduations, my marriages, break-ups, the births of my children, and any other major events. We had many conversations, road trips and adventures. She listened as I struggled through my master's thesis and Ph.D. dissertation, always encouraging me and lifting me up. She didn't just love me, she put in the work to show that she loved me. Because of her love-work, my mother across the ocean could sleep peacefully.

It was my honor then that when her misdiagnosis of chronic fatigue syndrome turned out to be stage four breast cancer that had already spread to her vital organs, I was able to work and hold the space for her. That first night after she had entered the emergency room with shortness of breath and she had to spend the night to await the outcome of the testing, I raced to her side and relieved her husband. We knew it was bad, but not exactly how bad. Not having the words to adequately express what was happening to us, I sang to her. I sang all night, every song I could think of, and made up new songs, anything to bring some balm to her spirit. By the time sunlight arose, I started to fall asleep. Right as I fell asleep, her mother came in and waited with her for the consultation with the doctor. That's how this thing works, too, everything in divine order. Her mother needed to be with her when she received the diagnosis, while my work was done for the moment. She was expected to live for another six months but lived for another six years.

She allowed me to hold space for her and put in the love-work, after all she had done for me. That last year I will never forget. Together with another friend, we prepared and planned her funeral. From the obituary to picking out the coffin and burial plot, we accompanied and supported her as she planned her final days and funeral in great detail. Her funeral lasted three days. Three women and I stood guard by her coffin, dressed in white, with occasional bathroom and water breaks, as hundreds of people came to pay their respects. We held the space for her. There was a separate room where people reminisced and shared stories. There were laughter and tears, as she had expected, and we just stood there in silence, for her. We organized and directed the service that was a full production with African drumming, dancing, singing, and endless speeches by the many people whose lives she had touched from all walks of life. I had no idea how we were going to pull it all off, but through love-work we did.

Zambia Nkrumah, my godmother helped me grow. Inadvertently, she taught me that Holding Space requires work, love-work. She taught me that love is a powerful force and makes us stronger than we ever could imagine possible.

Gran tangi, godmother. Thank you, and may I carry the message that Holding Space not only requires work but love as well.

SINGING THE SPACE

Foundation — Ch.5

I was starstruck the first time when I saw her. Here she was: the voice. I attended the presentation at the Baltimore Museum of Art. During the 1990s, the independent film *Sankofa* had made as much impact in the black community as the television series *Roots* in the 1970s or the film *Black Panther* in the 2000s. This film, which chronicled the story of a young African American woman who went back in time to the days of slavery only to reemerge and find her true self, played to sold out film houses. I am sure we broke all kinds of fire codes, as people were sitting in the aisles when seats were no longer available. The soundtrack featured beautiful, haunting songs. And there she was on stage: the voice. I don't get giddy very often, but I was at the sight of seeing her.

The next time I saw her she was sitting on a sofa in a community center, either hand sewing or beading a garment. She looked up at me, smiled and said hello. She spoke to me as if she was a regular person! Here she was, that star from the movie! I had been invited to teach dance at an African American rites of passage program for girls and she happened to be one of the organizers. I tried to be cool as I spoke to her but had to work to contain my enthusiasm. From this first real meeting our relationship grew.

My memory bank is splattered with programming we did for girls, performances together, empowerment workshops for women, cultural events, and many talks about life, womanhood, natural healing and community. She gave me siblings. I got her to dance and she helped me to sing. She introduced me into her culture of Cherokee, Choctaw, and African American roots and taught me about her mixture of Pentecostal and traditional Native American upbringing with additions of Islam and Yoruba spirituality and a sprinkle of militancy. She lives up to her name *Mama Wapajea* "Walks on Water".

When she formally adopted me as her goddaughter and committed to teaching me, she laughed at me when I showed up with pen and paper ready to learn. That is not how my learning was to take place. She taught me that spirituality is foremost about listening and obedience. I witnessed how from one moment to the next she would say, "Spirit just told me," and how she would unquestionably follow the instructions. From one minute to the next she would go silent because spirit instructed her to have a speaking fast. "Spirit told me we should go into the woods", and there we would go. And whenever we would go, there would be lessons to learn, things to witness; it never failed. I assisted her in the sweat lodge ceremony, helped prepare for pow wow give aways, and had so many magical experiences they cannot all be mentioned here.

The lessons were never hard in themselves. What was hard was the surrendering. After all, I had been trained with a Western mindset, and I was good at it. I was good at the analysis, questioning, searching for evidence. This was different. I had to learn how to give my Western mindset a place and embrace the rest of me. And no matter how much I was included in her traditions, she always reminded me that I had my own Surinamese traditions and that I should honor and embrace them, as well. When it was time for me to do a vision quest, she encouraged me to go to Suriname and do my own rites of passage via my own traditions. I will always be grateful for that.

Godmother Wapajea "Walks on Water" — Source: Mahatara Zubar Youssef

She was the one who held my back spiritually in the United States when my family was not near. She was the one who taught me I needed to sing when I was struggling with my dissertation, and she would sing to me on the phone. Grounded in the arts, spirituality, and cultural traditions, she has the sweetest laugh, but can as easily pull a tomahawk out of her purse and go to war. See, she is as loving as she is fierce, and fiercely authentic.

She taught me about walking the walk and embracing all of who you are, without apologies. She taught me about listening to the voices that guide you and that, when you choose to use your voice, it should mean something. She taught me that when you wake up, you should sing to yourself first because you deserve to start your day by hearing something sweet. She taught me that when you use your voice for justice, it should be as strong as it needs to be but come from a place of love. Our voices are vibrations and can change the atmosphere. Our voices are a source of power.

Gran tangi, mommy. Thank you for using your voice to strengthen and support my path. I am committed to use my voice to change the atmosphere.

HOLDING THE SPACE
IN SPITE OF

Foundation — Ch. 6

When I was a teenager and my male friends would come to visit, if they were black my father would make them sit down and would ask them to play a game of chess. If they didn't know how, he would teach them, because his position was that every man needs to know how to play chess. I knew better not to voice any objections. I thought it was racist that he never asked my white male friends to do the same, but I didn't question him about that, either. He was just as courteous and kind to my white friends as my black friends, but he just wasn't that invested in them, so I left it at that.

It was just my luck that my first boyfriend was a member of the chess club, hence many a romantic encounter I had hoped for was wasted on him playing chess with my dad, or so I thought at the time. However, there was a message there, an unspoken message, which I did not get until much later.

Similarly, one night when I must have been seven or eight, he woke me up from my bed and made me come and watch tv, something unheard of. We watched a documentary about South Africa and how black people suffered under Apartheid. To this day, I remember that people had to have passports in their own country, that they had to get off the sidewalk when a white person would approach them, and that the garbage truck workers would have to run constantly because the truck would not stop and wait for them. The in

Dad — Source: Family Cairo

justice of it all made no sense to my young mind. I remember just crying and crying as he held me. He never explained anything. Then he put me back to bed and tucked me in. Apparently, he thought it was important that I knew. There was a message there too, which I did not get until much later.

When you walked into our house, my father would sit to the left in the corner, across from a tv and with a chess computer in front of him. We were the first in the neighborhood with a VCR. He loved Disney animated movies and would laugh heartily at Tom and Jerry. The only time I have ever seen him cry is when Kunta Kinte was being beaten for not wanting to say his slave name in the tv series *Roots*. It was a monumental event, both *Roots* and watching my father cry.

My father was sick. That's how I was raised. *Your dad is sick. Don't make too much noise, your dad is sick. We probably can't do that because your dad is sick.* We hardly went on family vacations because dad was sick. The sickness was always present, it was our normal. Weekly visits to nurses, doctors, clinics, extended hospital stays. I still have certain feelings about being in a hospital, having spent so much time there as a child.

Like my mother, my dad grew up poor, only he grew up in the city, not the countryside. When he got hit by childhood diseases like mumps or rubella, there was no money for medical care. He survived but had a damaged heart as a result. As an adult, he had a stroke which left him half paralyzed, but he eventually recovered. He had more than one heart attack, one I actually witnessed, as I was the only one home with him at the time. He ended up with three artificial heart valves. He would show me his 'zipper,' and as you sat close to him you would hear the ticking of a watch, which was actually his heart.

In spite of all of this, he worked at the university in the publishing department. He loved writing and books. When his health prevented him, he would work half days for as long as he could. To this day, when I visit the Free University of Amsterdam I have special feelings going inside that building. He was a member of the community chess club and would play multiple people at a time. Often, we would come home and there would be strangers, newfound people he had invited to play chess. Amazingly, he never complained about the weekly shots, the regular prodding, or his incredible health regimen. Instead, he taught me about pride, commitment, the arts and loving black people. He was the one who would read stories to me and sing Surinamese songs to me. He was the one that taught me how to read at age two. He was the one that inundated us with classical music as well as Stevie Wonder. We dreaded the classical music, but we put up with it, something I appreciate now. He was ever so patient but determined that I learn.

There were things he wanted for me, like he wanted for the black young men that entered our house. I can see that now. His heart finally did give in, at age 50. I had been in the US for only six weeks when I had to return for the funeral. The man that lay in the coffin did not resemble my father at all and I am glad that image did not stay with me.

What has stayed with me is his stoic presence, his stubbornness to live and claim space and recognition in spite of. In spite of the poverty that denied him good health, or the negative messages about black men and fatherhood, he was here and made sure that he contributed lessons about self-worth to me and so many others.

Gran tangi, pa. Thank you for your demonstration, never giving up and for persevering for as long as you could. May I be as determined and committed to walking a decent path in spite of anything that may come my way.

BOUNCING
DOWN THE PATH

Foundation — Ch. 7

There is not much that you can remember from when you were two or two and a half years old. There is a picture of me standing next to my new baby brother in his crib, however, and the picture displays this sense of pure joy within me. Here was this incredible gift that was bestowed upon me, and one thing I knew for sure is that he was mine. And mine he was.

I must have smothered him with surrogate motherly attention. I remember making him play things I wanted him to play until he wouldn't comply any longer. My brother was fiercely independent about finding his own way in the world. The best metaphor for him would be the Tigger character from Winnie the Pooh, who joyfully bounces down the path in the pursuit of simple enjoyment. When it was time for his early reading lessons with my father, he cried and kicked and screamed. I had loved those sessions. For my brother, however, there was no greater torture than having to stay inside reading when you could play outside and have some real fun. Are you kidding me? My father gave up after three days.

My brother was fiercely committed to living life to the fullest and enjoying every step along the way. Friends, playing outside, exploring; those were things to be valued. School did not always appreciate his spirit and he was quickly labeled as having ADHD and needing special attention. Thankfully, due to my mother's constant watch and advocacy, he made his way through the school system without too much damage.

Whereas I would make myself sick fighting to make the highest grades, my brother would make sure he got the minimum he needed to pass. Mostly, you could find him outside somewhere playing, exploring, daring life. He was a regular at the emergency room and the doctors knew him on a first name basis. I remember when he and his friend went fly fishing and he came home with a hook in his head. Off to the emergency room once again. I also remember when we were in Suriname at the pool and he went to the edge of the diving board and looked down, too scared to jump off. I remember watching him from the edge of the pool as he went back again and again, each time trying to push himself a little bit more. Within an hour, he was doing front flips and backflips off that same diving board, because life is an adventure to be explored, and why not? I have similar accounts of him teaching himself how to skateboard, break dance, ice skate or snowboard, always ending with him reaching near professional proficiency.

I remember being envious about his ability to be so carefree, to not worry about high grades or what people thought. From very young, he had that wisdom on lock down. It was also his protection, as my father could be very critical of him, whereas my mother would always come to his defense. My father's calm nature and my brother's rambunctiousness clashed at times. Yet I see how the appreciation for music and the commitment to fatherhood lives on in my brother.

My brother, who once was part of the number one Dutch rap group, is now a teacher, coach and mentor to young people. He is a devoted husband, father to a daughter and the knowledgeable uncle to my three sons and hordes of other nieces and nephews. He has taught me that besides seriousness and commitment there needs to be room for joy, fun, and relaxation, because why the hell not?

Gran tangi, my brother. Thank you for teaching me about balance. May I not only embrace but teach others about balance on the path, as well.

Brother — Source: Family Cairo

BEGINNING

In the beginning...
She created the earth, moon, sun and the stars
Mother Moon, Father Light
Waxing, waning, energies entwined
Endless possibilities, potential inclined
In the beginning the work was done,
with elements of love and alchemy
In the beginning things were formed
Things took shape, Thing things came to be
In the beginning we roamed and danced
In and out of potentiality
In the beginning we were free,
Until we were set
In stone
Or so it seemed

ABOUT
THE "D" WORD

Beginning — Ch.1

The year was 2007 and my first born was accepted at the top arts university in the US. Actually, he had been accepted at each of the three institutions he had applied to. He chose the top one. I tried in vain to steer him to another one that was cheaper and closer, but he wanted that one, so I let it go. It would be at least a 10-hour drive to this university. Of course, my godmother Zambia was part of the trip. She and her husband both were going to come with us. I didn't bring my other two boys, ages eight and three at the time, because I needed to have all my attention for my son.

My little Toyota Matrix was a great road car and cheap on gas, but for this trip we needed some room. So, I rented a Big Toyota SUV. We loaded it up and the four of us took off. The ride was smooth and comfortable. The gas costed a little more, but I was glad we had the nice ride. We had fun in the car, laughed and talked. But honestly, I was nervous, too. I was feeling all kinds of emotions. I was taking my baby away to college, and if everything was to go as planned, he would really never return home to stay. I pushed the thought away and drove on.

When we arrived, I gradually started to feel better. There was the hustle and bustle of new students. Having worked at a university, I had seen it every year, the tangible excitement. Now I was here myself, as a parent. We stood in various lines for various registrations. Each time, they would address Zambia as my son's mother and me as his sister. My son's skin tone is a shade lighter than mine and Zambia is caramel colored too, so it didn't surprise me. It didn't bother me, either. I knew who his mother was and that was all that mattered. We did the rounds, received lots of trinkets and information. There was a health booth. Zambia's husband said, "Let me take him." I saw them wander off together. He took him straight to the bowl of free condoms and told him to grab some. They had some more private man talk that I wasn't privy to. I was glad he had a man there.

A few weeks earlier, I had asked several of the men in the community if they could have a ceremony for my son. He was about to go out into the world and leave the nest. As a woman and a mother, a single mother at that, I had given him everything I could to get him ready, but there were some things he could only get from men. Therefore, I asked them to do whatever they felt was needed to send him on his way. They showed up and did their thing. I will never know exactly what they did because my son would not tell me, but I knew it was good. I did not need to know or ask. I felt my father's spirit as he reminded me that there are just some things young black men need to receive from their male elders. Several of the men thanked me: "I wish I had had something like that when I went out into the world." Traditions of old refurbished for the new still resonate and touch. Somehow, we still know. Zambia's husband was there then, too. I stood there looking at them at the health booth, assuring myself that I had done everything I could to get my son ready for this next step.

In the evening we went to Walmart and shopped till we dropped buying things for his room. The next day was the big assembly and then we would leave. The assembly was a show, a spectacle. At least 1000 eager new students from all over the world were there with their families. The excitement was palpable. It was so enjoyable to look out at all this young potential in this space. You almost forgot that this was

66

about education; it felt more like a sports event. Here we were in the big basketball arena. There were flashing lights, music, and overall loudness. It was crowded with people from all over the world, eager students with their families. All the African American students stand up! Latino, Asian, Native American, stand up! International students stand up! Look at how diverse we are! I had to admit that it was a beautiful mix of ethnicities, something to be excited about. There were some more sermon- and cheerleading-like comments and then they were off and officially started as university students.

After the assembly, it was time to leave. Here was the hard part. I didn't cry. I think that didn't happen until after I got home. I was sad but also excited for him as he was to start this new adventure. There were a whole bunch of feelings mixed into that moment of goodbye. I kept it together for his sake more than mine. I know that as the oldest child of a single mother he had a sense of responsibility for his mother and brothers that perhaps wasn't always fair, but that is what the universe had dealt him, and he had carried it well. Now it was his time, this great – great grandchild of Ma Po. She had carved the space through which her granddaughters, great granddaughter and now great – great grandson had left home, never to return. At some point, you have to let go, know that you have done enough, have provided enough, and have to trust that he can do his thing. So, we hugged and kissed one last time and off we went, back on the road in the nice big SUV.

He did his thing as a university animation and sequential art student and did well. The roommate was rather immature, so again he was in the big brother role, but he dealt with it. Three weeks after starting he called me: "Hey, ma, guess what. In our arts history class we are skipping African art, Asian art and Oceanic art. We are only studying

European art." So much for all that diversity that was celebrated in that first assembly. So, this is how it goes at the top arts university in the US?

I have shared this story many times publicly. At the time, I debated whether to do something about it, to voice my complaint to the school. But I would just have been one of those annoying parents. So, instead, I took my hard-earned money and went scouting for some good secondhand art books on art history from various cultures and sent them to him. Many years later, as I moved into a role where I had some power to address this issue – first as a diversity officer, and subsequently as a research professor in inclusive education – I would use this experience as the foundation in my "diversity and inclusion" work. You see, just because I didn't act at that time doesn't mean I wasn't going to act. Sometimes you have to wait, be in that space of incubation and be patient, until the time is just right.

Now I use my son's story to illustrate the underlying nature of diversity and inclusion. We see what happens when, out of the range of stories that are present in a space, a particular story keeps rising to the top as being more important, valid, trusted, unquestioned, and so on. In this particular example, by choosing only European art history to be taught and skipping the others, the university sent a message that only European stories were valid, or at least highly favored to be studied. And why? More importantly, we tend not to question why. It is the norm, and not just in art history. Out of all the stories, the range of knowledge representations, one keeps rising to the top as dominant, most valued, important, exalted, the 'go to,' the obvious or default story.

There is nothing wrong with that particular story. European art history is a very interesting and worthwhile story to be studied. What is wrong is what happens to those other stories, and inherently the messages students receive about those other stories. Those other stories become... less or not valued, overlooked, silenced, marginalized, ignored, unimportant, ridiculed, extracurricular, "oh, if we have some time left over", and more. Being different from the norm, then, automatically means less. And not only did my son not learn about his African heritage in the arts, neither did any of the other students.

This is the pattern that has become the norm. We approach diversity by focusing on the variety of visible stories in the room, or the lack thereof. We don't address the inherent inequalities that are affiliated with how that differential came to be or how it is maintained through our conditioned behavior. The quest in addressing diversity, better known as inclusion work, the love-work, then becomes this: Can we value and honor all the stories that are present in the space?

Gran tangi, my son. Thank you for allowing me to use our story to teach what the real love-work concerning diversity and inclusion is all about.

THE OTHER "D" WORD

Beginning — Ch. 2

You know that feeling when you are in a meeting with people and you speak, and it is as if people did not hear you? They speak right over you, barely acknowledge you, and at worst you might hear your words echoed by somebody else and then all of a sudden people seem to listen? I bet many have this experience. It might be because you are the woman, the man, the person of color, the disabled, the junior, the senior, etc. in the room. It is not as much about what you represent; it is about the status of the majority of the people in the room, those representing the *dominant* story.

Within academia, we have a wealth of analyses about this phenomenon talking about power differentials, hegemonic relations, or modes of oppression. I like to keep it simple. I prefer the concept of *the dominant and the other*. From the indigenous knowledge perspective, we have the first principle that we are all related. Our stories are interwoven with one another. This is important to take with us in exploring this concept. *The dominant and the other* refers to the fact that, out of the range of stories that we have, one has risen to the top, while the others have remained below. However, given that all stories are interlinked, when one rises to the top it has effect on the others. *The dominant and the other* is not a static model where one story stays permanently at the top. Instead, depending on the gathering, those of *the others* can rise to the top, even if only momentarily.

The *dominant* position is an interesting yet precarious status. The dominant position is inherently a position of power. Those in the *dominant* position have been raised with their story being presented to them as valid, unquestioned. Their story is always told first and the loudest. After a while, they end up believing that their story is actually truly more valid than those of *the others*, and herein lies the crux of the matter. Through reasons we actually can explain, their story has risen to the top out of a wealth of stories. But their story is only one of many stories. Their sense of superior value is thus based on a fabrication and the confrontation with that fabrication can be extremely unsettling. That superior position, then, is in fact a very fragile position. My cousin once told me wisely, "Don't put me on a pedestal, because the higher you put that pedestal, all I have to do is sneeze to fall off."

Being placed in the *dominant* position leads to having a sense of entitlement. Those in the dominant position should have access to all information at any given time, preferably without any difficulty. Their story is so valid that they don't need to bother to learn anything about those other stories. They can be in decision making positions over others without knowing anything about those other stories. They get to speak first, loudest, and can speak for others. They should be comfortable at any and all times if possible, and so on.

The other has learned about being overlooked, silenced, ignored, marginalized, and has developed coping skills ranging from covert plotting of resistance to total acceptance of their position. They have learned that in order to move up they will have to learn everything there is to know about the *dominant* story. In this aspect *the other* is then stronger than their *dominant* counterpart. Whereas *the dominant* only needs to be cognizant of their own story, *the other* knows both their own story and the story of *the dominant*. Similarly, when those in *the other* are confronted with denial or exclusion of some kind, generally they are so used to it that it doesn't faze them. *The dominant*, however, will show their fragility when they are confronted with a situation that destabilizes their position.

Something as simple as being asked not to speak or not to speak first can result in great indignation or disbelief for those so used to always having the floor. At the macro-level, we see how during the COVID-19 pandemic in the early spring of 2020 those in Western nations had a harder time dealing with imposed restrictions than their counterparts in African, Asian, and South American countries. Equally, having to resort to advice from these nations and following their example also was met with resistance, with fatal outcomes as a result.

The dominant and the other model is a dynamic model, rather than a static one. The oppression model, which easily explains racial or gender hierarchical differences, is too rigid and limited in scope. It allows too easily to posit the oppressor in opposition to the oppressed, leaving fighting the oppressor as the only and logical option in the pursuit of change. Or one gets caught up in moral condemnation of one party and pitying the other. Interestingly, change has been pursued by focusing on informing the offending party in the hope that, once people are informed and gain insight into their ways, they will instantly make an effort to change. Now, gender inequality and white supremacy, for instance, are real things that affect people's lives in significant ways. However, these constructs are not that simple. It assumes a schism between opposing parties, male versus females, or whites versus people of color, that must be fixed or overcome. The schism also allows you to dismiss the offending party. What if there is no schism?

The dominant and the other starts with the principle that we are all connected at any given time. *The dominant* is not separate from *the other*, and vice versa, even if it might seem like that. Instead, this unequal division has grown out of specific efforts started over hundreds of years ago. Throughout those years, mechanisms became practiced, oiled, and solidified to the point of conditioned normalcy. *The dominant and the other*, then, is a well-oiled and well-maintained machine. The only way for it to continue working as efficiently as it does is if everybody participates. Participation is not voluntary but conditioned. When people are confronted with its workings, they react in abhorrence, saying that they had no idea. That is exactly the way it was designed. This is also what makes it so treacherous. Mutual responses and reactions that invoke discomfort are all part of the mechanisms that ensure that *the dominant and the other* model remains intact.

It explains why changing the system remains such a challenge, and why focusing on making people be "nicer" proves least effective. A model incorporating the complexity of our relations is needed. An alternative to the 'us versus them' approach has been attempted in the academy through the concept of intersectionality. Intersectionality specifically posits that people are more than just one assigned category and hence that engaging them requires consideration of multiple axes of analyses. The concept of intersectionality was introduced by Crenshaw and has been explored in greater depth by Hill Collins but remains mostly an academic analytical tool. In spite of efforts by Hill Collins and others, it often remains watered down to a "multiple boxes checking" exercise. I believe that *the dominant and the other*, which offers a more dynamic approach, offers easier access to grasping the complexity of *the dominant and other* relationship.

I arrived in Suriname in 2003 with my two boys, ready with a two-year plan to pursue research for my anthropology dissertation. I had looked forward to the familiar Surinamese food and sunshine, but somehow it didn't suit me as it usually did. After a few more weeks of feeling out of sorts, I came to the horrifying realization that I might be pregnant, something that was indeed confirmed. Prior to leaving for Suriname, I had said goodbye to the man with whom I had spent the summer. Having met more than a year before in the Netherlands and having talked with each other on the phone for well over a year, we decided to spend time together to see if a relationship was possible. It wasn't necessarily horrible, but it was clear that we were not as compatible as we had seemed on the phone. We had said our goodbyes, both with the unspoken understanding that we would not see each other again.

So here I was, about to be a single parent to baby number three at age 37. On top of that, I was supposed to start doing research. I had intense tearful pleading sessions with God, promising all kinds of things if She would only magically undo my state. I received no confirmation. I considered abortion for a full two minutes, and although glad that I had that option, it simply was not an option for me. This was my responsibility. I was 37 with two master's degrees. And even though my sense of self-esteem was at an all-time low, I had enough sense to know that I had enough to make it work, somehow. The first person I told, with a deep sense of shame and tears streaming down my face, was my oldest son, then 14. He listened, grabbed my hand and told me not to worry, that he was there. We were going to be okay. That was all I needed.

As the news of my pregnancy became more known, several women in my circle would approach me and ask me if I was sure that I wanted to stay in Suriname to have the baby. Did I not want to go back to the United States and have the baby there? I did not understand their concern. Don't people have babies in Suriname every day? Furthermore, here in Suriname I had relatives, while in the United States I did not. So,

I moved forward as planned. When I further engaged the health care system, however, I understood their concern.

I noticed a pattern as I went to the consultations. Most of the women were there with partners, except for the Afro-Surinamese. Now, it is quite possible that the partners of those Afro-Surinamese women were working and not able to come, but it still was interesting and somewhat depressing that the Chinese, Javanese, and Hindustani women, and also some of the Maroon women, almost always were accompanied. The doctor was a light-skinned man, a *dougla*, meaning of mixed descent, and generally of the higher class. He was kind, but very information oriented. I was quite aware that I was in a different medical culture than the United States, one where doctors have a quite high authoritative status. They instruct and you follow orders.

It was then, with the same informative tone, he informed me one day that my blood test showed I had Hepatitis C. This would mean that I would not be able to breastfeed my baby when it was born. But I shouldn't worry about it too much yet. With that, my session was finished. I left the hospital stunned. I had just been informed that I had an incurable disease. Determined not to give in into the despair I felt creeping over me, I went straight to the internet café. One thing I could do was research. I searched the websites of the CDC in the US and the GGZ, the Dutch equivalent in the Netherlands. I found out that, indeed, you can breastfeed if you are infected with Hepatitis C if certain medicines are given to the mother right after birth. I found out that those medicines were not provided at my hospital, but they were at the public hospital because more poor women came there who needed to breastfeed. The explanation given for this discrepancy was that the hospital I was using in Suriname was apparently a hospital where more affluent women could afford to buy formula.

I subsequently called pharmacists and the hospital to ask about the possible cost of the medicine and how long it took to deliver. I made two packets with all of this information and gave one to the pediatrician assigned to newborn babies, an older doctor, as well as my doctor. The pediatrician was very grateful and thanked me for all the hard work I had done. My doctor was outraged and yelled at me. What was this?! This was unnecessary! I had overreacted. Didn't he tell me not to worry?! And on he went in his temper tantrum. I sat calmly and stared at him as he raged, backed up by my female ancestors, I'm sure. There was nothing this man could say to move or shake me. This was, after all, about the welfare of my baby.

You see 14 years earlier, at age 23, I was married, a graduate student, and pregnant with my first child. I lived in student housing and had gone to the clinic where a midwife followed my progress. In Kentucky, where I was living, midwives are not allowed to deliver babies in the hospital, thus as time got closer, I would have to see the doctor. This doctor was specifically assigned to work with poor people. The waiting room would always be packed, and you had a maximum of 15 minutes with the doctor, the total opposite of the loving care I had received from the midwife. The doctor would barely look up from his file and never spoke more than a few words to me, except one time when he realized I was from the Netherlands and he proceeded to tell me how his son had died on a trip to Europe walking along the railroad tracks. That was a very awkward one-sided conversation. During the delivery he came in told me to push, caught the baby, and handed it off to the nurse. They didn't let me hold the baby, but immediately took it away. You will see him later, I was told. The doctor left, too, and didn't come back. I never said anything. I regret to this day that I did not demand to see or hold my baby right after he was born. I was young and poor and that is how they treated me.

This time however, things were different. I was 37, a mother of two, and had a degree in medical anthropology. I knew what I was talking about, but more than anything, my age and life experience made it so that I was not fazed in the least by the doctor's dominant status. He gave me the option to have my blood retested at an independent lab, but I would have to pay for it. I left and got tested again. When I returned, there was a different doctor in front of me. He apologized profusely for his behavior and what I went through, something he would do each subsequent time he saw me. It turns out I was not infected with Hepatitis C, but that the hospital sample had been contaminated. There were six other women who had already started treatment, whose blood results were also contaminated.

Three weeks after my son was born, the secretary of the pediatrician called me to let me know that, due to my research, the hospital policy was going to be changed. Women were no longer going to be told that they could not breastfeed if infected and the medicine was going to be made available to all women as part of standard procedure.

I share this story to demonstrate the complexity and dynamics of *the dominant and the other*. As a single, dark skinned woman in a culture where doctors are generally not questioned, my advocacy for myself and my child were seen as an affront to the doctor. However, there was another doctor who did not see my contribution as offensive at all, but in fact welcomed it. This doctor was much older. Perhaps his maturity allowed him to focus on the information I was giving and thus not take my initiative personally. It is all speculation on my part, but it does show that even in a culture where doctors have God-like status, not all doctors are alike. As far as my own response, I was well aware of my position as *other* in this medical system. My age and academic skills conversely, made it so that I could step out of my subordinate role and face whatever consequence I encountered, such as the raging response by the doctor. My age, skills, and maturity empowered me. This was something I could not do at age 23 with the doctor who attended me at the time. I was not happy with my care then, either, but was too intimidated to say anything. I was told this was the doctor for poor people and thus I accepted the care that came with that classification.

I use *the dominant and the other* model to highlight a basic structure that underscores the difficulty we have with diversity and inclusion. Diversity and inclusion are not just about difference, but about the inherent inequalities that are embedded in that difference and the mechanisms that maintain the system. Like an iceberg, this system has deep implications and maintains the superficial lack of diversity we encounter. Diversity and inclusion endeavors are thus not just about who is present or absent, but more about what the mechanisms are that are contributing to continued inequality patterns in our interrelations. *The dominant and the other* model also usefully demonstrate that anybody can be in the *dominant* position at any given time. This forces us to honor the connections between us and extend compassion to the other, even when rejection would be a more desirable course of action. The *dominant* position is about power. What do we do with that power? How do we use our power to change those unequal relations? Changing inequalities requires understanding how power works, and then carefully but courageously negotiating those power relations within.

Gran tangi. Thank you for the insight. May we be brave and bold enough to examine our own dynamics and power potential across *the dominant and the other* divide.

POSITIONS
WE CANNOT ESCAPE

Beginning — Ch. 3

Mother, mother, may I travel? As elementary school children, we played this game often. As mother, you stood on one end while your children stood at the other. With the call of each country or city your children would take big steps corresponding to the number of syllables. Me-xi-co, that was three. It seemed there were always those who would win with their abilities to take big jumps or just because they had long legs. Or sometimes they would run by you just as you were ready to win. It seems it was an easy game at which to cheat.

There was something about playing this game and always have somebody jump past you at the last minute. Something about not being able to escape changing your position in relation to the winners, no matter how hard you tried or how hard you strategized. They must have been cheating.

In the *dominant* narrative, we are inundated with stories about the individual. Me, myself, and I, is all I have to worry about. You are special. If you just work hard enough you can be anything you want to be. You can separate yourself from those others and achieve, unlike in that pesky *Mother-may-I-travel* game. If you did not achieve, you must not have worked hard enough. In addition, we inundate the space with narratives of heroes and sheroes who broke the mold. They who were able to aspire, outgrow their circumstances and triumph into higher realms. Those are the feel-good stories. The stories that make you warm on the inside and inspire you to do better, be better. Within the field of diversity and inclusion, this narrative exists, as well. Everybody is welcome and has equal opportunity to participate; hence, if they just work hard enough, they will achieve. Teachers pride themselves on saying that they don't see difference between their students and treat everybody as equal. It is a commendable ideal that is undermined by the fact that everybody, including teachers, is influenced by the larger narratives in which we function. Even though our indigenous knowledge has as its primary mandate that we are all related, and even though our 21st century globalized living proves to us daily that, indeed, we are connected, the story of the special, triumphant individual remains a *dominant* cultural trope.

One time, I attended a workshop about how to use stories in scientific reporting. The workshop was rather enjoyable, but I kept noticing how they kept presenting a certain storyline for us to follow. They presented a protagonist who had to encounter and overcome some type of obstacle, and ultimately achieved resolution. There was something that bothered me about this scenario. As always, when something does not feel right, my belly starts to burn. My belly would not let up until I figured out what it was, at which point I raised my hand. I told them, "I notice that your story line is very individual- oriented." In Native American storytelling, for instance, there is always a person, animal or spirit that comes along and gives guidance or assistance. The message is that you cannot overcome anything without some help. They also always have an element of sacrifice in the journey. You have to sacrifice something in order to achieve your goals. "Yes, we are aware that there are other stories out there, but this is what we use as the standard and the norm." And with that, the story of *the other* was wiped off the table. Which story rises to the top as valid, without question? I kept quiet and continued with the workshop, but with less enjoyment, tired of once again having to deal only with the *dominant* story. I was bothered also by the fact that participants would leave this workshop thinking this was THE way to do stories, rather than one of a range of ways. But it was not my show, so I let it go.

Another thing that counters the narrative of the sole triumphant hero or shero is the concept of *positionality* as defined by Icaza and Vázquez. Positionality is a term within academia that generally is mentioned in research as a word of caution. For those engaging in social research with people, researchers have to understand that they occupy a certain position in relation to their study subjects. No matter how equal they may feel to their informants, they must always remember that they do represent a university and hence an institution of power and wealth. Although they might not feel like it, this automatically puts them in some type of dominant position in regard to their research informants.

This is an important awareness, but Icaza and Vázquez's perspective on *positionality* takes us further. Rather than taking an individual approach to positionality, they base their positionality on the indigenous-informed concept of an extended, relational and communal sense of self. Similar to *Mother-may-I-travel*, they present positionality as a position in relationship to others that you cannot escape. That you are connected to others is a given. They state that, in fact, from the moment you are born on this earth and exude breath, you are born into a narrative that places you in relationship with others in a certain position without any effort or fault of your own. This narrative is shaped by a certain history, more than likely by a certain colonial history fed by communal narratives. Hence, the idea of an equal playing field is a myth, because this grander narrative that we are born into determines the kinds of obstacles we face or privileges we receive on our paths. How we negotiate the extended parts of ourselves that we are connected to also affects how we traverse our paths. Thus, it makes no sense to judge how people traverse their paths based only on their individual capacities without also taking into account the obstacles they may face on that path and/or the support they receive along the way. It also does not mean that one is locked into that narrative for life, it is just that the journey to escape or transform this narrative is different for each of us, and many are just not able to do so.

As an 18-year-old, having been born and raised in metropolitan Amsterdam, I left for adventure and went to pursue my education in rural Kentucky in the United States. The culture shock going from a metropolitan, international city to the foothills of the Appalachian mountains is beyond anything I could put into words. I cried for three days after I arrived, wondering what I had gotten myself into. But I adapted and adjusted and actually came to love my experience there.

I stayed in the residence halls. In my first year, we still had only one telephone for the whole floor. Throughout the day you would hear girls running up and down the halls, waiting and hoping for phone calls, mostly from boyfriends. Pretty soon we had a Friday evening routine, however. We all knew that on Friday evening at a certain time Peggy Sue would receive a call from home. "Peggy Sue don't answer the phone, you know who it is!" Peggy Sue did know who it was and would always dutifully answer the call.

Peggy Sue was born and bred in Kentucky, raised on a farm not far from the college. Every Friday night her folks would call her to ask her when she would come home. "Peggy Sue, ain't you ready to call it quits yet? A girl ain't got no business getting an education. Just come on home to the farm and get married." Peggy Sue would listen and be ever so polite. "Yes ma'm, no ma'm. Yes sir, no sir", while tears would be streaming down her face. Every Friday we would beg her not to answer the phone. Every Friday she would stand there crying, until one day she didn't. Peggy Sue gave in and went home.

I often tell this story to my students to tell them about the complexities of diversity. I was black, female, international, and across the ocean from my family, by all accounts clearly *the other* and perhaps in need of special attention and assistance. Peggy Sue was white and local, yet Peggy Sue was farther from home than I ever was. When we hold space, we don't know what kind of stories are present in the space. We do not know the kinds of sacrifices people have made or are making to be in the space.

I graduated from college and went on to pursue my master's degree in a nearby city. One day I was walking and ran into Peggy Sue. She shared that she had gone home and had married, as desired by her family. Her married life had been difficult, however. Her husband was involved in drugs, something quite common in rural Kentucky with a desperate economy. She had two children in the marriage, and eventually chose better for herself and her children. She divorced her husband and went back to college. "I am back and am determined to finish this time." I looked at her, saw her confidence and knew that she meant it. I am convinced that Peggy Sue is somewhere out there with a college degree.

I also share this part of the story to show that even though Peggy Sue's path was confined by the story she was born into, a narrative in which women should not pursue education, she was able to transform that narrative. She might not have done it in a way we would normally expect. She had sacrifices to make and obstacles to overcome, far greater than many of her peers, but she did. I am sure she had helpers along the way, seen and unseen, that inspired her to make some changes in spite of. I would like to think that even we, her college peers, in our encouragement and example placed some seeds of inspiration that sprouted later. But, I expect that more than likely her children were her ultimate sources of inspiration. It is all speculation of course.

The lesson here is that we step into these greater, communal narratives just by drawing breath. Not only does it shape the obstacles we encounter or the privileges we receive, but it shapes especially how we stand in relationship to each other. Consequently, the "just work hard and you can become anything you want" trope is an idealistic myth. We are not necessarily locked into our positionalities, but our positionalities surely affect the struggles, choices, and sacrifices we need to make to walk our paths. Similarly, understanding our positionality will also help us understand some of the behaviors we encounter when we interact with each other.

Mother, mother may I travel? Yes, my child you may, but heed all the gifts and obstacles you will encounter on your path.

CONSUMPTION JUNCTION

Beginning — Ch. 4

During the COVID-19 lockdown, I started a new morning routine. I would go for a walk for up to an hour or so through the urban landscape. Purposefully, this was not a fitness walk. I did not set out to sweat or lose weight. Instead, I walked purely to affirm my connection with the world. I could breathe and I could walk, and in a time of intense uncertainty that certainty was appreciated. I was also aware that in many other countries people were not allowed the luxury of walking outside at all. Images of people singing to each other on balconies in Italy, or stories about police fining and beating people for being outside in Spain had reached us, so this was also a walk of appreciation because things could be worse. And so, I walked with a purpose to connect, be aware, and be appreciative. I walked in awareness of my steps, my breathing, and the natural sounds of the cityscape. But most of all, the trees and the water served as my nourishment during these walks. After a while, the birds became part of the repertoire too.

I would watch them, listen to them and eventually started carrying pieces of bread with me, always making it a point to stop along the way to feed some of them. As spring progressed, nests were built, and eggs were hatched. There was one pattern that kept getting my attention. As I threw the bread, one of the parents - which I assumed to be the father, but could as well have been the mother, as many do equal opportunity parenting - would immediately come and eat their fill. The other one would stay with the chicks and would then come and eat. But after eating she would fill her beak with more and take it back to feed the little chicks. Time and time again I would see the parent go back to feed the chicks. The species of bird did not matter. Those little ones were insatiable. Their beaks would be open, and they would scream. Once the food would go in, they would swallow instantly and immediately scream for more.

There was no repose, no moment of satisfaction or stillness, no appreciation, just the constant insatiable hunger for more. Now, of course these are biologically, animal - driven needs and behaviors on display, yet it reminded me of people. This is a long and arduous way to get to the image that is invoked in me whenever I am confronted with the consumption behavior embedded in *the dominant and the other* model.

You see, one of the aspects of *the dominant and the other* interaction is that of consumption. Those in *the dominant* position are generally unaware and or uninterested in all that the dwelling in *the other* position entails, especially in regard to experiences of marginalization. Because of the interrelatedness of *the dominant* position with *the other*, stories of experienced marginalization are inherently uncomfortable, "niet gezellig" as we say in Dutch. Thus, avoidance or dismissal of storytelling with that particular theme is preferred. But there is an exception. If the stories of consumption have entertainment value then they are allowed, even if the stories are about experienced marginalization.

It was during my first year teaching as an assistant professor. I was co-teaching a course. The university had developed a requirement for seniors where they had to take a course presented from two different perspectives. Representing anthropology, I was assigned to co-teach a course with a colleague from the business department. This man was older and experienced, and we clicked immediately. His ease and frank wisdom provided guidance and mentorship, not just in this course, but in my budding career as a university professor, as well. We had at least 60 students in this class, predominately white males, whom I had the pleasure to convince that there was value in understanding culture when doing business.

It was a hard sell. Somebody sent me an anonymous note that business was about Xs and Os, nothing more. They were polite enough to listen to me, but their body language did not hide the fact that they found me irrelevant and slightly entertaining, at best. Now, I also have to mention that this was the class where often the international students, gay students, and students of color would wait for me after class to thank me because they felt represented or saw themselves in the material, often for the first time. So, oddly enough, as tough as this class was, there was also something very gratifying about teaching this class.

But I digress. Now one day, I can't recall why, but I decided to share a story with them about what had happened to me the day before. Somehow, I thought it would make a connection to the material I was about to teach. The day before, I had scheduled and reserved a classroom to teach in the gym. I came loaded with a boombox and other material, ready to teach the course. Upon arrival, however, something had gone awry with the scheduling. Rather than assisting me, I was dismissed from one person to the next for at least 20 minutes, all the while lugging my stuff around. When I had had enough, I literally kicked open the door of the person in charge - because my arms were full - and demanded to talk to them.

I declared in no uncertain terms what the issue was and what I demanded in terms of full attention. Of course, I added drama to the retelling of my account, especially the kicking in of the door. The story ended with the message that the indifference I had initially encountered instantly disappeared and that my situation was resolved in a few minutes. Ma Po had shown her spirit and had been effective.

It was a silly story to prove some point, but what happened was phenomenal. For the first time I had this majority white male audience with me. They were focused, leaned forward, hung on my every word and laughed, especially at the part where I kicked in the door and scared the director to death. I had them with me. The rest of the class was way easier than any of my previous classes had been, except for my loyal students who were always with me.

I felt good about my accomplishment with the class that day— until I debriefed with my colleague and mentor. "Did you notice what happened?" he asked me. "They loved your story. They ate it up because you finally fulfilled their stereotype of the angry black woman. They have a hard time connecting with you as a professor who has something to teach them, but this tickled their fancy. And the fact that it came out of you being treated poorly, makes it extra sad."

Wow. I was kind of deflated after his revelation, but I could see what he meant. I learned a lot from him, and not just that one day, but many other days after that. I also started to pick up on this notion of consumption of our stories, in particular stories of marginalization and pain. Now mind you, we often do tell our stories to entertain. The issue is that on those occasions when we tell our stories to really share something of ourselves and make a connection, more often than not those attempts are rejected, minimized or ridiculed. Hence, we have learned to keep our stories to ourselves. So, on those rare occasions when we are brave enough to tell our stories, it is unfortunate when the stories are merely consumed. They are consumed, gobbled and swallowed, as if by those little birds, and afterwards *the dominant* move on to the next morsel, leaving a potential relationship by the wayside.

Those in *the other* position engage in consumption behavior, as well. Like those little birds, they swallow one bite after the next. Slights, insults, dismissals, insensitivities and plain stupidities are part of an ongoing daily buffet. These interactions that are part of maintaining *the dominant and the other* divide are consumed and swallowed as if they are nothing. They swallow and just keep it moving out of necessity. They consume mindlessly not for the sake of nourishment, but for survival. They mindlessly swallow in order not to taste, not to feel, to let go instantly, and it becomes normal. And yet...

There is something that happens when one consumes without proper digestion. There is something that happens that is not right. True nourishment is supposed to transform and make a person grow. Two people in particular taught me lessons about the importance of true nurturance. My African dance teacher would hold big Kwanzaa gatherings at her house and would always prepare a feast. The first time I went, she spoke to us about the importance of slowly cooked and prepared food as opposed to fast food. Fast food is not meant to nourish you, but the time and love that is put into slow-cooked food will be beneficial to your body. Similarly, my anthropology mentor, a Native American elder whom I met at my first national conference, counseled me from time to time throughout my graduate school journey. He took it a step further and talked to me about the importance of intention when you cook food and how songs are prayers that rise up to the spirit world. He talked to me about the importance of singing while cooking and the importance of taking in properly prepared food with intention to nurture your soul.

It may seem a far stretch from the consumption of food, but there is something to be said about being mindful about what and how you ingest information, and to become mindful of the intention that is affiliated with that ingestion. When *the dominant* merely consume stories of pain of *the other* without proper digestion, they fail to grow and transform, but most of all they fail to connect to *the other* and hence an opportunity is missed. When *the other* consume the unpleasantries from *the dominant* mindlessly, it might contribute to bearable numbness in the present, but in the long run will lead to indigestion.

Of course, there are those in *the dominant* sphere who are generally interested, but if upon hearing the stories the impact does not evoke more than a feeling and fails to incite any transformative interaction, then the interaction remains merely consumptive. And, of course, there are those in *the other* position who realize that consuming disrespect is unacceptable but are so caught up in normalizing and minimizing for the sake of survival that they don't know where or how to start disrupting the consumptive behavior.

This act of consumption that seems so natural and part of our normal survival has, in fact, been detrimental and has contributed to the formation and maintenance of *the dominant and other* divide.

Gran tangi. Thank you for the lesson that when we consume mindlessly without proper intention or digestion, we are not nourishing ourselves, but in fact are harming our individual state of being and our relations.

TO BE OR NOT TO BE SUSTAINABILITY

Beginning — Ch. 5

Greta Thunberg age 20, Sweden; Licypriya Kangujam age 8, India; Artemisa Xakriabá age 19, Brazil; Autumn Peltier age 15, Canada, Jerome Foster II age 17, USA; Melati Wijsen age 18, Indonesia; Jamie Margolin age 18, USA; Misimi Isimi age 13, Nigeria; Ayakha Melithafa age 19, South Africa; Isra Hirsi age 16, USA; Lilly Platt age 12, Netherlands. These are ten names of ten youngsters dedicated to fighting for sustainability of the planet. They are committed, driven, and by no means the only ones. They represent hordes of young people who are looking to the elders of the world and are demanding more, better.

How do we make this world last? We admire their spunk and energy, but let's be frank. We also get tired just by thinking about all that stuff. Aren't they asking for too much? Do they understand the lifestyle that we have? What would the cost be to make all those changes they ask for? What would the cost be not to, they answer.

Time and time again I see young people stepping up when it comes to recycling, thinking about the environment, and demanding changes. From access to clean water to plastic bags or pollution, they are on it and better informed than many of their elders. The argument seems logical. Our global lifestyles are not sustainable as is. Hence, we need to change it. For some reason it is not that simple.

I read an article once that stated that we shouldn't worry so much about recycling because our individual efforts didn't

92

mount to much. The true pollutants were the big corporations. Responses were vehement and swift. Apparently we do value the idea that we can make a difference even as individuals. Yet, we remain removed, distant somehow. We take our time while the clock keeps ticking.

Our Native American teachings teach us that we are connected to all, and that includes nature. Yet we have become more separate as we indulge in the lifestyles we have developed. What does all this have to do with inclusion?

If we are the extension of each other and the world and the world is sick, we are affected as well. We are not at our best. We do not function at our best. If we take a laissez faire attitude with our environment and all we are connected to, we will take a laissez faire attitude with each other and ourselves.

I had a valuable learning experience while doing research with a number of community centers in The Hague. This research was part of a larger project to investigate the impact of Covid on citizens in the city. My research partner and I noticed that the public discourse about certain communities were extremely negative or absent all together. "Well, they are by nature more communal, so they will naturally engage in high-risk behaviors. These are the kind of people that don't stick to the rules, so...." These communities, which were mostly lower income and multi-cultural, were generally highlighted in the media for things that go wrong there or are lacking. In this City of Peace and Justice, which also happens to be hailed as the most segregated city in the Netherlands, this trend was disturbing. We knew that the story of the city as it was presented was incomplete and flawed, and we wanted to use our research to do something about it.

Whereas initially we set out to collect stories of solidarity of certain communities with the help of community centers, we quickly changed course. Rather than doing and pursuing as traditional research required, we took the more indigenous approach and focused on "being with". Being with and joining changed our perspective. We no longer focused on collecting stories. Who said we had a right to those stories? Were we going to utilize those stories to prove that they had a right to be seen and heard differently? Did they have anything to prove, or did they have the right to just be? So instead, we started to focus on being with and then learned about how they do stories and how they included us as part of their stories. Our stories became intertwined. After all, the fact that their stories were present and valid was already a given. They had nothing to prove. The learning was about the power of stories and our stories interlinking, as my mother had taught me. The lesson was about transformation through the sharing of our stories.

On numerous occasions we were able to witness the power of the interweaving of our stories and its potential for transformation. One profound lesson for me was that of sustainability. Actually, first I learned about the concept of "matter of fact-ness", and secondly about the concept of "fighting for" that totally changed my view of sustainability.

My research partner and I worked with three different community centers. Each of the center directors led their centers with dedication and compassion, but what stood out was the 'matter of fact-ness' with which they navigated and handled situations. In one of the centers everybody is a volunteer. People come for different reasons; some to get out of the house, while others might be court-ordered. It doesn't matter, and nobody needs to know. What matters is that you are there and can make a valuable contribution. Hence there is great pride. The director is very friendly but will immediately encourage stragglers to think about how they can contribute. He is matter of fact about it. That you have something to contribute, that you will be of value is a given.

The other center is not run by volunteers. People come to learn and socialize. The coordinator of the women's program works relentlessly for her patrons. Her commitment to the women is strong. She is always trying to empower them, yet not in a patronizing way. Like her male counterpart there is a matter of fact-ness about her. That you matter is a given. That you want to learn is a given, and she will provide the means to do so.

One time, at the end of a presentation, one young woman stepped forward and sang three songs in three different languages. She shared that she had discovered that her true passion was singing, not school. Each of the songs were laments and she had taught herself some of the languages. My research partner and I were moved and thrilled. It would be perfect to ask her to sing at the social gatherings we wanted to organize. When we told the coordinator and told her about our plans to ask her and that we wanted to pay her, she corrected us. We should not offer her money. Money would set her apart from the group. We could maybe give her a gift, but as a member of the community she should be willing to share her gifts to benefit the community. We stood corrected.

Coming from a feminist perspective on social justice and equity, wanting to be vigilant about not being extractive and exploitative, we felt it important to pay the young woman for her contribution. However, we were reminded about what it means to be within that space of solidarity, and that an economic remuneration could actually do damage as it would signal separation. So, we quickly had to shift to what we had learned from our experiences with North American and Mesoamerican first nations and indigenous communities, regarding knowledge, dignity and justice. We were so focused on making sure we were correct by "doing for", that we forgot we just had to "be with." Again, I was struck by her matter of fact-ness. That we do for each other is a given.

The second aspect was that of "fighting for". Each of the directors held the space for their constituents simply because they mattered, but they also fought for them. One of the centers that hosted social lunches for the elderly, upon hearing that closing due to the pandemic was eminent immediately started planning and organizing so the food could be delivered to its elderly patrons. "If they can't come to us, we will bring the food to them." Volunteers were mobilized and food was delivered. The other center's director went as far as going to court to fight to keep the center open during the pandemic, because in his community the support that the center offered was crucial. He won and they remained open during the whole pandemic.

In addition, directors engaged and utilized the media to fight the negative stereotypes about their neighborhoods and constituents. Government funding for summer programs for the neighborhood were cut and these funds were steered toward security. Consequently, or incidentally, riots broke out. The director publicly criticized the municipality for withdrawing funds from the community and laid the link to the public misbehavior of youth that had nothing to do. In his criticism he also provided an alternate view of the community, and reminded people that rather than looking at the young people for acting out, the government needed to be reminded of its responsibility towards them. He refused to let the young people be seen as separate, but instead showed how interconnected we are and how destabilizing underlying support structures can have far reaching effects.

This "fighting for" in combination with "a matter of factness" attitude gave me a new appreciation of the concept of "sustainability". Up until my experience with this research I had always thought of sustainability as the concept of "How do you make something last." In the case of organizations, it would translate into "How can you gain and set up financial and logistic structures so your programs can continue." In terms of materials, one looks for the resources needed to make a product recyclable or durable. In terms of nature, "How do we prevent extinction and how do we stop depleting our finite resources? How do you make it last?" This research gave me insight that there is an important step before one needs to look at what needs to be done to make something last. First, there needs to be a deep and sincere appreciation that something is worth preserving. That appreciation will lead to the motivation to do something, or in this case "fighting for" with a "matter of fact-ness", just because it matters. That it matters has to resonate deep within you.

We live in a throw away society. We consume and move on. We don't invest in rebuilding or fixing. That is not just about the consumption items or about nature, but also about our personal relationships. We live in an era where time has been sped up. If we don't figure things out quickly we move on to the next thing, the next situation, the next person. I am not just saying this to lament. I am saying this as a reflection and an encouragement to slow down, take stock and savor the moment. What is worth preserving in this moment? What is worth the effort?

Now I am not talking about abusive relationships. I am not suggesting that people should stay in relationships that are damaging or violating at any cost. What I am saying is that there is an appreciation for living, being that should or could count for something. When we look at those young people who are fighting to preserve the earth there is something to be learned there.

So, as we start with the premise that we are connected and that we all matter, we need to add to that a moment of reflection. What is so precious to us that it is worth preserving? We see people sacrificing their health and sanity in order to belong. What is worth preserving? What is worth preserving in the relationships we have and what price do we pay not to? What is worth preserving in this world that we live and what price do we pay not to? What risks and sacrifices are we willing to pay for something that is so worth preserving?

Gran tangi. Thank you for the lesson that we and our extended community are too precious and valuable not to be preserved and are worth the effort.

APPROPRIATION AS COLONIZATION

Beginning — Ch. 6

As a postdoc student in the U.S., I had the honor to present at a conference in the Navajo Nation. After landing in a remote airport, it took another three hours by car to get to the town where I would be presenting. The Arizona landscape was beautiful yet desolate at the same time. I would pass remote little houses, wondering how the people survived with no other houses or people in sight. I passed through one-stoplight towns until I got to the college town that was my final destination. There was an odd familiarity, although I had never been there before. Then it hit me: this was like Appalachia in the desert! Appalachia, where I spent my formative years in college, had left a big imprint on me. And thus, a homecoming sort of feeling overcame me in this browner, drier version of my youth.

The Native people, too, were different yet familiar. Their way of speaking was different. I had to get used to a different sense of time as people would refer to the past in the present and vice versa. People spoke about experiences of their ancestors as if they happened yesterday, highlighting the connection in their communal experience. What really stood out were the introductions. People introduced themselves by first stating the linear tribes of their fathers' and mothers' people. Instantly, I was taken back to both Appalachia and my Surinamese roots. From "Who's your kinfolk" in Appalachia to my cousin introducing me as, "This is so and so, she is from my *bere* family", meaning womb family. She announced that we were related through the mother's side, descendants from one womb, which is considered stronger than the *brudu* family, the blood family, the members of the father's side. In Suriname too, then, you generally are not fully acknowledged until people have an answer to "Who's your mother and who's your father?

Across Native American, Appalachian, and Surinamese introductions, the affirmation of lineage, and connectedness stand out, but so too does a sense of honoring where you come from and whose shoulders you stand on. This sense of connectedness and honoring translates into a tradition of giving and exchanging seen in each of these cultures, in particular in their art forms. These three cultures also share a history of being under resourced and experiences of outsiders coming in and exploiting their resources.

In the dynamics of *the dominant and the other*, there is a practice that reflects the paradigm's colonial roots, namely appropriation. Similar to the act of consumption, *the dominant* takes from *the other* for their own good. However, while the purpose of consumption is for temporary nourishment or enjoyment, in appropriation what *the dominant* does takes this practice a step further. *The dominant* takes elements from the story of *the other*, and not only uses those elements but claims them as their own. *The dominant* does this to enhance their own story.

Now, there is nothing wrong with taking or borrowing from each other's stories; after all, our stories are connected anyway. In many cultures, this is even encouraged. In the African American juke joints where jazz and blues are played, people are encouraged to take what is given in one another's music and to elaborate on it. The Blues Aesthetic acknowledges the important role of enhancing and elaborating on what is given. It shows our capacity to grow and excel through sharing stories. Similarly, in tap dance or even break dance challenges, one presents their work in the circle as a statement and the opponent is invited to elaborate on it. Each can use parts of the other's dance to bring their own performance to a higher level. It might be constructed as a challenge, but also functions as a gift. In Hip hop, sampling of classic R&B music has led to the younger generation reconnecting with the older generation and validating their musical roots.

In the Appalachian culture, there is a strong tradition of storytelling. The region is known for its skillful ability to entertain through oral mastery. In this region that has been marginalized and under-resourced, storytelling has not only served as entertainment, but also as an important social bonding tool. Stories and the story telling tradition are gifted and passed down through the generations. As such, the idea of individuals honoring who they are as a people is always present. Similarly, when I was on the Navajo reservation, people showed me their blankets as heritage heirlooms. They weren't just proud of their craftsmanship but of the tradition itself that had been passed down through the generations and of the way this represented their family.

This is the difference I see between the indigenous and colonial approaches. Among the indigenous, there is an honoring of those whose stories have been gifted. The colonial version of this interaction is where somebody comes and simply mines the stories of others. They don't ask, they just take. There is no reciprocity or even consideration of reciprocity. They may justify their actions by claiming to preserve history, but this is hard to prove. Usually, nothing is put in place to support that claim.

This colonial act of appropriation is about taking – unasked and unsanctioned – without giving due credit and in order to enhance one's own story. At its worst, the perpetrators of this cultural theft also make significant financial profit. We see this particularly in fashion and in museums. Indigenous groups have seen their art displayed on fashion runways without receiving any credit, financial compensation, or even inclusion in the production process. Museums are the bastions of thievery and display. They are a whole industry unto themselves.

There are those who lump hairstyles like braids and dreadlocks in the category of appropriation. I personally don't necessarily see it that way. I don't think one particular group has the patent on certain hairstyles. However, what happened with Bo Derek in the 1980s was appropriation. Bo Derek wore her hair in braids in the movie 10. Now, everybody instantly knew that that was an African hairstyle. However, this hairstyle hit like a bomb. People, meaning white women, ran to the salon to get "Bo Derek" hairstyles. "Wait what? Bo Derek hairstyles?". Yes, and people were dead serious about it. No mention, no acknowledgment of the African heritage represented in the hairstyle. This was a new cultural phenomenon. Black women were left scratching, or rather patting their head, wondering what just happened.

The phenomenon of appropriation is so painful because it takes place in a particular context, a particular story. Again, there is nothing wrong with gifting, borrowing, and exchanging stories. However, in the case of the "Bo Derek" hairstyle, there is a historical story of African exploitation and colonization, of centuries of oppression and being mined for environmental as well as human resources. Having one's story taken once again and then being displaced, as if you never existed, is not only disrespectful, it is just painful.

This appropriation is possible because of the sense of considering oneself as disconnected from others, as a separate individual entity, which is one of the biggest mythological pitfalls of Western philosophy. Our indigenous cultures teach us that we are connected at any given time to everything and everyone. What we do affects others. It imbues us with a certain responsibility, whether we want it or not.

Even when you act and progress through life solo, you never know who is watching, listening or inspired by what you do. Hence, appropriation – especially within a context of historical marginalization – can be so painful. A simple "oops", or "oh well, that is my blind spot" does not touch the gravity of the damage and disruption that appropriation might cause.

I experienced this with my own young staff when I was a lector. As lector, I lead a research team dedicated to inclusive education. From the beginning, I felt it was important to have a unit specifically dedicated to students. If we were to work on changing the culture of the university, we could not do it without its biggest constituents, students. I created the Student Branch and hired young people to lead it, all recently graduated but close in age and experience to the students.

Their story was immediately complicated by the fact that people kept referring to them as students. No matter how many times we informed people – both via verbal and written notice – that these individuals were not students, people kept referring to them or introducing them as students. There was a message of marginalization there, of not being regarded as equal to the other employees, even though they had earned their diplomas and their position. We talked about it, joked about it, and were at the point where we would give each other the look and roll our eyes whenever it would happen again. We would vent to each other when necessary, but addressing it became so useless that we hardly bothered. It is within this context that they had their experience with appropriation.

One time we were invited to an event where the work of the Student Branch was heralded and displayed. It was obvious that the presenter had not done two minutes of research on what our work actually entailed, but they were more than happy to brag about it. The presenter started by referring to my young staff as students. We looked at each other, gave a deep sigh and an eye roll. But then it went on and got worse – way worse. Every piece of shared information was wrong. I wasn't surprised or even hurt, though annoyed maybe. This was nothing new: appropriation in action. Of course, it is great when people want to celebrate your work. But I got the feeling that because it was about students it was not taken as seriously. It would have been so easy to have involved the Student Branch staff in the presentation or at least consult with them. It would have given them their due respect, a respect they deserved. None of that had happened. As the only black lector, I was used to the tokenism and appropriation. For me that was par for the course, an unspoken part of the job description. What did strike me here, though, was how by affiliation to me, these young people were also negatively impacted. I felt bad for them. Their work was diminished and pimped.

I turned out to be right. I watched as horror materialized in my staff's whole demeanor as they realized what was happening. I saw how all the theoretical insights they had gained under my tutelage suddenly became real on a very visceral level. And it did become real. At that point, the violating party was no longer of interest; the only thing that mattered was how was I going to help them get through this.

As we left, we checked on each other and talked a little bit, but not much. The first call came while I was still in the train on my way home. "I am sorry, but I just have to talk about what just happened, because I am so upset!" And so, I listened and affirmed their feelings. "They just raped our work, and I feel violated!" ... and on and on. And I listened and held their hand through the digital divide. The Blues Aesthetic teaches that you have to go through the ugliness in order to resurface in a better place. So, I let them swim through it and held the space for them, as these young people had done for me many times.

One has a tendency to think of appropriation in terms of intercultural experiences because those are the easiest to notice. Someone wears or performs black culture. Somebody steals Native American dress for the fashion industry, etc. But appropriation can happen in any setting. Appropriation is about using and taking without honoring. On the work floor, then, this can be a major issue. Appropriation is like that little insect that bites, that you swipe away and makes you think "What was that? Oh well." The next morning you wake up with a swollen, infected hand. No matter how innocuous the act seems, it always leaves pain in its wake, and that pain can linger and fester. A workplace where some people tend to take and appropriate the work of their colleagues or subordinates has a different atmosphere than a place where people honor and celebrate each other's gifts. Distrust, dissatisfaction and resentment are sure enough ingredients for a nasty relationship or workplace climate infection.

Gran tangi. Thank you for the lesson that taking without honoring, as innocently as it may seem, has the capacity to do serious damage.

TO SPEAK
THE UNSPOKEN

Beginning — Ch. 7

There is a part of indigenous knowledge that talks about the space of not knowing. There is an element of knowledge that you might not have access to immediately. Even in Western science, you can never know all there is to know. You work with an α of 90 or 95, meaning that you are 90% or 95% sure. There is no study that will claim to be 100% sure. And so, I imagine it as this dark place, this place of unknowing. The darkness is not dark because it is bad, something we get from Western culture, but because it is a place of incubation.

It is a humbling place. When you go into a sweat lodge it is dark. The sweat lodge represents the womb. You humble yourself, kiss the ground and crawl in. It is easy to get frightened in the dark, but the key is to stay calm and patient. When it gets too hot you might have to humble yourself once again. "If it gets too hot, bring your face all the way to the ground." Mama Walks on Water told me. "The air is cooler there and you can breathe. Mama (Earth) will take care of you."

All that to say, there is a space of not knowing and the challenge is to be okay with that. The challenge is to be humble and to be in incubation until you are ready to receive or understand the information. The information will come when the time is right and when you are right. Of course, this goes against all our Western sensibilities, especially those of us with formal academic training. We are in search of facts and would like to have them yesterday. We are expected to make plans, frameworks and predict what we are going to find. That is how we get our work approved. That is how we receive funding for our work, which ensures our academic and financial survival. Hence, that also means an embedded sense of insecurity and fear when it comes to "what if...?"

You can counter that sense of insecurity and fear with an approach that says it will come when it will come. This means you have to go into that dark space and trust. You might have to meditate or pray, or just be still and patient until the answer comes. It is a different way of walking in the world, and it is a different way of doing academic work. I learned this when I was doing my dissertation research in Suriname. Financially, it was a serious struggle. I was hired by the government to work for the department of culture, but like any government position the wait for the paycheck was at least six months. One male co-worker told me. "You are a beautiful woman; you can get a man to take care of you in the meantime." So much for cultural sensibilities. I was hired by the University as well, but they also had a six-month payment waiting period. The money I had brought I had used to pay the rent for the year up front and my son's schooling at the international school, so I was between a rock and a hard place. My oldest son's father had not sent money for years so there was no need to ask there, and my second son's father felt that since I wasn't in the United States he wasn't obligated to provide.

I did not tell my family about my situation. We could always visit and eat and sometimes we did, but I was not there to be a burden. Somehow, we got by. I had one dear sister friend who offered me a place to teach dance at her dance studio. We ate pancakes quite a bit and a lot of popcorn. Flour was cheap and you could buy single eggs. There were days when the refrigerator would be near empty and I would worry how I would manage the next day.

It would never fail, though: somebody would be at the door.

"You know, I was in my garden today and something told me to bring you some of my vegetables."

"You know I was cooking and thought let me bring you some of my soup."

My auntie, a friend, an acquaintance even, they all listened and obeyed that little voice. They have no idea how much they meant to me and my children and how much they taught me. And it was not just women. There were two male friends in the US, two of my poet friends whom I confided in. They immediately sent money or a care package, no questions asked. To be okay in that space of not knowing, of not panicking and be humble and knowing that spirit has your back was an incredible lesson.

The lesson was not limited to the daily struggle of survival, it extended into the research as well. In formal university education, you are trained to construct your questions and methods of inquiry and then are expected to execute as planned. Well, in real life, a lot of things go very differently than planned. People don't show up, different people show up, different topics get addressed, etc. etc. The challenge is to not panic and instantly feel like you have failed, but to dwell in that space of not knowing and trusting that whatever is being concocted is going to be okay and probably even better than what you had planned. It took work to learn that, physical work. I was not trained as an anthropologist to include my bodily senses as part of my personal radar system or guidance mechanism. Furthermore, as academics, we are expected to be these lone rangers, something that is also misleading. I learned the reality of an extended sense of self as my Surinamese culture had taught me and to trust that what I was connected to things seen and unseen.

In my dissertation I devoted a whole chapter to the idea of *spirituality*, not as a concept, but as part of the work we do and something worth paying attention to. I had a wonderful mentor who encouraged me in this. They told me that, indeed, I needed to include these insights because my spirituality was present all throughout my writing, but that if I were serious about this, I needed to place myself within the literature of spirituality in academia. Another member on my committee was not as open and understanding and asked me if I wasn't proselytizing. I searched for others in the literature who had addressed spirituality as part of their practice in academia and didn't find much of anything until I found that *one* piece. It is hard to describe how it feels when you see things so differently within academia and then you finally find someone else who feels the same way and confirms what you are feeling. The article by Islamic Shahjahan, who was born to Bengali parents in the United Kingdom, raised in Kuwait, and completed his dissertation in Canada, rocked me to my core. He held up a mirror to me and, in his words, I finally found the affirmation that how I walked my path was not as odd as academia made me feel I was. I will quote him here as I did in my dissertation.

> *As academics we need to be aware that spirituality is not a part-time thing but rather it is something that penetrates who we are. To have a spiritual way of knowing, we need to constantly work on ourselves to maintain our life in the spirit, during the process of knowledge production. But I raise this point to highlight the point that our spiritual worldview should permeate everything we do, which it does, but we forget and need to reclaim and remember that (2005: 698).*

Why do I mention it here again? I use indigenous knowledge as my go-to model for approaching the work that I do.

It is a marginalized knowledge field within academia but has claimed its space. Not many people know about this approach to knowledge in academia and I want to share it, as it might offer refuge to others who are seeking for a way to do storytelling within academia that resonates more with who they are. Inherently in this approach is a space of not knowing, which entails a sense of patience and humility not often found in academia. In addition, it facilitates embracing one's spirituality. Within academia, we are generally careful to keep that part hidden out of fear that it will be condemned, ridiculed, or otherwise be used to lessen our credibility. However, it is part of who we are and of how we bring all of ourselves to do the work we do. For those skeptical of all things spiritual, the space of not knowing can also be regarded as a perspective of being open to wonder, inspiration and curiosity. It is a state of humility that reminds us that we don't know everything there is to know, and probably never will.

I write this book from outside the academy, so there is a freedom here. Yet for those still inside the academy, I want to send the Morse code that your spirituality is not an anomaly. That your sense of wonder is not an anomaly. That you are not an anomaly. On the contrary, our indigenous approach to knowledge provides us with tools to access untapped resources that can help you do your work. What better way to show up fully, when all of yourself is present?

Gran tangi. Thank you for the concept of not knowing. May we be humble enough and brave enough to embrace that dark space as part of our daily and academic practice.

ABOUT COMMUNITY AND SUPPORT

Beginning — Ch. 8

As it became clear that my oldest child was going to go to college, I was starting to become concerned about my other two sons. They were extremely attached to their big brother. His leaving would be hard, especially for my second child. He was eight by now. His father and I had separated since he was three. He did have a good relationship with his father, but his father was not a constant, stable presence. That is not to talk ill of the man. Stability was just not something he could offer, but love was definitely there.

His big brother was there all the time however, and exuded stability, the stability he needed. Since he was born, my second son was very unsure of his place in the world. And since he was born, his big brother was there to hold his back. It was his brother who held my hand during the homebirth of my second son and never let go. It was big brother that, when my then husband said, "no thanks" and stepped out of the room at the opportunity to cut the umbilical cord, stepped forward and cut his brother's cord. He was the rock. Now the rock was leaving.

There was this one part of town where I would drive by, where a church stood, the Unitarian Universalist church. I kept being drawn there and spirit kept telling me to go there. In those days I was still questioning. I didn't have that listen and obey thing quite down yet, as Mama Walks on Water had tried to teach me. "Y'all want me to go to the white people, for real?" I had been there a few times with my dance group a number of years before. I knew they were very open minded, we had performed there, after all. It was still an all-white gathering, I was sure. So, I avoided and ignored the voice. But the voice would not let up.

One day, I looked at my altar and looked at the bottle the medicine man in Suriname had given me a number of years before. He had spoken to me about walking my path in the white man's world and he gave me that bottle of protection. I didn't really get it. I was born and raised in the Netherlands and had been either the only one or one of the few black children wherever I went in school or sports. In high school, it was the same and when I left for college in the U.S. not much different. That I was walking in a white man's world was nothing new. But I listened to the lesson, took the words of protection and kept that bottle. Sometimes you just store the lesson until you get it later. It was one of those incubation things.

So, spirit was telling me to go to the white people. Damn. That voice was so strong I could not avoid it anymore. And wouldn't you know? From the moment I walked in and had the first meeting with the female pastor, I had found the home and support my children needed. In this church, all faiths were welcomed and celebrated. Children did not have Sunday school but Religious Education where they learned about the different religions. When they become teenagers, the children come out to the congregation and can use art to do so. I have chosen to become a Christian. I have chosen to become a Muslim. I have chosen to become a Humanist. And then the congregation would embrace them and commit to support them whatever their paths may be. This was truly the only way I could do church. I ended up teaching a few of the Religious Education classes and even a few sermons. During Kwanzaa I had children dancing Lamba down the aisles. I enjoyed the fellowship. Most of the time I wasn't necessarily moved spiritually, feeling more like I was attending a college lecture rather than receiving spiritual nourishment. But, what I needed was the openness and the acceptance of all, so it was good. The unconditional kindness and the commitment to be of service resonated with the treatment I had received from my auntie.

My second son did have a hard time when his brother left. He felt lost and unsafe in the world. He was allowed special phone calls to his brother while at school, just to make it through the day. This church made a difference. They provided the support and community that we needed. When we moved to another state, I immediately sought out the Unitarian Universalist church again. I did not have much of a connection with this new church, although I met some wonderful people there. My youngest loved it, but mostly because there was potluck after almost every Sunday service. "Ma, I like that church with all the food."

This would be a theme throughout his young life. When he started in Catholic school he asked me: "Ma, how can I become a Catholic because they get to eat crackers during service." "Yeah, son, that is not how it works." But I digress.

Thus, I was in search of supportive community once again. My neighbor, who became a very dear friend, invited me to go to her church. "They do missionary work!", she told me enthusiastically. She did not know that I have the strongest allergic reaction at the mere mention of the "M" word. I do not get happy at the thought of white missionaries. I have seen what they have done firsthand in terms of destruction of people's cultural traditions in the name of Jesus. When you go into the interior of Suriname and you ask if they can share a traditional song they start singing about Jesus. They don't sing the traditional songs nor play the drums anymore. The deeper you go into the interior, the less chance that has happened, but where the white missionaries have settled the damage was surely done. And it is not just about losing singing or drumming; the associated disdain for one's own culture, and thereby oneself, is very painful to witness.

When you go to Africa you meet people who have come to hate their own traditions and their beautiful dark skin. Don't get me started on what missionaries have done to Native Americans. So, the word 'missionaries' fills me with much trepidation. But she was so kind and enthusiastic, and I liked and trusted her, so I went with her. Once again, spirit led me to a congregation full of white people – oh, wow. And this time it was not a church open to all faiths, but a Christian one. Hmmmm. But when the pastor started to speak, he spoke of love so deeply that it moved and touched me. I had found community, love and support in the Unitarian church. I had been enriched but was hardly ever moved. Here I was moved and not just by the words, but by the love that poured from this man's pores. He and his family practiced what they preached in their daily lives. From day one I have felt and seen the love-work that Zambia Nkrumah taught me about. Perhaps that is why these people resonated with me.

The pastor not only embraced me and my children, he allowed me to be me and to question freely. When I introduced myself to the congregation I spoke freely about my hesitation with "missionary" work and we spoke about that. I even joked about coming into a church where everybody..... wore jeans. "You all thought I was going to say something else." We could laugh about it and like the pastor these congregants exuded love, something I would encounter again when Ferguson erupted several years later 20 minutes away from us.

My children instantly found a home here. My youngest really connected with the church and especially the pastor and his family, even though they did not have potlucks every Sunday. I remember when he was about six or so and one morning I didn't feel like going, he flat out told me "That's okay ma, I know where it is, I can go there by myself." "Hold up, hold up I am coming!" The associate pastor and her husband, then our neighbors, became the uncle and aunt he adopted. These people have been there for me and both my children at the drop of a hat, no questions asked, consistently. Now that my youngest has moved back to the U.S. the pastor's family and the associate pastor and her family are his bedrock again. "It has nothing to do with race", my son told me. "They are white, but I have a connection with them. They are my family." In his wisdom, he reminds me of my mother who taught me how our paths are stronger when they are linked.

I do not write this piece to write some kumbaya story about racial harmony. I write this piece to talk about trusting that voice that provides guidance. Listen and obey, Mama Walks on Water would say. I hesitated because that voice sent me to the white people. I had to get past that and trust. Neither one of these communities expected me to act white or anything other than what I was. And together we explored racial differences when necessary. But their love showed the deep humanity that mattered and that we are more than the limitation of our ethnicities. As a 16-year-old black young man in the U.S. my child knows firsthand about racism. But he also knows about family, true family.

Gran tangi, church communities. Thank you for the lesson. May I pass on the lesson that community and support may come from unsuspected places and might not even look like you.

SEVEN
DIRECTIONS

Beginning — Ch. 9

One of the benefits of being a speaker is that you often are part of a lineup of great speakers and thus you get to learn a lot yourself. One night in 2020 at one of the art institutes in the Netherlands, I had the honor to listen to a professor who was in charge of the master's art education program at the institute. He shared a picture of an art class from the early 1900s probably. The picture was jarring. Like robots all the children in the crowded classroom were drawing the example of a leaf. Their hands were all at the exact same place. They must have moved in unison in accordance with the teacher, although you can only assume this because the teacher is not even in the picture. "You think this is horrible?", he said. "That was then, but they still teach art the exact same way today." He then shared how in Britain as of recent, newly arrived African children would have a different way of seeing the world, and thus had a different way of drawing. If they didn't draw exactly the way the teacher and the other children had done the drawing, their artwork would be ripped into pieces and thrown into the trash. Where is the room for creativity?

My mind went far beyond the question of creativity, however. What did it do to these children to have their artwork ripped up? How many times would their artwork have to be ripped before they learned the lesson that they had better adapt and adjust to *the dominant* norm in order to survive? How much of themselves did they have to sacrifice to belong? When I look at the picture, I see children copying a drawing of a leaf. Rather than taking the children outside in

nature and exposing them to leaves, they are cut off behind walls, learn to imitate abstractions and are denied a possible connection to the real world.

Children still learn about abstractions of the real world, rather than the world itself. One of the greatest fears teachers have is that children will bring the real world into the classroom. They are not that concerned about the beauty they might bring but fear the potential darkness from the outside that might filter in and settle into the classroom. *You know who you are and where you are when you can orient yourself according to the seven directions* the Native American teachings taught us. Within that wisdom is also the knowledge that you are the extension of the world. You are connected to everything and the extension of everything, including nature. What happens when we consistently cut young people off from their connection with the outside world and force them to deal with abstractions within the safety of artificial school walls? What happens when we only offer them controlled access to the beauty of the outside, but fail to help them cope or equip them to deal with the darkness? The Blues Aesthetic teaches us that we have to deal with all of it, the painful stuff as well as the good stuff, and that we have to be honest about it.

In 2014, when I worked at a university in the U.S. as an anthropology professor, I lived in a school district 20 minutes removed from Ferguson, Missouri. When unarmed Michael Brown was killed by the police and riots broke out, I was in its back yard and witnessed firsthand how intertwined our stories are. Everybody was affected by this story. Yet the superintendent of my school district, was the only superintendent who instructed all of the district's teachers not to discuss the Michael Brown incident with their children. A concerned parent called me and asked if I would organize something for students to discuss this and help them understand what was going on. I contacted the love church, which immediately offered to host the gathering. I also contacted several colleagues from work, one of whom was a psychologist, and all immediately agreed to participate. Together with a local lawyer, we hosted an event where children were the focus and adults if present could speak only with permission of the children. They discussed many things and had profound questions. One of the things that stood out was their confusion about the police. They were raised to think of police as a safe haven, yet they were inundated with images of police in combat military gear, with heavy artillery and tanks moving against citizens rather than protecting them. Their sense of safety had been profoundly shattered. It was our job to help them understand and deal with that new reality. I am glad we were able to do that for them, even if it was only for a small group. What happens when you are disconnected and cut off from the seven directions? What happens if you can't find your footing?

Since the release of various reports in 2018, there is heightened attention to mental health among students in the Netherlands, a sentiment echoed in other nations across the world. Depression and anxiety are normal. Suicidal ideation is common. There are a number of reasons why this is so, but what is clear is that our institutions are falling short in helping our students connect with the world around them in ways that can help them gain their footing. I see young people who are either bringing the world inside the classroom or who are forcing their teachers to deal with the stuff outside the classroom, something our teachers aren't always prepared to do. There is a hunger and need for a connection. There is a demand to bring the two worlds together and to become grounded within the seven directions.

As institutions, we often send conflicting messages to our constituents. We want our students to be global citizens. We want our employees well rounded and embedded and committed to our causes. Yet our structures and policies don't facilitate those notions. In the Netherlands, in one higher education institution – which according to their public relations messaging is dedicated to being an extension of and resource for the multicultural city in which it resides – the education students (and their concerned parents) frequently request not to be assigned to so called "black schools" (schools with high numbers of children of color generally from lower income communities) for their internships. And those requests are honored. Similarly, there are reports of minority staff experiencing verbal abuse, bullying or other exclusionary mechanisms by other staff or even students. Rather than taking steps to correct these types of occurrences and implementing new structures, these staff are generally offered individually oriented pacifying messages of consolation or encouragement. An attempt might be made to address the issue among colleagues, but actual steps towards lasting change are hardly ever taken. There is greater emphasis on following existing policies and thus hiding behind the wall of information, or preventing negative media attention, instead of correcting a destructive pattern. The violated staff who are aware of the superficial action will end up feeling lost and will soon start to think about going elsewhere.

Whereas anxiety and depression have become the norm for our students, so has "burn out" become the norm for the staff. Our stories are intertwined, my mother reminds me, and when our students or members of our staff feel lost it has an effect on everybody's stories and the overall climate. These stories of disenfranchisement do not remain unheard, regardless of silencing efforts, but instead become part of the lore. Worse still, they become a normalized part of the lore.

> "Oh, that's just how this place is."
> "Oh, yeah, that doesn't surprise me."
> "Well, you know where you are."

And so on. Failure to provide consistent footing can contribute to a disoriented and unhappy community.

I have always loved learning. As a child, I loved reading books and could get lost in them for hours. Figuring things out was like puzzling, and hence I loved math. I wasn't great at it, but good enough. Whereas I loved the opportunity for intellectual growth at school, my little brother predominately loved it for its social opportunities, always enjoying the path. I, however, didn't mind spending time figuring out assignments, spending hours at the library, or any academic pursuit. Yet, as much as I loved it, it didn't always love me, or so I felt. And at times it even disoriented me. I loved learning about other worlds, but my world was hardly ever encountered. One time it was, only to have it yanked away from me. I had started on my second Master's in anthropology while working as the coordinator of the Martin Luther King Jr. Cultural Center at the University of Kentucky. As an employee I had the option to take classes for free and I joyfully took advantage of that opportunity. I took a class here or there and loved it. After a year, the department offered me a scholarship to pursue my studies full time and I accepted. I gave up my position at the Cultural Center to return to school full time. Here I was back in school, still loving it – except this one class. Theory of Anthropology is mostly about old dead white men with Margaret Mead and Ruth Benedict sprinkled in. Anthropologists of color were nowhere to be found at all. There were some, it turned out, but they were not mentioned in this class or any other class for that matter. I was struggling, not because the material was hard, but because it was deadening my soul. I had a hard time making a connection and the seven directions eluded me.

At some point we started to read a book about young, teenage boys from a working-class community in England. We learned about how they behaved in school and their social circles, basically being predestined to work alongside their fathers and uncles on the shop floor. For some reason, I loved this book. I could relate to these young white men, more so than the old dead people. Even though they were portrayed in a rather negative light, I felt an affinity with their young lives being so strongly shaped by their communities and families' circumstances. I connected with the working-class culture of these European youths. Finally – something that linked to *my* life. I truly enjoyed the book, until I came to the last chapter. The author, who had been a member of that particular community and who had diligently given us access into their lives, turned around and chastised these young men for not trying harder and working their way up and out like he had. I was so disappointed. Once again, the story of *the other* was berated and diminished by *the dominant*, even a *dominant* who was a former *other*. What made it harder was that my fellow students and the professor did not see my point. Wasn't the author correct in his conclusion? Wasn't it a tragedy that they didn't try to work their way up and out? I felt alienated and truly wondered if I was going to be able to make it. The one time there was a story that linked to my life, it was degraded. And this story was about young white men. The few times stories of black women passed in review throughout my courses, they were always stories about suffering.

And then she came... Patricia Hill Collins. Patricia Hill Collins with her book *Black Feminist Thought* gave me affirmation that I had a right to exist in this academic arena. She highlighted that there were other ways of pursuing knowledge that were equally legitimate. She explained that in the black community when we seek knowledge we go to our elders, in particular our aunties and grandmothers. She talked about learning through exchange and assured me that it was okay to be passionate. In this world where you are supposedly meant to be objective and emotionally removed – while your story is being dismissed, silenced, or invisible – here was a woman who told me it was okay to have feelings about that. She also told me it was okay to celebrate the morsels of knowledge I could find that were part of my world and to share that passion. I am sure I could have struggled through my academic trajectory without her, but she contributed to my being able to do so with a strong sense of validation intact. She allowed me to be grounded and know and hold my own. I did not meet her until I was in graduate school, but she became my lifeline. I wrote her four main points on a notecard and carried it with me in my wallet as I went out and did field work in Suriname. If ever I had any doubts about who and where I was, I would pull it out and read it. She was my compass as she provided me with the seven directions. I was fine as I was, wherever I was at any given time. I wish a Patricia Hill Collins for every student that pursues their education.

If our organizations and institutions are not grounded and in alignment with what they claim they want to be and how they enforce those claims, they cannot offer solid ground and direction to their members and constituents. We are interconnected and to create artificial spaces that disconnect us from the extended world creates people who are cut off and do not function to the best of their abilities. How are we cut off from the world out there? How do we excuse structures and behaviors that interfere with people's sense of self and groundedness? How willing are we to provide clear directions to who we are as a community and not hide behind window dressing? How committed are we to create structures that hold people up instead of letting them fall through the cracks and disappear out of sight?

Gran tangi. Thank you for the lesson. May we learn to commit to people and, on their behalf, create institutions that honor the seven directions so our people may feel at home and confident and thus able to thrive.

MIDDLE

There is a Dutch children's song that
has the refrain

Hi Hi Hi, Ha Ha Ha,
'k stond erbij en ik keek ernaar.

He He He, Ha Ha Ha,
I stood by and I watched[1]

As I was attempting the inclusion work,
this refrain would often pop up in my
head, and not for nostalgia's sake.
There is an awareness now that things
are not as they should be.
There is shock, concern, and compassion,
yet somehow things continue as they are.
The issue is not with the outrageous,
obvious acts of trespassing, but with
the everyday normalized mechanisms
of exclusion and marginalization that
we not only tolerate but participate in,
knowingly or not.

Hi Hi Hi, Ha Ha Ha,
'k stond erbij en ik keek ernaar.

 1   Ik zag twee Beren - Loulou & Lou - kinderliedjes
www.youtube.com/watch?v=5PLVdLI5AgQ

TOKENISM
STEPPING STONE

Middle — Ch. 1

My son taught me about the *Women in Refrigerators* trope. In comic books the catalyst for a male superhero to step into his identity, is generally the injuring, murdering, maiming or depowering of a female close to him. Stricken by this horrific calamity the male superhero will then step into his true power.

He also taught me about the Rule of Three. In any given story, whether in comics, tv or film, if there are three or more black characters, the story will automatically be categorized as a black story.[2]

Especially in superhero stories, which are generally white male power fantasies, the underdog can be cheered for unless that underdog is of color. And again, there shouldn't be too many of them and any presence of three or more automatically presumes they want to get rid of white characters.

In 2017, students at the School for Oriental and African Studies in London demanded that the majority of philosophers should be African or Asian, and that European philosophers be presented from a critical perspective. Response was vehement and swift. Staff was outraged and poured their hearts out to the press. "Students want to remove philosophers because they are white! Ignorance, ridiculous, political correctness out of control", were some

 2   Dwayne McDuffie on the realities of the Black writer in comic books
www.youtube.com/watch?time_continue=131&v=u16sKK-10LQ

of the panic-stricken messages that were expressed in the media. Mind you, these were words from professors, people hired to inspire, nurture and instruct our young people. It is easy to get sucked into the injustice narrative and to get caught up in the distraction of questioning the students. What should be the focus here is the level of outrage and fear. Again, the request for the presence of *the other* is interpreted as a threat and removal of *the dominant*. The instant kneejerk reaction and vehement response is the mechanism that is automatic and generally not questioned.

The other can be present here, but they should know their place – namely down there – and they should not threaten the security of those in *the dominant* position. Time and time again that narrative is enforced by immediate outrage or some fear fueled response. And the leveling mechanism works. Those in *the dominant* position can react freely and those in *the other* position learn how to silence themselves. That has become our normal, and this is how diversity initiatives generally work. Companies are open to improve the visible lack of diversity. They welcome people with open arms. But there should not be too many and they should adapt and adjust to *the dominant* narrative 100%. *The dominant* might want to taste and consume what *the other* has to offer, but never too much, and never to the point of true absorption. In other words, the unequal relationship between *dominant* and *other* should remain unchallenged and unchanged. The addition of *others* should not necessarily mean equality in status and thus sacrificing one's power. And *the other* learns that in order to be present or to move up one needs to shed one's *otherness* and adapt to *the dominant* story. There might still be a limit as to how far one can rise, because there is only so much *otherness* one can shed, especially if the *otherness* is visible.

I myself have learned to silence myself and not challenge *the dominant and the other* dynamics directly. Well, for the most part. I am the great-granddaughter of Ma Po after all, and sometimes that machete comes out. I can't help it.

One time, as a new college professor, I was informed by my then-mentor that I did not receive a grant because of how I had submitted certain materials. My answer was machete swift and direct. I told her in no uncertain terms that I did not mind not getting the grant, but that I had followed their exact procedures according to the training I had received, and that I did not appreciate when people wasted my time. She paused, turned pale, and stuttered "Well... you know... you should be happy because people like you usually don't get positions like this." I just looked at her but didn't answer. The next day I was informed via somebody else that she would no longer serve as my mentor because I was difficult to talk to. Now, luckily, I did not mind. I moved on and got a different mentor but note the lesson here. I had dared to question and voice an opposition thereby stepping out of my quiet *other* position. The spirit of Ma Po would not allow me not to, and breaking the silence came at a price.

Similarly, in another college position I was expected to give an inaugural speech. When I questioned the practice, the standard answer I would receive was that I could make it into something nice. However, that did not answer my question. The message was, you received an answer, now remain quiet. I did not remain quiet, and when I questioned again one person in particular was so incensed that they raised their voice and yelled at me. These were the norms of the organization and they did not appreciate me questioning them! The anger was instant and intense. This person had conveniently forgotten that I had in fact been hired to help change the culture, and that questioning the norms was actually part of my job description. The fact that I might have a legitimate reason to ask the question was lost in the moment. I had stepped out of place and they were setting me straight.

Now, both of the people at the center of the anecdotes I've shared above are rather nice people. If either was confronted with their behavior as being racist, they would both object in horror. Whether their behavior needs to be labeled as racist is not the issue here. These examples are shown to demonstrate one of the mechanisms that maintains *the dominant and the other* divide, and how conditioned behaviors are part of this mechanism. When *the other* dares to step outside of that *other* position and challenges *the dominant* order, the reaction is swift and vehement and seems to go from zero to 10 in an instant, without thinking. The reaction is palpable. There can be bewilderment, shock, or outrage, or all three combined. But more interestingly, one can see an instant physical difference. The breathing changes resulting in gasping or the words just falling out, stuttering "Yes.. but...". The person becomes visibly unsettled, as seen in their facial expressions or body language. Their tone of voice changes.

I am sure some study could be done about the link to the flight or fight response in panic attacks. After all, this is about a reaction to a perceived threat, the threat of destabilizing the status quo. But that is not the goal here either. The goal is merely to become aware of this mechanism, and to learn how to detect it in the dynamics of our relations. As my mother taught me, our paths are inextricably linked. We need to understand some of the dynamics of those links. We all participate in those dynamics. *The dominant* have learned that it is acceptable to respond like that. *The other* has learned to avoid, be silent, or lash back equally. Now lashing back might be gratifying in the moment and seemingly a way to fight the inherent inequality of the situation. Yet, being in the position of *the other* also means less power, and thus there might be serious repercussions. When I spoke up, I was instantly labeled as difficult and lost a mentor within 24 hours. Let that sink in. It did not stop me, but it could have been a major career setback for a beginning professor.

Thus, before we can start looking at how to change things, we need to really understand how our relations are structured. We need to understand, without judgement, the power of conditioned mechanisms and how they shape and affect all of us.

Gran tangi. Thank you for the lesson. May we take a first tentative step on the path of understanding how the dance between *the dominant* and *the other* works.

FORTRESS OF INFORMATION

Middle — Ch. 2

When I used to teach anthropology there was a film that I would show every now and then. The name of the movie is *Turtles Can Fly*. It is a haunting, gripping, moving movie about Kurdish children in a refugee camp on the border between Iraq and Turkey after the fall of Saddam Hussein. I show this movie because in anthropology children are an often-overlooked population group. The movie shows the lives of children who collect artillery shells and detonated landmines to survive. Their lives are harsh, and the brutality of their existence is normalized, but I also show it because of the many layers of symbolism in the film. The main character is a boy called Satellite. He installs satellites and antennas in the village and functions as the mayor of the children, most of whom are orphans. He also speaks a little bit of English and thus is often requested to translate the news. Now, his translations are often (if not always) wrong, but it doesn't matter. He has made himself invaluable because he holds access to information.

One day, a boy and his sister join the camp. The boy is disabled because soldiers have shot his arms. But this boy has a special skill because he is psychic. He knows, for instance, where the live artilleries are, an invaluable skill for children who rummage through minefields and such. Instantly, then, he is a threat to Satellite. Hence, you see intuition pitted against reason and information. You see competition because Satellite is no longer the sole keeper of information. They who hold the access to information hold power. The movie has a lot more that I will not get into. I recommend seeing it, especially as it is about a marginalized population within a marginalized population. The reason I bring up the story is the similarity I see in *the dominant and the other* divide, and another particular mechanism that keeps the divide in place, namely that of information.

We live in a world where information is valuable currency. Many people carry a telephone that serves as a computer and grants people access to incredible amounts of information at any given time. In academia, especially, status is measured by mastery of information. Information holds power as it provides access to knowledge, and access to knowledge – the right knowledge – contributes to being included. One way the divide between *the dominant* and *the other* is maintained is through that ownership of knowledge. The ownership of knowledge sets *the dominant* apart from *the other*. Their approach to and cache of knowledge have become heralded as most valuable. In addition, they police who has access and to what extent people can partake of these information resources.

Let me draw on my background in medical anthropology to explore this idea further. In the early development of the United States, a variety of approaches to health care were in evidence. The many different groups present in U.S. society brought many different styles of attending to health, including African, Native American, manual-chiropractic, European homeopathic, eclectic, and allopathic (the precursor to biomedicine) care. Out of the variety of health treatments, biomedical medicine eventually rose to the top, incidentally along with and supported by the rise of capitalism. This rise to a dominant position was assured by the establishment of the American Medical Association (AMA) and other such associations. These associations regulated who was in and who was out. Black people, Jews, and women, for instance, were not allowed access. They were not allowed to attend the medical schools that were sanctioned by the AMA. Certain forms of medicine disappeared unless they were willing to conform to the medical model. The rise of biomedical knowledge did not happen by happenstance but was strategically organized and had more to do with power and control than purely health considerations. There are powerful mechanisms in place to steer and control the medical establishment and its knowledge base. But this control of knowledge is not limited to the medical field.

Access to knowledge, then, serves as currency for entrance, and as protection to keep those out who are not deemed worthy. They who are "in the know" belong to the in-group. Hence, taking the opportunity to gain knowledge, as in education, can mean the difference between staying in *the other* category or working one's way up to *the dominant* realm. Knowledge has become such a valuable currency, especially in education, that we tend not to question it. Now, there is questioning that can lead to shifts within *the dominant* norm, such as believing the earth was at the center of the universe until the invention of the telescope debunked that notion. But still, questioning is done and respected *within* the realm but not as easily *across* the divide. We have difficulty accepting that there may be as many different ways of doing knowledge as there are people. Knowledge produced by *the dominant* realm has become accepted as true, most trusted, or more valid than that from *the other*. Notice I have made a jump here from information to knowledge. It is easy to do. Having information translates to being "in the know". Although information and knowledge are not exactly the same thing.

Information is tricky to define, as it refers to content, stimuli, stuff even, that when combined gives one insight into things. Yet knowledge assumes an understanding. One can be informed and have ample information but have no understanding of what the information means. Thus "being in the know", which means that one has gained certain information, does not necessarily mean that one is knowledgeable. At its worst, knowledge or purported knowledge might be totally unsound, but because of its ampleness in size or who has the power to control it, it can be used to do damage.

In the 17th century there was the belief in New England that women had a propensity to be witches and hence were a threat to the community. After expedited and forced testimonies, women accused of witchcraft were thrown into the water. It was reasoned that if they were not witches they would drown, if they were they would float, after which they were burnt at the stake. This was evidence-based knowledge 17th century style. Based on biblical and mystically informed precepts, this knowledge base was accepted, sadly at the expense of many unfortunate women. All the checks and balances normally in place were removed and people were allowed to hide behind information and knowledge that went unquestioned. Actually, there are reports that people did have doubts about the knowledge this movement was based on, but things rapidly went haywire and there was no room to fight those in power. Those in power used knowledge as a tool to control. Reflection shows that these trials were the result of an attempt at religious control and the subjugation of independent women within the context of a politically unstable situation. It was not until those in power's own wives were starting to be accused that they were willing to question the knowledge and the practice came to a stop.

In addition to using knowledge as a power base, we see knowledge used in two particular ways in *the dominant* versus *the other* paradigm. First, as a mountain of information behind which one can hide. Secondly, as a mountain of evidence to excuse not engaging with the story of the other. Like a good barrier, it divides the space and always keeps the other at bay. Like a fortress, the amount of knowledge provides comfort and security. And like a moat around that fortress, one is protected from having to reach beyond the divide.

Having to navigate my three black sons through various educational systems in both the Netherlands as well as the U.S. has given me ample experience with the fortress of information construct. I would rank the Dutch system as a little worse, as it blatantly and notoriously steers children of non-Western immigrant backgrounds into lower levels of education in comparison to their Dutch heritage counterparts. Although people are aware of this inequity, parents are regularly and easily offered explanations that are based on policy and information as to why their children are better off in a lower education track. However, the United States has its own means of alienation.

When my second son went from elementary school to middle school, he went from a school with a maximum of 300 children to a school with 1500 students. For a child with attention issues and a hyper-sensitivity to stimuli, this was a nightmare in the making. Coming from an elementary school where teachers and administrators had been sensitive and willing to work with his particular needs, he now basically entered an industrial complex.

Having to navigate his way through crowded hallways to different classrooms proved to be a torturous exercise and we received a note after three days that he needed to go to detention for arriving late in class. I was understanding of the fact that such a big school needed regulations to keep things running smoothly. However, I also knew that for a sensitive 12-year-old who already felt he did not belong, being punished for not being able to keep up after only three days would only make matters worse. I went to bat for my child and initially ran into the wall of procedural information. The "Yes, we hear you, but..." response was encountered time and time again. Policy mattered, even when it was obvious that for a child with these particular needs the outcome would not be worth it. "If only he would stick to and learn about the rules, he would eventually catch on", they assured me. After all, that is what the rules were for. Suffice it to say, I persevered and won that battle, but not because they ever saw my son as a person, but more because of my relentless stance, I will be honest. Ma Po's spirit was with me that day.

I encountered experienced educators, people familiar with children, who easily hid behind procedures and did not bother to look beyond and connect with my child as a person. I tried to work with that particular system, but it would not budge. The fortress held strong. My son's head would hang lower and lower every day, and after repeated utterances of "I am never going to make it there anyway", I decided to remove him. But this story did not end badly. I arranged for him to attend a small Catholic school where from day one they saw my child and totally enveloped him with love and support. They utilized their policies to provide the best care. Like the spirit of my auntie, they offered nothing but unconditional support. They saved him and they saved me. The fortress is not an inevitability, it is a choice.

The fortress of information also gives the false impression that there is nothing behind the obstruction, while in fact there might be a valid story there, worthy of engagement. The fortress of information, then, obstructs the flow of communication that could reveal the common story. I have seen this phenomenon in higher education's student activism, where students and administration end up squaring off against each other, while in fact they are participating in the same story. Unaware of this fact because of faulty, mis- or incomplete information, they stand yelling at each other, one group inside the fortress, one outside of the fortress. They yell within the comfort of their limited perspectives and self-righteous insulation, while all they really have to do is lower the drawbridge to see that they are, in fact, engaging in the same story.

At one of the universities where I worked there were hardly any trash containers that separated the trash based on recyclability. Students concerned about the environment addressed this issue with the administration. They received an answer that the matter was being looked into. It turns out that in the past there had been recyclable containers but that they were not used diligently enough. The administration then decided to work with a contractor who would separate out the trash after collecting it to assure that the trash would be separated. This arrangement was not only more efficient, but also proved to be more cost-effective. Seen as a purely administrative decision, this information had not been made public. As a result, the students were seen as intrusive and bothersome, while the administration was seen as not caring or willing to work on this issue. Neither was the case.

Similarly, at another university students were adamant about making the building fully handicap accessible for their fellow students, which it was not. They engaged in several campaigns to make campus members aware of this issue. They found it extremely hard to gain traction and see change and thus became disillusioned. A conversation with the administration revealed that indeed change had been taking place, but because the building was listed as a heritage monument, the bureaucracy was complicated, but it was being worked on. The students saw the administration as being resistant and unwilling to change, while the students were seen as unnecessarily radical and unconciliatory. Neither was the case.

The thickness of the wall makes it hard to hear, let alone listen to the story of the other party. As our voices bounce off the interfering wall, we become more and more convinced of our being right, all the while ignoring that we are dealing with an insufficient information base. We don't see the other. We don't deal with the other. All we deal with is our information wall. It provides a sense of security and comfort because it confirms what we think we know, and it allows us to not have to go beyond and make an effort to connect with the other. Reaching beyond that fortress is not an option however, not if we want to impact change. It is a must.

What makes the fortress so effective is that we have a built-in reward system for those who collect and display their wealth of information. It provides status. It overshadows the fact that it lowers the ability to see and connect with the person across. It almost justifies it. The right amount or right combination of information can be transformed into standards by which we can condemn and dismiss others. "If we allow their story in, what will happen to the quality?". In the end it is all about the choice, about how much value we place in information and how much value we place in the relationships we have with each other. That fortress of information has become such a normal and valued part of our culture that it pops up regularly in any kind of situation at any time without us even thinking about it. Like a whack-a-mole game it will take considerable effort to make a dent in its practice.

Gran tangi. Thank you for giving us the lesson that thát what seems so valuable can in fact be our greatest obstacle.

POWER LANGUAGE

Middle — Ch. 3

"We introduce our students into urban education," the document read. "So that they can learn about poverty, delays, and criminality." I stopped reading and went back to the beginning of the sentence. "We introduce our students into urban education." This was code for... we introduce our students into education for brown and or poor children. And when we think about brown and or poor children, we think about.... poverty, delays, and crime. I sighed, grabbed a highlighter and highlighted the sentence. Then I closed the booklet. I had lost all interest in reading further. A few minutes earlier, an administrator from the education department had enthusiastically handed me the booklet, stating that this was what they were going to share with the evaluation council that was going to stop by. I was going to have to talk to her about this, but not today.

Language is very powerful. I had the joy of being able to study linguistics after I started working as an anthropology professor. As a professor, I was allowed to take classes for free and committed myself to pursuing a certificate in Teaching English as a Second Language. I had worked with a wonderful ESL teacher during my post-doc position and was going to Ghana regularly where I worked with teachers. Colleagues who had followed the program raved about how good it was and that it made them better teachers in general. I was excited about being in class again after so many years and learning something new. I was also nervous. Here I was as a professor among students. I still had a full teaching load. Could I do well, despite my regular workload? How would my fellow students look at me if I didn't do well?

It was indeed hard work, but I learned so much that I am glad I made the sacrifice. I learned about the power of language, from syntax and grammar to sociolinguistics. About how you can structure language just to get your message across most efficiently. Or how language speaks to us on so many levels, from the direct meaning to the intonation, to the symbolism, to who speaks when and where, and under what conditions, and so on. It has been very helpful in this pursuit to hold space, because language is a major player in *the dominant and the other* divide.

We learn language by picking up what we hear, by what is said to us. We are inundated with language constantly. In anthropology, we are taught that language is the main conditioned aspect of culture. That means that through listening, engaging and modeling you all of a sudden know it, are in it. When I arrived in Kentucky with my schoolbook English, I was not prepared for the sing-songy dialect of rural Kentucky. My college was a college specifically created for poor Appalachian people. The early students in the 1800s literally paid for their education with eggs and chickens and whatever they could bring. Everybody at this college worked to cover their tuition, room and board.

My labor assignment was in the kitchen where I worked with quite a few local employees from the mountains. I don't know how many times I would stare at them and ask them to repeat what they said. And it wasn't just how they pronounced things; it was also the expressions they used. It all sounded like a beautiful cacophony in my ears, but I didn't understand a word. And then one day I just did. Similarly, the majority of black students came from Birmingham, Alabama. The southern black vernacular and drawl sounded uniquely beautiful but often unintelligible, as well – until

144

one day I could understand it. To this day, the moment I hear a southern drawl, I get a warm feeling of familiarity. Because language can take you there. Language creates atmosphere. Language does more than just communicate words, it communicates place, belonging, or exclusion.

Gloria Wekker has laid out how in the Netherlands language affiliated with government policies has influenced educational policies and has trickled down to the classroom. Immigration policies from the 1980s that stressed integration and assimilation contributed to a language linking immigrants to deficit, delay, and failure to adapt. This language has become normalized and continues to this day to shape the attitudes towards those in *the other* position within education. Children with immigrant heritage background are more likely to receive lower high school advice than their original Dutch heritage counterparts with similar grades. The standard explanatory language stating they received lower advice "just to be sure" is not questioned and in fact ensures that they stay 'down there,' and are systematically delegated into the position of *the other*. Countless are the stories of young people who have been told that their academic struggles must be because they are Moroccan, Turkish, Surinamese, Caribbean or other. "It was never about my test taking anxiety, always about me being Turkish", one student lamented.

Language shaped in the halls of academia is accepted and not questioned, representing *the dominant* and affirming the lower status of *the other*. Terms such as superdiversity, micro-aggression, or evidence-based, easily become infused in diversity and inclusion discourse. Closer observation shows that there is nothing super about superdiversity, nothing micro about micro-aggressions, and evidence-based means validated according to norms determined by *the dominant* party. Similarly, words such as *decolonization* and *woke* are thrown into the arena as badges of honor for those defending the cause of *the other*, without questioning the true depth and meaning of these words. Ironically then, these badges can contribute to one's own dominant status by marginalizing those deemed not *decolonized* or *woke* enough.

Language can be wonderfully excluding by creating enclaves for those speaking in elite or academic styles, subtly but easily ascribing *other* status to those with accents, whether regional or international, and especially those using street vernacular. Most powerfully, language can serve as a mechanism of enforcing *the dominant* and *the other* divide, while offering a distraction at the same time. My linguistics class taught me that words have power because we ascribe power to them. The words by themselves are totally arbitrary. We call something a table because we all agreed to call it that, but the word itself could be anything. Similarly, you can take a word, any word, but because it is used in a certain context and we all agree that that means something, that word then becomes loaded. Curse words, which we agree on as emotionally loaded, are perfect vehicles to affirm the lesser status of *the other*.

A number of years ago I spoke with Jerry Afriyie, one of the well-known anti-Zwarte Piet activists in the Netherlands. Zwarte Piet is a controversial character. He is a person, and part of a holiday tradition with a role of servant to the Dutch Saint Nicholas. Since 1850 white Dutch people have celebrated this particular character by donning black face. Activists have been fighting this character as they see it as a racist image. Anti-Zwarte Piet activism goes as far back as the late 1920s but Jerry's brutal beating by the police while participating in a peaceful protest in 2014 stirred something in the media and social media to give the movement impetus. He shared with me how his child had come home crying from school one day because they were teased and bullied at school over Zwarte Piet. "As a parent I just had to do something," he told me. I thought about that and my first thought was: "Yeah, we didn't come home crying in our days." But then I thought about it some more.

I did come home crying, quite a bit actually. I grew up in Amsterdam South, a very white community, especially during the 1970s. I didn't play outside that much when I was little. Girls just wanted to play house or school and just wanted to boss you around, which I thought was incredibly stupid. And boys, well, unless you could play soccer, you didn't play with them too much. So, I would play mostly in the playground on the equipment or engaged in some other type of physical activity. At times, I would come home crying because children called me names. My father sent me back out there with a simple "Kick him in the shin" message. My mother decided to put me in judo. There I went at age five, learning to "man up". This was the 1970s. Our parents did not have time to protest. They were busy surviving, best as they could.

I shared Jerry's account with my older cousin. Working at the same university, we enjoyed sharing lunch together. "Remember those children in the playground?", she retorted. Growing up my brother and I would relish visiting our cousins in Apeldoorn, a very white town which seemed on the other end of the world. We would look forward to the trip for days. Our parents would pack as if we were going on a month-long journey, while we would generally just go for the weekend. The drive seemed to last forever, but only lasted an hour I found out in my older age. We had special Apeldoorn music for in the car, Toots and the Mytals, Mighty Sparrow, Bob Marley and other Caribbean greats.

Going to visit my uncle and aunt and their seven children was for sure the highlight of our youth. It was like visiting the Waltons. We slept on air matrasses, ate Apeldoorn chips and other foods, lots of food. I later found out that they actually sold the same chips in the stores in Amsterdam, but for some reason my mother never bought that brand, so Apeldoorn chips it will remain till the day I die. Their back yard had a little path that led to a big communal playground where you could swing on the swings very high and play on all types of equipment. This was like paradise to us. We would play outside until we were called in to come home. I adored my cousins, still do, and at night, like the Waltons, you would hear all kinds of noise from the various rooms. I have nothing but good memories about those days, until she brought up those kids. Oh yeah, those kids.

"Do you remember those kids who would always curse us in the playground? Darkie, nigger, sambo, black moor, Zwarte Piet,.... They would be relentless and make our lives hell. Sometimes it wasn't just name calling but they added throwing rocks or other such behavior. We couldn't go home with that. Our parents didn't have time to deal with that. So, we handled it. We would beat the crap out of them. Then it would be quiet for a while. After a while they would start up again until it was time for the next beating."

Oh yeah, I remembered. Interesting that I had forgotten about all that. My cousin and I laughed, kinda, even though it was not a laughing matter. It is insane the things we come to accept as normal.

Recently, my youngest son dealt with an incident at his high school in the U.S., where somebody wrote on a car in the parking lot "We hate Niggers". It was out in the open for anyone to see. This was followed by a threat on social media to all the black children in the school. It made the news.

Typical for most schools, leadership assured the public that there was zero tolerance on the use of the "N" word and that everything was under control. Similarly, uttering "Zwarte Piet" also has become controversial. My linguistics teachings taught me that the words themselves are actually innocuous. The words "nigger" or "Zwarte Piet" are arbitrary symbols. The words themselves do not hurt or do anything. It is what the words stand for that is hurtful. The word nigger in the United States is affiliated with slavery practices, lynching, persecution and the overall ability to communicate the power to terrorize and even kill somebody. Prohibiting the utterance of the word nigger does not address the message that black children can be terrorized and should fear for their safety.

Similarly, Zwarte Piet is not only linked to the character of a Moorish servant, but additionally has served as a derogatory character of a black person in a predominately white country with a specific colonial history, and where black people have consistently been relegated to the marginalized place of *the other*. In addition, it has contributed to an atmosphere where children are emboldened to terrorize their black peers and remind them of their lower status.

Focusing on the words and the immediate emotional experience affiliated with these words distracts from the real issue, namely the untouched and continued divide between *the dominant* and *the other*. Furthermore, the words have become so emotionally laden that people are afraid to utilize them, a mere slip of the tongue can lead to condemnation or the loss of a job. But while we are upset about the use of the word, we fail to get to the needed discussion of how to dismantle the unequal divide between *the dominant* and *the other*. Heed the power of language as a dividing mechanism.

Gran tangi. Thank you for the lesson. May we be wise and alert enough not to get distracted by the power of language, but to use it as an effective tool.

"GEZELLIGHEID"

Middle — Ch. 4

All people have cultural norms for making others feel like they belong or not. In anthropology we study what those rules are. What are the boundaries? The best informative lessons do not come from studying from what happens inside the circle, but from what happens at the boundaries. What happens with those who break the rules? The risk of being cast out of the group can be so great that people focus on and adapt to the behaviors that assure that one can be part of the group. After a while these behaviors become norms and nobody questions them. People just do them, and those who are new to the group are expected to pick up on those behaviors and adapt accordingly.

I was born and raised in the Netherlands and am well aware of the Dutch cultural concept of *gezelligheid*. Dutch people are known for valuing down to earth earnestness, but *gezelligheid* adds something to that. *Gezelligheid,* the noun or *gezellig*, the adjective, is hard to translate in other languages. *Gezelligheid* is a certain kind of comfort level and could be compared to a sense of coziness. However, it has strong social and or environmental connotations. *Gezelligheid* is not really referred to for a person who is by themselves. It requires social interaction, but also social commitment to contribute to a common sense of pleasantness. In a group activity as innocuous as people drinking coffee, the one person who chooses not to drink coffee, or worse not to drink at all can cause one to be chastised for not being *gezellig*. At the same time, a location can be deemed *gezellig* because of the ambiance or the people who are present.

You learn about *gezelligheid* through enculturation in Dutch norms. After you live in the Netherlands long enough you know what is *gezellig* and what is not. It is such a common cultural aspect that people don't question its value and practice. *Gezelligheid* has become a Dutch norm and a powerful tool to get people to conform to who is in versus who is out. *Gezelligheid* is powerful because it promotes social buy-in, but also – and perhaps especially – because it promotes a sense of feeling good. Certain parts of the Netherland are particularly known for embracing *gezelligheid* as part of the local culture. I have not found an official theory for why this is so, but I have my own musings on the phenomenon. I was born and raised in Amsterdam South, a borough of Amsterdam known for middle and upper-class housing. However, there were some working-class pockets too, including the street where I grew up. I went to school and lived in close proximity to the Dutch elite, however, and learned that they were really not that different from my working-class family and friends. Yet, their lifestyles were significantly different. In my experience, people in upper-class communities were polite, but they tended to keep to themselves. They could afford the space and the boundaries to do so.

For lower income and working-class communities there is a different code, however. They cannot afford to have distance from each other, especially in the Netherlands where space is a valuable commodity. *We are in this together* is the undercurrent because that is the working-class reality. As a teen, I spent a lot of time in the Jordaan, a borough in the center of Amsterdam, then still predominately a working-class neighborhood. Now it is a gentrified area and most of the original Jordaan residents have left, but when I was a teen they were still there. This community was proud and loud about its working-class history. The organization in the Jordaan that I was a member of – a youth circus – displayed black and white photos of its past and people did not hesitate to tell you how it used to be. It is also a community known for its cafés and accompanying singing culture. Some of the best Dutch life-song singers had their roots in the Jordaan. I truly learned about Dutch *gezelligheid* while spending time in this community. *Gezelligheid* was not just about feeling good together, but especially about participation. The social control was strong, and as a teenager I learned that if I wanted to belong, I had better be *gezellig*.

Another part of the country in the Netherlands that is known for its *gezelligheid* is the southern part of the country. Carnaval, a traditional Catholic celebration, is a serious part of the culture. At one time it is said that one could draw a horizontal line through the Netherlands and the southern part would be Catholic and the northern part Dutch Reformed. The national school calendar is adjusted to accommodate the Carnaval celebration. One time I was invited to give an inspirational keynote in the South at a university of applied sciences to a mixed group of Dutch students and invited international students. It came as a surprise and a reminder that I was in the South when, as a welcoming activity, the Dutch students jumped up, dragged their international guests in a line, put their hands on each other's shoulders and started singing and dancing in a line. Instant laughter was all around, and people were not allowed to sit and watch. Of course, you wanted to join in: *gezellig!*

There is nothing wrong with *gezelligheid*, especially when it can stimulate a comfortable atmosphere of bonding and fun, like with those students. However, it has become an entrenched part of the Dutch psyche and has become so prominent and normalized that it often functions as a levelling mechanism, serving as an incentive to curb one's behavior. "I had better not do that or say that, or people might think I am not *gezellig*." Alternatively, one might use it to bring others in line: "How dare you say that or do that. That is not *gezellig*."

The concept of *gezellig* has contributed to an entitlement

and fragility that, although forceful, is totally unwarranted. It has given the false message that one has the right to have it *gezellig* at all times, and that when not, there must be something wrong. This has been especially detrimental for those in *the dominant* realm.

Being in *the dominant* realm inherently implies a certain level of privilege. One's story is always upheld as valid, is told first and the loudest. It is a comfortable position, and given that it is a socially sanctioned position, it is a *gezellig* position. Because the message has been cultivated that this position and its accompanying *gezelligheid* are normal, it gives the false message that this is how it ought to be. Confronting the realization that the experienced *gezelligheid* is, foremost, a gifted privilege, rather than a right, can be quite painful and difficult to swallow.

Gezelligheid can be an innocuous state of slight discomfort, but it can be such a powerful force that it paralyzes everyone in the room and severely disrupt relationships. I have experienced more than once situations where I chose to speak up about something that didn't fit or wasn't right. As a result, all those present withdrew into silence. Not only were they silent, they averted their eyes, and only later would come to me and almost in a whisper share their support or concern, long after the incident had passed.

One such incident was when I was in graduate school for my Master's in Clinical Psychology. I had to take an elective and since I had had a double major in psychology and physical education as an undergraduate, I decided to take a physical education course. I decided on sports marketing. At the time I had a teacher's assistant position as an assistant swim coach. The coach called me over. "Don't you know who this man is teaching the class? He hates blacks and he hates women. Don't take the class." I didn't even think about it for a split second. Of course I was going to take the class. After all, if I am a good student it should not matter what I look like. I will just deliver excellent work and it will not make a difference. Well, I cannot say that I wasn't warned.

The man was as stereotypical *ol' boy Kentucky* as ever was possible. Think big white stereotype of the old South, gentleman like, but very set in his ways. This was his last class teaching before he was to retire. He started every class reminiscing about American football from the 1940s and 1950s and complaining about how Title IX had messed things up. I knew I was in trouble. Don't say I wasn't warned. I just focused on doing my best and tried to ignore the rest. One day he came to class carrying a box with yellow stained papers. He started handing them out. *101 Ideas for fundraising.* As I received my paper and started reading my eyes stopped at nr. 73... *Slave auction.*

"Slave auction?!" I said out loud as the teacher was still walking through the class handing out papers. I said it not angrily, but with an incredulous "Are you kidding me?" tone in my voice. "How old is this piece of paper anyway?", I continued. I looked up and around, for sure expecting my fellow students to be as shocked by this as I was, but it seemed as if time stood still, as if the air was sucked out of the room. The room was dead silent, and everybody stared intently at their paper. I know because I did a 360 looking around the room expecting somebody to make eye contact with me and join me in this questioning.

"Aahh, don't make a big deal out of it. It just means that you rent somebody out for the day. Don't be so sensitive." And he continued handing out his papers. I was quiet for the rest of the lesson. So were my fellow classmates. When we left the class, most people didn't look at me and seemed to walk away from me a little faster than usual. A few came up to me and sheepishly whispered that they thought that what had happened was awful. That whispering thing again. I wasn't mad at my teacher. I knew what he was about. I had been warned after all. I was deeply disappointed in my fellow students, however, and something shifted in the way I looked at them and how I related to them. If before I had feelings of being part of the group, that illusion was totally shattered.

Whereas an initial fleeting thought crossed my mind that, apparently, they must agree that slave auctions were appropriate activities, I changed that into theorizing that by my speaking out, I had made the situation quite *ongezellig* in that moment. It was a confrontation that they wanted no part of. Actually, there was no confrontation, it was just an honest question. I was really incredulous that somebody would propose a slave auction post-1950 something. I was also incredulous that I was the only one who found this odd. I wasn't, as their whispering showed me, they just chose not to speak out. So, instead, I came to the conclusion that they were just weak, punks, and useless to me. Did I mention that I was the only black person in the class? Should it matter? If I had not been there and there were only white people, would anybody have objected to a slave auction as a fundraising activity? I would like to think so. That is not the point of this musing, however.

The point is that *gezelligheid* is such a powerful concept that it can paralyze people from stepping up, speaking up or taking a stand. We freeze because the feeling of *ongezelligheid* signals that something is wrong. That is indeed true. But somehow people have also received the message that they ought not feel *ongezellig* and hence they withdraw and fail to engage. In the fight to overcome *the dominant and the other* divide, this is a major stumbling block. Ironically, many academics have wanted to focus on supporting *the other* in their development of resilience, so that they can become better equipped at dealing with the inequities that affect their lives. It would be far more effective to help *the dominant* group face their fragility when it comes to *gezelligheid*. For instance, directness is another element of Dutch culture on which they pride themselves. Dutch people are quick to tell you that they like being direct. However, that directness is mostly from a sending perspective. Receiving directness is quickly experienced as *ongezellig* and elicits all kinds of fragility related responses. Again, this is especially challenging for those in *the dominant* group.

Rather than allowing *ongezelligheid* to serve as an excuse to disengage, we can do two things. First, we can acknowledge that *ongezelligheid* is an unavoidable factor of Holding Space and, instead of trying to avoid it, we can recognize that it has to be traversed. This is an essential message of the Blues Aesthetic. The blues is not just about suffering, but about the message that one has to go through the painful stuff in order to resurface better at the end. Not only does one have to go through it, one has to be brutally honest about it and face it. Rather than suppressing or dismissing feelings of discomfort, from a Blues Aesthetic perspective, one makes room for the lament. On the other side of pain is always goodness and vice versa. There is a balance. We cannot go through life by avoiding the uncomfortable parts, the *ongezelligheid*. The lesson of balance that my brother has always demonstrated to me, holds stock here too.

Secondly, if one accepts that *ongezelligheid* is an inevitability, one can make the choice to utilize it purposefully and strategically. As a diversity policy worker in the Netherlands, I attended a national diversity officer's meeting. My partner and I were the only temporarily employed staff there among the officers of the various universities. As such, we did not have any decision making power, and I wondered why we were there. We were also the only two people of color there. Well, there was a third person who was an immigrant and non-Dutch but made it known that they did not want to be regarded as a person of color and was against any kind of ethnic labeling. An interesting take for a diversity officer, but I was just there to listen. As the conversation progressed, I was not impressed. People talked about their respective policies which were scant, non-existent or addressed gender only, meaning the presence or absence of white women. My belly started to burn the more I listened, my ancestors' way of signaling to me that I would have to speak up. I knew they were right. I also knew that it would be an *ongezellig* moment for sure if I did.

I looked at the time and decided to speak at exactly 10 minutes before the meeting was about to end. I listened and started to get ready for what I was going to say. I just focused on the main message I wanted to pass on. It was not my goal to slam them or to hurt them, but they needed to be aware. Mama Walks on Water had instructed me on how to come from a loving place but to use my voice unapologetically to make a difference. This was one of those moments. Tapping into the compassion demonstrated by my auntie I opened up at exactly 10 minutes before the end stating: "Before we go, there is something I need to share." I didn't talk too long, just stated what needed to be said. I started by saying how painful it was to sit there and listen to them. I told them in no uncertain terms that when they talked about gender they were talking about women and not women who looked like me. I also told them that they would need to think about that when they went back to their respective campuses and needed to figure out a way to address that. It was eerily quiet after I finished talking, and then it was time to go. Sometimes you need to take the opportunity, and in this case use a moment of *ongezelligheid* to create a crack to make a statement.

All and all, our understanding of *gezelligheid* is that a cultural construct that is so focused on feeling good, can be at the same time a force to help maintain *the dominant and other* divide. *Gezelligheid* is here to stay, however, and therefore its opposite, *ongezelligheid* will continue to work as a restricting force, if we let it. We have to learn how to work with it, go through it, or learn from it, but never ignore it.

Gran tangi. Thank you for the Dutch lesson of *gezelligheid* and our ability to navigate and transform spaces of disempowerment into empowerment.

INSIDIOUS DOMESTICITY

Middle — Ch. 5

When we were young in the times of rotary phones, when we still just watched tv between prescribed hours, sometimes the phone would ring. Often in the middle of a movie or some other special event. On the other side of the line, an eager auntie or uncle. Did you all see? Turn on the tv! Having a limited choice of channels, we would quickly find the treasure they wanted us to find. There was one of us in a Hollywood movie. There we were! More than likely as a chauffeur or some domestic worker, grinning from ear to ear, making white people happy. We didn't mind, we didn't care, we were there, right on the screen! And if we were lucky, they would do a song and dance number too! Forget the fact that we never saw our people that happy and subservient in real life, but we were there on tv. We were there in a way palatable, enjoyable and consumable to *the dominant* party. Sweet loving darkies, created to make their lives better.

We didn't care, I tell you. We were too happy to understand the dynamics that were playing out here, not only in the film but in the larger discourse as well. *The dominant and the other* were in full effect. We could be seen, but only in a way palatable to *the dominant* narrative. Now, there were exceptions. Sidney Poitier, Harry Belafonte, Lena Horne, Dorothy Dandridge were exceptions to the rule. We saw them too, but not as frequently. And remember, if there were more than three than it would be a black project, so *the dominant* party is probably only aware of Sidney Poitier in this line up, who was allowed to hold his own in white films.

Another major exception, especially in my house, was the Greatest of All Times, Muhammad Ali. When he would fight, and boldly claim his space not only in physical strength but in words, for a very short time he offered *the other* a view from above, even if it was for the duration of 12 rounds. Whenever an Ali fight had taken place, the next day one or more uncles would come by the house to reflect on the match. They would walk into the living room, turn left, address my dad and go... "Ey kitto fa! Did you see?!" Of course he had, and off they went, discussing every move, every action, every punch and counterpunch in great detail. They revisited the story of the night before, dove in, tasted, re-tasted, savored every morsel, and for that time soared along with Ali.

And thus, the image of the subservient domestic was not constant, but it was a story that was and continues to be deeply embedded in the narrative of *the dominant and the other*. Not only is *the other* palatable in the role of the domestic, it is a desirable role. Quietly as it is kept, there are those among *the other* who have embraced their positionality of domesticity. And here lies lesson number one, *the other* is not a homogenous group, just like their dominant counterpart is not. Within the group classified as *other* there is a range of ways that people have accepted, embraced, survived, rejected, or simply chosen to live with that positionality. Thus, there are those who have embraced their positionality of domesticity fully. Regarded with suspicion, wonder, rebuke or disdain, they are not always understood.

Aware or sometimes unaware, through careful conditioning this particular *other* holds up *the dominant* and serves to protect them from their presumed fragility. And here comes lesson number two: this positionality of domesticity is not to be confused with the position of a domestic. A domestic is a person who is paid to serve in a particular role, and who is often knowledgeable of all matters of the house. Their subservience is a role if not a mask. These others seem to go out of their way to silence themselves, bend, twist and contort themselves to please *the dominant*, or at least not to make them uncomfortable, make it *gezellig*. They smile and excuse the trespasses, the insensitivities that are hurled their way. There is the chance that if one performs well one might gain access, or at least feel like they belong up there, up in the realm of *the dominant*, if even for a moment. But the slightest trespass can send one soaring down.

Dedicated to their position and their relationship with *the dominant*, they become excellent gatekeepers. They are the ones who call their brothers and sisters to order, who reinforce that people toe the line. There is an urgency and necessity to their work. They understand what it takes to gain entry to *the dominant* realm and are very serious about protecting that entrance.

I had my encounter with somebody who embodied domesticity while I had my post-doc position. I had received a Lyman T. Johnson post-graduate fellowship. It was a great honor to receive a scholarship in his name. Lyman T. Johnson is the person who integrated the University of Kentucky in 1949. I even had an opportunity to meet him in person at one time. He was a legend not only for the institutional racism he battled, but also for the racism he endured while doing so.

So, for two years I had an opportunity to do some good work at the University of Kentucky in Mr. Johnson's name and I enjoyed every minute of it. One time I was invited to a women's meeting. I don't recall the purpose of the meeting. There were about 12 to 15 women there, one of whom was a black woman like me. We saw each other and gave each other the nod, the silent acknowledgment that we had seen each other. Sistahs were in the house and accounted for.

The tables were organized in a rectangle with an opening in the middle. The black woman was sitting across from me. Informal introductions revealed that she had recently obtained her Ph.D. in nursing and also was at the university on a post-doc fellowship. There was another friendly nod, we were in this together.

The meeting had not started yet and women were talking amongst each other, friendly banter getting to know each other. We did the same, across the gap, a physical gap that would soon prove to have strong symbolic value. She shared with me what she had been working on in her post-doc, the number of publications she had submitted. She then asked me what I had been doing. I shared about my work with refugee children in the school and that along with school staff we had been developing programming to support the children and their families. We were also helping the school adapt and embrace this new population.

The more I talked, the more her face soured. She finally interrupts me. "So, you haven't been writing? You have been working with people? It sounds like you have been having fun!" Her face was disgusted by now. Her voice was getting louder too. That is not how you are supposed to use a post-doc! She was flat out angry now and getting louder. As in slow motion, I see this woman in my mind's eye, across the gap just focusing in on me and being so angry. A post-doc is supposed to be used for the further development of your academic career, not to have fun with people! I am not sure if she slammed her hand on the table or not. I might have made that part up. I do recall that the rest of the women, all white, had become eerily quiet as they watched our interaction.

I don't know what I said. I probably mumbled something. I was too shocked to be embarrassed. This woman that I barely knew, this woman whom I had instantly connected with as a sistah, was really angry with me. Why was she so angry? She was so angry that it literally spilled out for all to see. If she could have foamed at the mouth she would have. After she spoke, she folded her arms, with the greatest look of disgust. Whatever I had said or done really upset her deeply.

Luckily, her abrupt closure also gave the host room to jump in and start the meeting. I don't remember much about the rest of the meeting or how I left. I do remember that she reached out to me a few days later with an email. She didn't apologize for her outburst. Instead, she wrote me to remind me again that the proper way for me to do a post-doc was to spend my time writing and publishing, not wasting my time developing programs. As a matter of fact, she was willing to help me. Even though she came from nursing she had done some qualitative research and had submitted a journal article with her qualitative data that had been rejected. If I liked I could work on the rewrite of the article and we could resubmit and publish as co-authors.

The gesture was nice, though a little bizarre. I must have said that I would take a look at it because I remember receiving her article. The article was one of the worst pieces of writing I had ever seen! It was incoherent and mostly a listing of answers. In order to rewrite I would have to go through the original data, reanalyze and write the article from scratch. I found my nicest vocabulary to tell her thanks but no thanks. I am sure she probably cussed me out for my stupidity. I don't know, but I never heard from her again. She did not finish out her post-doc and was gone before the year was over, I learned.

The experience was unsettling. The level of rage she generated in such a short moment, and so publicly, is something I had never experienced before. But, I had another similar experience with a black woman in academia, although the expression was not rage. When I had completed my master's research on mental well-being in a low-income African American community, I was set to present my work at my first American Anthropological Association national conference. These annual conferences are the largest gatherings for anthropologists. I was nervous at the prospect.

Before I went to the conference, however, I decided to give the presentation in the community first. I wanted and needed their blessing; after all, it was their story I was going to share. I organized an evening at the YWCA in the East End. The room was nicely decorated. All the people that I had interviewed were invited as special guests and anybody else from the community was welcome to come. And they came. My godmother Zambia drove 1.5 hours and she was there. She would not have missed it.

I was nervous, incredibly nervous in fact. I was going to share my work, their words, and it wasn't all positive. Here we were in the gym of the YWCA. I had a big plant which symbolized the earth. I started with a song and then poured libations for our ancestors. I poured water into the plant, symbolizing water, the life force that connects us with the earth. At each pour I encouraged the audience to call out the names of their ancestors, to invite them in. This was going to be our evening. We were going to tell our story.

They called out the names and then I was okay. I told my story and opened the floor for questions. I had talked about mental health in our community and the stigmatization. I had talked about the fact that we do not do a whole lot for our community members who need that kind of help. We send them to church or simply ignore them. As long as they are not too disruptive or destructive, they are contained in the community, but we don't really help them. We had our own informal ways of support, women doing somewhat better than men, but still we could use more help, and our pride and denial were in the way. I had laid it out there. This was not my story; this was our story. Now there was silence.

"You know, what you are saying there is true...", one person started. And then it was off. People started sharing stories, testifying. One story followed after the next. They were appreciative of the opportunity and space to be able to do so. I received their blessing that night. I felt emboldened and empowered to go to the conference. It was good.

The next day one of my mentors, an older white male who had been present, called me over. He told me he had not seen anything like it before. He had the best time. He said: "I call that Academy Church!" We laughed and I thanked him for his compliment. That same day, or perhaps a day or two later, I ran into a black woman who had a very high-ranking position. She was a vice dean or something. She called me over. She said, "I understand that you gave a public presentation in the community." Wow, word traveled fast, apparently. She continued, "You really should not be doing that. As a graduate student you need to make sure that you present on campus or at conferences, but don't waste your time doing that kind of stuff in the community. It will not help you." I was stunned and instantly came down from my self-congratulatory high. Here, too, I was too shocked to be angry.

Looking back at the interaction with both these women I am struck by their embodiment of domesticity. I am also struck by the complexity that is involved in that embodiment. This embodiment is not about having a lower-level job or position, it is about how one positions themselves in alignment with *the dominant* realm. They were clear about what was needed to make it into *the dominant* realm. But what was also clear was that they had sacrificed to get there themselves. Both these women had achieved a lot. Both these women had made sacrifices to be where they were, hence, the fact that they were willing to share their advice with me meant something. Looking back, I am sure it came from a place of concern and kindness, although I experienced it as offensive. The nurse also showed me that there is pain involved in reaching and even operating in that dominant realm. The thought of me having fun with people and not following the rules of *the dominant* order that she so diligently had followed almost blew a fuse in her head.

People in these positions are easily dismissed as "sell outs", "oreos", "Uncle Toms", and so on. The challenge is to leave their stories in their value. We might not understand, but we can at least acknowledge that there is a reason why they chose to position themselves in that way in their story. Those in *the other* position are not a homogenous population. There are some who will do their utmost to make it into *the dominant* realm, even if it means severing themselves or turning their backs on their fellow *others*. Some are admired but are often misunderstood or condemned for their actions, especially if their actions include a separation from their fellow *others*. The challenge is to appreciate that their chosen position did not come without sacrifice. Similarly, those who break rank from *the dominant* to truly join with *the others* also may have to suffer major sacrifices.

Rather than focusing on and condemning the people who chose to navigate this *dominant and the other* paradigm a certain way, it is of greater importance to grasp how the setup of the system contributes to certain people making choices that involve pain, sacrifice and rejection. For us the challenge, then, is to use compassion rather than condemnation, see beyond the obvious and appreciate others' particular choices for survival and adaptation.

Gran tangi. Thank you for the lesson and the insight into the plight of those who have embodied domesticity as a coping strategy.

166

POWER
OF SILENCE

Middle — Ch. 6

One of the most powerful mechanisms that maintains *the dominant and the other* divide is the use of silence. Always having the right to speak, to speak first, loudest and not be questioned, *the dominant* assures that *the other* is silenced. By affirming *the dominant* speech as valid and something to strive for, *the other* gets silenced. Furthermore, *the dominant* often also receives the power of setting the agenda and determining which story gets told, in what form, and what order. The power to silence *the other* is great, indeed.

Those of us early generation *others* were deliberately taught how to silence ourselves. It was seen as a form of protection, even survival. Do not question *the dominant* norm. It might cost you participation, your job, your safety, or your life. Those of us from immigrant backgrounds are familiar with *The Talk*. *The Talk* first starts around five or six when you are instructed on what your skin color or ethnicity will mean in terms of how you will be treated, and that it will be different from your white playmates. More importantly, you are instructed how to behave.

At a very young age, you are taught that you carry the responsibility for all your fellow ethnic brothers and sisters. "If you are late the white people will say that all black people are late all the time....", but more importantly you are taught to be quiet, to suck up the insults and harassment which inevitably will come your way.

In the Netherlands during my youth, the issue of Zwarte Piet, the Moorish character that accompanied Saint Nicholas as his servant, and for which white Dutch people gladly donned blackface, was not discussed in our house. Sure, it was offensive and racist taunts would go up during this period of the year, but this was their country. This was a Dutch people thing. Suck it up and let them do their thing, by December 6 it will be over. Keep silent and do not rock the boat. Our parents' message was clear. Their guidance came out of a sense of survival and protection. As outsiders, we had to live here and adjust. They dealt with their share of discrimination and violations but they would hardly ever talk about those experiences with us. It was silenced.

Their advice, though it might have come out of concern for survival, did contribute to a pattern of silencing. You keep your pain to yourself. You adapt and adjust and don't rock the boat. You will be judged differently, that is a given, but you have a chance. Work that chance. Make sure that you are 10 times better than your Dutch counterpart so you can get where you need to go. They were not necessarily wrong, but the self-silencing that resulted from these lessons became part of a normal aspect of *the dominant and other* divide.

I understood and appreciated the protection of silence. Silence served as a layer of protection. However, that layer of protection can also serve as an insulator and prevents one from breaking through. Over the years I have learned a lot about my own uses of silence. Audrey Lorde once said that we wait in silence for the fear to disappear before we speak out. I am not sure if I ever experienced silence in that way. For me silence has meant that I am listening, reflecting, healing, contemplating an answer, waiting for the most appropriate time to answer, that I am tired, protecting my audience or rejecting. It is those last two, silence as protecting and rejecting that have been most stifling for my own growth. I learned this through my experience at the Love Church.

The year was 2014 and the killing of Michael Brown had happened. I lived in a town across the Missouri river on the Illinois side, a mere 20 to 25 minutes away from Ferguson. Ferguson was in our back yard and we felt it. "Are you going to the protest?", was something you heard daily. People were going daily, bringing their children, friends. I didn't go. I had my reasons. The killing of Michael Brown was bad enough, but the fact that they left his body lying on the ground in a residential area for hours, for everyone to see. The disrespect of black life, not just his but the whole community, was so evident. As a black person and a mother of three black boys, this hit me deeply. And even though we did talk about it amongst each other, the level of disruption within me was so great that rather than speaking out, I withdrew into silence. I had to sit with what it meant, how I chose to share what was happening with my boys, and how to restore some sense of healing to my spirit. Until that phone call came.

"This is the pastor [from the Love Church]. I see what is going on, and I think I understand, but I am just a white guy and my understanding only goes so far. I really would like to understand. Would you be willing to talk to me, and I will just listen?" The request was sincere, it was also different than I had ever had before. So, I agreed, and we met.

We met and we talked for at least two hours. Well, I mostly talked, and he listened. I had not talked to many white people like that before, with that honesty and freedom. There are a few that I am close with, with whom I can be totally honest, but mostly I censor myself, something I think most of us do. At the end he asked me if I would be willing to talk to the congregation. Now that was something else. If I don't talk to white people on an individual basis about how racism affects my life, you can imagine that I don't talk to crowds of white people about this. But I agreed because of my experience in that meeting and because I trusted him.

That Sunday I was the second speaker. I sat on the podium next to the pastor. On the other side of him sat the first speaker, a white woman who was a principal of an elementary school in Ferguson but lived in our town. She shared how she missed her babies and how her heart went out to them. Because of the protests the school had been closed but she had gone by and had been able to hug some of them. It provided a touching humane story of connection. Then it was my turn.

I started out by saying that I normally don't talk to white people about racism because I don't think they can go there with me, but that the pastor had asked me if he could listen to me and in doing so became my brother. It was my brother's request that I was there, so that is why I was willing to share this time. I connected with the previous speaker's story about how we want to hug and love on those children. "But", I told them, "when they are 15 or 16 they are not cute and cuddly anymore. Just because of their color and size they are seen as suspect or a threat." I talked about what that was like for them and for me as a mother. I talked about the talks I would give my boys when they would venture out in the public space by themselves, the behavior codes they would have to abide by. I told them about the anxiety we as parents are left with when they do go out and the relief when they come home. I talked about the fact that racism is not about nice or not-nice individuals, but about a system that is maintained because it benefits some of us. I talked and told, brutally honest about my life as a black woman in America, to a sea of whiteness. And they listened, some cried. The Blues Aesthetic demands that we are brutally honest about our pain and I was that day.

Afterwards many came up and talked to me. For the first time in the several years that I had been attending the Love Church, I felt a real connection. Something had shifted, not just for the congregation, but for me too. For years I had told myself "I do not talk to white people about racism because they cannot go there with me." This attitude did not come out of arrogance, but out of experience. During the 1990s, I had attended several diversity and anti-racism trainings, trainings which I started to refer to as the "waiting for the white people to get it" trainings. I had been in trainings where the people of color would nod in recognition of the presented material or would send each other knowing smiles and nods while the white people went deeper and deeper into shock by learning about our experiences. By the end they would come to us, quite traumatized, emotional, wanting us to know that they were not aware, that they were not bad people, etc. They would come to us in the hope we would make them feel better, absolve them, who knows. All I know is that it turned me off. And, thus, I silenced them because I could not be bothered with the fragility of it all. I don't mind you getting emotional, but do the work, don't come to me to do the work for you.

Part of my silencing was out of protection for myself, but also out of protection for them. For if I were to really let loose and express from the depth of my soul what I had experienced and bottled up, it would only hurt them. The Blues Aesthetic might require brutal honesty, I had no faith that they could handle mine. So, silence worked, it was fine, until this day. With the trust of Ma Po and Zambia and my dad at my back, and my church-brother at my side, I talked and opened up honestly. I did not censor myself but spilled my truth. What I learned is that, in order to do so, I not only have to rely on and trust those who held my back, but I have to trust my audience as well. Sure, there were some who might fall into their fragility and make it about their feelings, but not all of them. I had to give them the benefit of the doubt that there were some who were willing to go there with me, even if they didn't know how. By blanketing all of them as "not being able to go there" and automatically re-jecting them, I was denying some of them the opportuni-

171

ty who could and would go there with me. That realization shifted something in me and forced me to grow. By opening up, I made a deeper connection and, with some, a real connection for the first time. I also grew as I broke through my self-imposed limitations. I can connect to any human being, regardless of their story if I connect to the essence of who they are and not their story.

Silence can serve many functions, one of which is to cocoon ourselves in presumed security and safety. They cannot get to us. But we also cannot get to them. And we don't need to get to all of them, but we might be missing out on some of them. Traversing *the dominant and other* divide requires at some point that we have to take a chance to trust each other with our stories. Silencing prevents us from doing so. My church-brother and the Love Church provided me the opportunity to learn that.

Gran tangi. Thank you for walking me through the lesson to learn about the power of silence and helping me understand how this false sense of security, in fact, maintains *the dominant and other* divide.

GENTRIMIWAH?

"Have you heard that podcast yet? *Nice White Parents*, you should really listen to it. It really explains a lot." Several people had told me about it. Apparently, the podcast was about public schools and the roles of white parents in what happens there. I had been in white schools my whole life and so had my children, except for a short stint in Suriname and Baltimore where they had different experiences. The bulk of their school experiences were in predominantly white schools in predominantly white communities, so I had an idea of what the podcast might be about.

I listened to the preview, a 2.5-minute section in which the host shared her own experience as a white parent visiting a public school to which she is being asked to consider sending her own children. She and a group of fellow white parents received a tour. Nobody mentioned that the vast majority of children they saw were of African or Latinx descent. Whites were in the minority. Nobody mentioned that when they went to the gifted class they saw a class full of white students. In the end, they all decided to enroll their children elsewhere. A school like this in the Netherlands would be called a "black school". This might be an American story, but it could have been a Dutch one just as easily and the story could equally represent the Dutch school experience.

The tone of the podcast reminded me of the many National Public Radio documentary programs I had listened to and enjoyed throughout my years in the U.S., so I decided to listen. I came back later in the day and started on episode one. I only got about 23 minutes in and then I had to stop.

I couldn't take it anymore. In the story, a group of white parents is being courted to have their children attend the local (predominately African American and Latinx attended) school. Given that the three white schools where their children usually go are over-enrolled, they are considering it. The father in the story who tries to convince his fellow neighbors to join him does so by agreeing with the principal that an intensive French program will be offered.

That semester a whole lot of new, wealthy white children entered the school. Nobody asked the students already attending the school how they felt about the newcomers, except the reporter. Some of the students didn't mind, but quite a few felt a little uneasy. The kicker was the Parent Teacher Association (PTA) meeting. The eager white father who was leading the effort to bring his fellow white parents along was also a professional fundraiser and had promised to put his skills to good use. The principal could not be happier. Unfortunately, she did not bother to inform her sitting PTA president, a social worker who had been supporting the school for years and who had focused on teacher appreciation, student support and other more bonding-like activities. At the end of the PTA meeting, the principal announced that the father had fundraised a large amount of money. There was shock. The PTA president and other lead members had not been aware. Protocol had not been followed. The man in question was not present, but one of the white parents assured that "He is a nice guy and has the best intentions." Aaahhh, the intention argument – I am starting to get queasy as I listen. There is unease all around. Feelings are obviously hurt. Yes, things should have been communicated. But the extra money is great, isn't it?

The reporter wonders aloud if the white parents are aware that they are in fact integrating the school. By now, my discomfort was so great that I had to cut the story off. I cut it off just at the point where the father entered the meeting. I did not even want to hear and feel more of the awkwardness, the stumbling, the attempts at restoring something, anything. The fact that the reporter wondered about integration added to the acidity in my stomach because this was not about integration. Integration is when you bring things or people together to create a new story. This was about gentrif* and that is something different. I find the practice so insidious that I don't even want to give the word its full due.

We know gentrif* from housing development practices. Affluent populations move into lower income neighborhoods. Housing value goes up, new businesses come in and inevitably the original inhabitants are expulsed. New populations are recruited into these neighborhoods because their economic and cultural capital is expected to revitalize the neighborhoods. Unfortunately, if the neighborhood is revitalized it is generally at the expense of the sitting population not with or for them. What we see in this scenario is one of the more insidious examples of *dominant versus the other* dynamics.

In this particular dynamic, *the dominant* is introduced into the realm of *the other*. However, they infiltrate like a parasite. Like a true parasite, rather than adapting to or co-adapting with the host, this particular dominant group takes over. A parasite may seem to live in symbiosis with its host, yet it lives and grows at the expense of the host. The reason why it is so effective is because it is publicly sanctioned, and the focus and distraction are on the cultural and economic capital that the dominant bring [doesn't the neighborhood look better?] rather than the cost involved. The word "gentrification" finds its origin in referring to the gentry, the noble class. The word itself then honors the process of conformation to the elite class. Massih Hutak, a Dutch hip hop artist, writer, and gentrif* activist is quick to point out that when newcomers come into the Netherlands (and other countries) they are required to take a course, making sure they know how to adapt. He astutely points out that there is no such request when *the dominant* class moves into the neighborhood of *the other*.

In gentrif*, *the dominant* is so assured and affirmed of its story that it never considers the story of *the other*, whose domain they are entering. They don't have to. Oblivious to the message it sends, they come in and immediately put forth their own story and expect *the other* to embrace it – after all, it is a desired story. They were recruited and facilitated to enter, were they not? But the practice of gentrif* is not limited to housing and urban development. It lends itself to education, as well, or any other field, for that matter.

Gentrif* is an interesting dominant vs. other dynamic because for once it is not about keeping the domains separate. On the contrary, it is about introducing *the dominant* into the realm of *the other*, purposefully. However, subsequently *the dominant* will start to take over with either absorption, but more often expulsion and eradication of *the other*. It is ingenious as it is tricky because this dynamic starts with the two domains coming together. Not only that, *the dominant* is introduced into the realm of *the other*, rather than the other way around. This introduction, rather than avoidance and distance, can appear to give some hope. City planners provide these plans of progress, although developers no longer fool the public that they care about bringing people together for the sake of revitalization. They are just in it for the money.

But outside of development, like in education, there is still some illusion of hope and morality at the introduction of *the dominant* to *the other*. As in the podcast story of the nice white parents. The story highlights how the school needs the white populations purely for survival. However, the story also touches upon the white parents' sense of moral responsibility to consider having their children going there.

It would be the right thing to do. Similarly, Hutak in the Netherlands has shared how, upon talking with the new artists that had been lured into the neighborhood with lucrative rent deals for creative spaces, and after explaining to them that the locals not only did not receive such deals, but were never invited into the new artist hubs, the new residents were sympathetic. Indeed, it did not seem fair and it should be brought up with the landlord. However, when discussion of this issue would lead to them having to make room for the local artists, then the new inhabitants changed their tune.

Gentrif* is a special dynamic in *the dominant and other* divide. In diversity work, we are used to *the other* being welcomed with open arms into the realm of *the dominant*, with the expectation that they will adapt 100% to *the dominant* realm. They can share some of their unique qualities, but only to the extent that it leads to pleasant consumption, not fundamental change. *The dominant* story remains *dominant* and it does in the gentrif* mode, as well.

What we learn from the gentrif* dynamic is that it clearly lays out a significant obstacle when it comes to bridging *the dominant and other* divide. Introducing *the dominant* to *the other* is one thing, but does one believe, at the core, that the story of *the other* can be equally valid to that of *the dominant*? Time and again, actions seem to prove the opposite. The dynamic is constructed in such a way that it entails enough distractions to not address this core message, or to ensure that the story of *the other* is perceived as meaning less or, at its worst, is insignificant. Every action, instead, is dedicated to forwarding and implementing the story of *the dominant* as valid, while minimizing or eradicating the story of *the other*.

Similar to the fortress of information, gentrif* provides a convenient way to thwart appreciation of the story of *the* *other*. The most basic ingredient needed to make a connection across the divide is omitted, hence a true connection can never be made, and the division remains. In gentrif* more so than the fortress of information, *the dominant* are facilitated in not making an effort to connect with the story of *the other*. No effort is required, and consequently no sacrifice has to be made. It painfully highlights how strong the conditioning is that affirms the superior value of *the dominant*. It demonstrates the intricacy and genius construction of a mechanism that not only provides you an out, but also a justification for that out.

Unlike the fortress of information, in gentrif* the presence of *the dominant* group is not by happenstance, they are invited in. This is also a significant difference with appropriation where people help themselves to other people's stories, without an invitation. In gentrif*, people are not only invited, they are welcomed with open arms. The joke is on the receiving party, however. Unlike appropriation, where the purpose of engagement is to enhance one's own story, in gentrif* people engage with the sole purpose of establishing their own story as valid, ignoring the story that is already in place. In the process they erase or remove *the other*. Again, what makes this unique is the justification of the whole process. Resistance to this process is generally experienced as highly unsettling and offensive.

I witnessed how the pushback towards gentrif* was experienced in just such an unsettling way. My friend is the leader of a transgender activism organization in the United States. After the 45th U.S. president was installed, government started to turn back the clock on hard earned transgender rights. They used existing laws to slowly chip away at their rights. Living in the Netherlands, I observed from afar and was concerned. I called my friend to share my concerns and to ask if there was something I could do, even so far away.

My friend told me that the group was withdrawing into themselves at this point. They needed just some time and space to get together as a group and to reflect on what they were going through, their sense of loss and unsafety, and more. But they needed to do it amongst themselves. My friend promised that they would let me know when I could be of assistance. I told them, no problem. My friend continued and shared that certain (white) hetero allies who had been supportive before had been incensed when they received this message. "We have been part of the Black Lives Matter movement. We have been part of the Women's March. What do you mean we cannot be present?!" I heard the weariness of my friend in their voice. "They want to help but it has to be their way. Not only do we have to deal with what is being done to us, we can't even have some peace to ourselves!"

I understood the plight. I felt their frustration. My friend held their ground. This group of allies was welcome but only on terms of the receiving group. They just had to be patient and humble. It was a bitter pill to swallow. I am not sure if they were ever able to do so. Although, ability was not really the challenge. The incredulity reflected the pitfall of gentrif*, the assuredness of wanting to be desired paired with an insensitivity towards the story of the party already occupying the space. The unfortunate side effect is the pain it causes.

Gentrif* is an intriguing yet highly effective mechanism that contributes not only to maintaining but also extending *the dominant and other* divide. Is it possible that gentrif* can be performed in a way that was intended, to enhance *the other's* story by introduction of *the dominant* group? I have not run across examples, I hate to admit, but I would like to think that they are out there. It requires a humility and patience that we tend to take for granted. It takes a curiosity and interest in *the other*. It demands a willingness to question one's own sense of superiority. It takes a mindset of being willing to invest in each other based on given stories. It requires a humility in understanding that, while there are certain elements that we bring that can be of value, it does not mean that what we are offering has *more* value. It does not mean that what was already there was not of value until you came.

Think of it as you being invited to a party where there will be soup served. People are aware that the home cooked soup is good but could be enhanced. You are invited because people know you live in an area where there are many gourmet soup stores, and people share that they would like for you to come to help improve the soup. (Work with me here). The hope is that you will bring some special ingredients and will come during cooking time so you can cook together while exploring together how you can make the soup better based on your ingredients. As my mother demonstrated, our paths are stronger when walked together. Instead ,you show up with a huge pot of gourmet soup. As you come in you remove the home cooked soup from the table and take it to the kitchen. You come back to the living room and start pouring everybody a bowl of your magnificent soup. Eat up and enjoy. Well, something like that. You get the point.

Gran tangi. Thank you for the lesson that progress can be disguised in the deadly mechanism of gentrif.

VALIDATION

My mother was born in the 1930s, a different time. She was born in a time when social control was an essential part of her culture. Being raised where interdependency and community were the norm, your behavior was not just for yourself, but for the benefit of, and a reflection on, the community as a whole. Hence the phrase "what will people think" was and always has been a key part of her vocabulary and how she raised us. There is nothing wrong with a sense of community and communal responsibility, but when in extreme it starts to become linked to shame and oppressive tendencies, then it becomes problematic.

What will people think is a strong influencer of behavior and is not limited to my mother's childrearing style. Many institutions, including academic institutions, have people specifically dedicated to public relations (PR), to make sure the institution is well received among the public. *What people think* goes a long way. Again, there is nothing wrong with wanting to be perceived and appreciated in a certain way, but when behavior becomes curbed or certain practices are purposely hidden, "What will people think" can become problematic.

Our behaviors can become so influenced by "what other people think", that they begin to function like conditioned behaviors. We focus so much on what other people think that we tailor our behavior accordingly and fail to question whether the behavior is, in fact, the right behavior. Our failure to question normalizes the behavior.

We live in a time of social media, endless selfies, the pursuit of likes, and where people with the press of a button feel free to spew their opinions on everything and anything without any restraint. Mishaps and misstatements are saved in perpetuity for all to see and for all to judge. Within that particular context, *What will people think* takes on a whole new meaning. People have lost their jobs in an instant after being recorded in a compromising act.

As a result, it is not okay to act and move freely and it can be scary to be yourself. We can be idealistic and say it does not matter and we should be ourselves regardless, but how does that gel with reality? One of the lessons I taught in my African Diaspora anthropology class was about the practice of skin whitening. In certain countries like Jamaica, Nigeria, or India, skin whitening is big business. Women and men invest in cremes and lotions to lighten the complexion of their skin. They even use it on children. It is believed that having lighter skin will contribute to a better life. Unfortunately, the grade of chemical strength is often so strong that it can do irreparable damage to skin and internal organs. It also sends the unfortunate message that dark skin is unattractive and undesirable. The fact that celebrities engage in the practice also impacts its popularity. Skin whitening practice is especially strong in formerly colonized nations with a history of European domination, but this practice cannot just be blamed on this colonial legacy. A contemporary social media-obsessed world, which constantly sends messages of white beauty being linked to desirability, success and wealth, also plays a significant role.

Counter movements have been designed to curb the practice with arguments about the danger to one's health or the need for self-esteem over external validation. However, the truth is that that lighter skin and a thinner nose will get you the husband you otherwise would not get or will get you the job that would otherwise be denied. This is the context, the

183

story that some of us live in. For many of us, it is not okay to just be.

At one conference where I gave a keynote, I was inspired to do a whole section on having participants greet each other with the saying "How you be?" There was some uncomfortable laughter, but people did it, after which they palpably relaxed. I felt it was important to take a moment to stop and recognize our being, not our doing, what we had done or should do, but just be. Especially for those in academia the notion of you being enough as you are is almost foreign. The whole system is based on and uses elements of competition. If only you had published more or in a higher-level journal. If only you had brought in more money. If only you had produced more. If only, maybe then... It is a treacherous slippery slope which has led to burn out becoming a common affliction among higher education staff. And this trend is not limited to academia.

Our goal is to live in a world where every story is deemed as valid, where it is okay to be as we are. However, we have to do that within a context where messages of invalidation are constant and relentless, especially for some of our siblings among us. In many Western societies our brown and black young men live in a world where every day they receive messages that they are perceived as dangerous, suspect, or untrustworthy. Ethnic profiling is for many of them not a question of *if* it will happen, but of how many times this month it will happen. Many of our girls will receive the message that they are incapable, unworthy or insignificant. Many of our young people receive the message that they are unknowing, 'green', and not yet capable. Many of our old people receive the message that they are obsolete, incapable or a burden. Many of our men receive the message that they are an oppressor, dangerous, and untrustworthy. Many of our women receive the message that they are weak, needy, and incapable. Pick your poison. All of us are in the position of *the other* sometimes. Of course the messages aren't always negative, but they are present enough that they affect our experience, curb our behaviors and affect our self-esteem. How you be?... in a context like this?

So, external validation matters and has the power to curb our behavior or diminish our sense of self. It even affects our educational experiences. Because of COVID-19, numerous schools changed their grading policies to accommodate the precarious school situations for many of their students. Unfortunately, academic achievement is so embedded in a system of external and comparative validation that not everybody embraced these shifts. In the US, Oregon parents protested the shift from letter or number grades to a pass/fail system. Part of the reason was the fear of the effect on their children's chances for college admissions. However, another argument was also that without this validation system their children would have no motivation to learn. Did the parents have such little faith in their children, or had they bought into the myth that external validation is a necessary factor for their children to learn?

In another educational example, this time from the Netherlands, validation also proved crucial. At a university where students had demanded change in regard to diversity and inclusion, several concessions were made and interventions were promised. Follow through was lacking, however, and students became disgruntled about promises not delivered. When the students demanded a conversation with the board, they initially received the run-around. Then there was the communication that a conversation would be possible, but definitely not a public conversation. The conversation never took place, but it was leaked that the board did not want to take a chance to be criticized publicly. Unfortunately, by choosing public validation over the students, the board damaged that relationship with the students and their credibility even further.

Our indigenous and spiritual traditions teach us that we are connected to everything and that we are worthy from the moment we draw breath. We have been sanctioned to be here and to learn whatever lessons we agree to learn. Somehow, that worthiness gets lost as we get caught up in all these stories in which we find ourselves. Our worth becomes steered by the context of these stories, which envelopes us. It is not enough to just boost our self-esteem with positive self-affirmation. Because even though the context consists of nothing but human-made stories, those stories have real repercussions. It is important, then, to understand and study those stories, like a true anthropologist, so one can navigate strategically and hold on to one's sense of worth.

One of my children, my Japanese daughter as I have grown to love her, had to make a drastic strategic decision to preserve her self-worth. She came to the Netherlands for a year as an international exchange student. She was housed in downtown student housing which would allow her to walk to school every day. Unfortunately, she was faced with racial jokes and remarks almost every day when walking to school. Sometimes even children while holding their parents' hands felt free to hurl their innocuous insults. It was the relentlessness of it that got to her.

In addition, she was taking a gender class at the time. "Here I am sitting in this class, listening to all these grand theories about gender. Yet there is nothing that relates to what I am going through on a daily basis because I am an Asian woman." There were days when she needed a reprieve and would not go to class because she just couldn't face it, something we refer to in my community as a "mental health day". Her participation in class became lackluster and her grades started to drop.

There were a few times she would yell back, question the

belligerents, or tell them to stop. This is something she could do only because she had lived in the US for a while, where she had acquired a way of being in the world, far bolder than her Japanese heritage would allow. Her fellow Japanese students on exchange in the Netherlands were not able to do that. They would just lower their heads and suffer through it. But even with her more "Western" coping skills it remained unbearable. She eventually talked with her teacher about what she was going through and received help that allowed her to pull up her grade. It was too late to engage with her fellow students in the class, however.

Finally, she decided to move. She moved to a student housing flat more on the outskirts of the city. From there, she would take the bus which would take her right to the campus, thereby avoiding downtown. It might seem extreme, but it provided her with peace of mind and spirit. She was able to finish out her year doing well in school. That story of looking at Asian women as animé characters is alive and well and shaped my daughter's daily experiences. A mere positive self-pep talk would not suffice, and even her feisty personality did not stop her from being affected by it. The casual normalcy of the insults can affect you to your core and, in this case, affected her school performance.

In the Surinamese spiritual tradition, it is believed that people are born with an inner self, a *yeye*. This *yeye* is believed to be the first gift from God and can be seen as a core self. This core self is infused by the *yeye* of the mother and the *yeye* of the father. Given that it is a gift from God, it can be seen as a pure self. It is comparable to the Rastafarian concept of *I and I*, which illuminates the physical and the spiritual self. This inner self, then, imbues one with innate value. This inner self is so valuable that it deserves to be treated with respect. It, in fact, demands to be treated with respect. Surinamese people believe that this inner self functions as a radar. If one is being mistreated or participates in an unsavory act, there will be an inner voice, a grumbling that one will feel. This is the *yeye* signaling "This is not right". So even when one does wrong at some deep level, if one dares to listen, there is the message that one deserves better, deserves to act better.

The *yeye*, then, is far stronger than any invalidating story one is presented with. The *yeye* is the inner source that one can tap into, far deeper than psychological self-talk. I believe this is what guided my daughter to make drastic changes for herself, because her *yeye* signaled to her that she deserved better and demanded better. According to Surinamese believes, then, the pain one can feel at the invalidation of one's being is in fact that *yeye* radar that is sending out signals. That pain, then, is a good thing. It is when one becomes numb and no longer feels the signals that there is reason to be concerned. In her, I saw the spirit of my father who so embodied his right to be, in spite of everything that was placed in his story.

So, what will people think? People will think a lot of things and what they think might even transfer into real life obstacles. What people think can even affect the way we value ourselves and prevent us from living and giving our best. However, tapping into one's inner value and carefully understanding and navigating our contextual stories should be the necessary tools to even out the score.

Gran tangi. Thank you for the lesson about how we have the right to be and how in order to fulfill that right we need to tune in and actively navigate the external systems of validation.

END

We stood in silence, dressed in white
and held the space for her
Women warriors, called to act
and we held the space for her
No question, no doubt, no fear, no discussion
We just held the space for her
Because we could, we did,
we trusted, we must
Just hold the space for her
And as we held the space
for her, for all
We stepped into our own
As women, warriors, nurturers
Protectors of the space
To let her know
And everybody else
That we got this,
You
And everything is fine
Love-work she had called it
Love-work she had given us
Are we up for the task?
I let you know
And everybody else
That we got this,
You,
And everything is fine

AHO METAKUYE OYASIN

End — Ch. 1

There are many preparations to do a sweat lodge. My god-mother Walks on Water guided me in the tradition as it was taught to her by her Lakota teacher. You have to make the prayer ties, placing tobacco in small pieces of fabric of different colors representing the various directions. They are tied to a string and will be hung in the lodge. Stones will have to be selected to be cooked. The stones are lovingly referred to as "the grandparents". Herbs will have to be selected for the ceremony. Water needs to be fetched. Of course, there is the building of the lodge itself and preparing the space and all that is involved with that. People will have to be instructed on what to expect, what to do and not to do. They have to be assured that they will be safe, that there is a way to handle the heat, and that we have built-in structures to assure their well-being. There is palpable excitement as we get closer. We check on the fire keeper who is cooking the stones, take off our working clothes and prepare to enter the lodge.

When it is time, we humble ourselves to the lodge, the womb, kneel down and kiss the ground, stating the Lakota words *Aho Metakuye Oyasin*, acknowledging all we are related to, and crawl in. A churchless ceremony facilitating cleansing, rebirth, and harmonious relations is about to begin.

In Suriname, the spiritual tradition is also churchless and embodies the pursuit of harmony through connecting with the elements. Rooted in African traditions, the first honor is for *Mama Aisa*, Mother Earth. We dance barefoot, shuffling and stomping, with bended knees, connecting with her, honoring her. This is where we start, to get our bearing.

As a dancer I studied African dance. I learned that the key to African dance is a bent knee position. Not only do you find it in African dance, but in dance of most if not all people of color. There is a spiritual orientation towards the earth, unlike ballet or other original European dances where the orientation is about going to the heavens. Now, of course, there are exceptions, like the Masai whose Adumbe dance consists of exuberant jumping to reach heights, but even here the dance is within a communal context and with a specific ritual purpose. A bent knee demonstrates your connection with the earth. A bent knee shows you are alive.

So that's where we need to start, with a groundedness and a connectedness with the earth that makes us feel stable and centered. Besides bending our knees, another thing we need to do in order to center ourselves is to breathe. Breathe in, breathe out. The oxygen fills the lungs, which keeps the blood flowing. We breathe in the connection to the ancestors and remind ourselves that we are not alone. We are, in fact, connected to all, *metakuye oasin*, all my relations, and never stand alone. And if all this sounds too esoteric then we just breathe to create a moment of silence, rest, let blood flow to the brain and embrace an opportunity to re-center ourselves.

When we deal with spaces that are off-balance, shaped by *the dominant and the other* dynamics, filled with confusion or direct conflict, we first need to take a moment to get centered. The conditioned response is to fight, fly, or freeze. The fear, rage or uncertainty take over and we react rather than respond. Whether defensive, offensive, or avoidant, we act or fail to act, but not effectively. The key is to find your ground and breathe. You don't even have to buy into the idea of being connected to forces unseen. Ground yourself and breathe anyway.

Being grounded and breathing brings a calm and allows you

to respond rather than react. It also communicates to others in the space that at least you have it together, even if that is not necessarily the case. You don't necessarily need to have the answers, but at least you need to communicate that you are present and ready to deal with whatever may come your way. Be steadfast in spite of, like my father was.

People are surprised after seeing me speak in public to find that, in general, around people I am rather quiet. I am quiet because I am listening and feeling what happens in the space. I generally pick up on incongruities, anomalies, insensitivities, or bold injustices that are present in the space. Because I have chosen to alter those incongruities as my calling and profession, I have to address them. My belly, steered from afar by my ancestors, functions as a radar, and will start to burn. And the more or more strongly the space gets out of kilter, the stronger my belly starts to burn, giving me the signal that the time is near for me to act.

As I have been walking this path and have committed myself to changing the space, not just for myself but for others, especially our young people, that radar has become stronger and stronger. It not only reminds me to act, but to be cognizant about how to act, because there is much at stake. Thus, I cannot react swiftly out of fear, indignation, or anger. Those types of reactions might be gratifying in the moment, but generally lead to unsatisfactory results. My goal is to alter the space by taking people with me in the process. It is not my goal to shut them down and show them how wise I am. My goal is to alter the space so we can hold it together the way it is meant to be. Engaging this space, then, requires restraint, compassion, and to find humanity in the offending parties within the space. This is not always easy to do, especially when the offending behavior is extremely grievous. There is a reason why they call this emotional labor. There is a reason why I call this love-work.

Ideally, you do not enter the space either wielding a machete, or just being soft and kind. You need a good combination of both Ma Po's and my auntie's sensibilities, an unapologetic clearing of the space, while acknowledging people's humanity. You do that by taking a moment to center yourself and breathe. Give yourself that moment to feel what needs to be felt, to see what needs to be seen, to have a moment of reflection and give a benefit of the doubt before you act. In this kind of love-work of holding space filled with the ramifications of *the dominant and the other* dynamics, it is easy to quickly label people as weird, jerks, ignorant, snakes, monsters, etc. and use that as the fuel for our reactions. Taking a moment to ground, breathe, and connect can make all the difference.

I implore you, then, with the utmost urgency, that when you take on this work of Holding Space, that you take as step one to ground-center yourself, breathe, and connect. These combined measures are the easiest and simplest but most profound resource. Take a second to find your bearing and take a deep breath. Draw in that oxygen, connection and strength. Relax your legs, bend your knees a little and feel the ground underneath your feet. Those few seconds can be the difference between you dehumanizing somebody and losing your own humanity, between you finding the right thing to say, or you finding the courage to say it. Practice this, often, for it is a necessary skill to have when entering this arena. The love-work and the emotional toll that comes with it is not to be underestimated. Most people who do this type of work get disillusioned and burn out. This simple exercise—ground-centering ourselves, breathing, connecting—is the first step in holding space and also the first step in taking care of oneself while doing this work.

And, thus, the work for us begins, for us and all our relations.

SAFE ENOUGH TO BE BRAVE

Ending — Ch. 2

When I was a professor, there was one thing I was fiercely committed to and that was the well-being of my students. The classroom was my space. You are now in my house. I tried to create a classroom where everybody's voice mattered. It was also the space where everybody's humanity mattered. At least, that was my aim. I am sure I might have missed some things or messed up along the way, but that's what I strove for.

When I took students abroad, it was no different, and that's when the momma bear was even more present. I don't play around when it comes to my children, whether I gave birth to them or not. I sometimes literally had to hold back and try not to be overprotective and stand in the way of their experiences. I might be the momma, but they were also there to explore and learn. The challenge was to find the balance, the balance between safety and yet having room enough to be brave.

When it comes to Holding Space, we want to create spaces where people can be safe, yet brave enough to express themselves. What does that mean exactly? At the most basic level, it means that safety assures that you will not be debased or devalued as a human being. It does not mean that people have to agree with you at all times or that it will always be *gezellig*. This is important to understand. People often confuse feeling unsafe with feelings of *ongezelligheid*. One is allowed to feel *ongezellig*, and it might actually be necessary in order to experience a breakthrough.

In my group work with people, I always start with a set of guidelines. I explain that I refer to guidelines rather than rules because rules can be broken, which only causes stress. I use guidelines because I try to create a certain atmosphere in which we will work together. These guidelines are used to create a sense of safety, knowing that safety cannot be guaranteed. However, if we are purposeful about our communal commitment to create a certain atmosphere, we are more likely to succeed.

The items on my guideline list include: Breathing (and grounding); Being open and brave; Having the freedom to "pass"; Being conscientious about one's use of silence; Not running from "*ongezelligheid*", Being sensitive to one's physical limitations; Being patient with oneself and the process; Being conscientious about language; and the Vegas rule – "What happens in Vegas, stays in Vegas". These are concepts I personally have chosen as key elements for a safe environment, but they are purely personal preferences. There is one I want to highlight here, and that is the attention to language.

When I gather with a group of people, I always stress sensitivity to the use of language. These days, it is more and more common to have gatherings with people of different language backgrounds. Generally, English will be the language of use, but I ask people to be aware that there might be multiple levels and styles of English that are spoken. I usually highlight the fact that I speak American English, and that when I get excited, I tend to speak faster. I encourage people to stop me and slow me down if necessary. I also encourage people to be aware and help each other with translations if necessary. Even when there is a group of same language speakers, there is variation, dialects, etc. We should not assume that we always have the same understanding.

There is the matter of address that can also be discussed

here. Based on gender or age, one might like to be addressed a certain way. There is a more pressing issue when it comes to language, however. There is a phenomenon referred to as *language* or *tone policing*. *Tone policing* refers to the condemnation of expressed emotion in speech, often reserved for women of color. Basically, through focusing on the emotional intensity of the speech, and the subsequent feelings of *ongezelligheid* it evokes in the receivers, those policing distract the audience from paying attention to the actual content of the communication, thereby diminishing or discrediting the speaker. *Language policing* refers to the condemnation of language that is not up-to-date or is expressed inappropriately in relation to the latest social justice lingo. It is another strong enforcer of the *dominant* versus *the other* divide, as those who label themselves as "woke" place themselves in *the dominant* category. This practice, too, distracts from the work that needs to be done and contributes to belittling people.

Why do I stress this? Because we need to be aware that in a space where people come together to create more validity for all stories, people enter with different skill levels. If one is not able or willing to accommodate that, this in fact might be contributing to the problems we are trying to solve.

In spite of all the agreements and assurances, it is still possible to not feel safe, because ultimately a sense of safety is in the heart of the beholder. Feeling safe then is not as much about what the outer environment might or might not do to us, it is about the inner environment. Do I trust that I will be able to handle it if I put myself out there? More than likely you can, but you have to try it to find out. Entering into the space to do the love-work requires some bravery, for some more than others. No matter how safe one tries to make the space, different people will experience it differently, and ultimately participation comes down to a level of risk taking. People bring their experiences, expectations, and fears into the space and thus we have to be careful in asking people to be vulnerable. All we can do is offer up the space as best as we can and hope that people take that step in order to make something happen.

In my early days of group work as a lector of inclusive education in the Netherlands, I did a series of sessions with students. I was assisted by my staff from the Student Branch. After several sessions, we did an activity where students had to pick up certain words from a selection of word cards, they could share their experience. When we came to one person they paused for a while. They asked if they could switch their word. We said they could. They then picked up another word and hesitated before they shared their story. We waited. It was obvious that this was not easy. They shared that they inadvertently had outed themselves as gay to their single parent. When the parent, who was extremely religious, found out, they locked this student in their room and berated them with religious doctrine. After a few days, the student finally consented and stated that it was a temporary phase and that they were over it. The parent accepted the explanation and released the student.

The student who had now returned to the university felt guilty about lying. "I am still gay. I lied to my parent. Should I be honest? Isn't it important to be authentic?" We were all kind of shocked by this story and were silent for a minute. I had some specific thoughts on the subject, but instead looked at one of my young staff members who was also a member of the LGBTQ+ community and deferred to them. I nodded that they should answer. I did not know what they were going to say, but I had to trust them. I could always follow up with some corrections if necessary, but it was not for me to lead in this moment. My young staff member took a deep breath and started with "...Well, the most important thing is that you are safe." My staff member then helped the student think through and work through various options and the repercussions of certain choices. I could not have been more proud of how they had handled the situation.

We had worked on establishing an atmosphere of safety. Apparently, it was safe enough for this student to share their story and ask for advice, something we later learned they had never done before. Secondly, when there is an atmosphere of safety there is automatically a level of trust. When you feel safe you can surrender. I trusted in my staff, not only that they could handle it, but that we could handle it together. It was not about having the right answer at the time, but that, in a safe atmosphere, connections grow which allow you to take chances, to say things, to do things. Even if those things evoke *ongezelligheid*, you can work through it.

Having a 'safe enough' atmosphere is a basic requirement to Holding Space. It is not something one can force, but one can strive for. Even in a one-on-one situation, by being fully present, one can create a space safe enough so one might be willing to take a risk to open up or engage. One can communicate that one's humanity will be respected. Striving for safety begins with intent and commitment. It is a small but precious gift to offer up a space in which we communicate that people matter.

Gran tangi. Thank you for the lesson that in order to Hold Space we first have to commit to making it safe enough so people can be brave enough to enter.

CARE

Ending — Ch. 3

In the 1990s in the US, there was a popular cartoon about a little boy aardvark on public television. My oldest son used to watch it. Now, there was this one episode that we watched together. Arthur as this (aardvark) boy was called, had a little sister, D.W., who could be incredibly annoying, often on purpose. In this particular episode, D.W. had hooked on to a favorite song, *Crazy Bus*. She had a cd player and put the song on auto-repeat and would listen and sing along with the song, over and over again, loudly, all with much irritation to Arthur. We witnessed his building irritation and we wondered out loud how he would handle it. Would he take the cd player from her? Would he hit her? Would he call his parents to deal with it? We waited in anticipation and watched Arthur reach his climax where he couldn't handle it anymore and he...... offered her headphones! My son and I looked at each other stunned. This was a solution we had not even considered. It was so simple and so compassionate and yet it had eluded us. Blame it on his other favorite shows Teenage Mutant Ninja Turtles or Mighty Morphin Power Rangers, which resolved every conflict with major battles in every episode. Perhaps it was about my faulty parenting. In our defense, in the next episode D.W. was at it again and that time Arthur did threaten to break the cd. However, it doesn't take away that that simple act of choosing compassion in a situation of tension and conflict moved us and stopped us in our tracks.

The Love Church had taught and challenged me to come from a place of love in my actions. My godmother Zambia had demonstrated that choosing love-work required diligent effort. You must consciously choose to come from a place of care and compassion when trying to hold space. In a space that is filled with elements of inequality, strife, misunderstanding and vulnerability, choosing to come from a place of compassion is a challenge when feelings of hurt or self-righteous anger prevail. It also does not mean that one should suppress feelings of anger or hurt. Arthur was justifiably angry with D.W. Coming from a place of compassion for the other does not mean one has to tolerate abuse or violation on one's own account. Can you feel what you feel and still incorporate compassion or at least validation of the other as a human being? But, just like the other deserves care and compassion, so does one have the right and responsibility to preserve care for oneself.

Self-care is a commonly heard expression and is easily translated into individualized self-preservation. However, when we start from our original premise that one is connected to everything and everybody, then self-care means something different altogether. We extend compassion to the other as an extension of ourselves. When those around us suffer, if we tune in, we can feel it. What we do with that feeling is what matters. Some of us have the tendency that when we feel the suffering or anguish of someone else, we immediately want to make it better. We want to console or take the pain away. Especially those of us who are parents or who have strong parental inclinations might be moved to do so. The hardest thing is to not immediately give in and respond to those feelings, but to take a big breath and just be present.

Why do I say that? When we care for others it is important to care for them as full human beings. Human beings have a full range of emotions. They experience joy, but they also experience sadness. Those emotions are there for a reason. Just like when we allow people to have their feelings of joy, we should allow them to have their feelings of sorrow. We don't know what lesson they are in the process of learning, which we might be interrupting when we jump in. Sometimes by immediately jumping in and comforting feelings of pain or sorrow, we unfortunately give the message that people are not allowed to feel bad.

I come from a long line of strong Caribbean women. As much as I love the women in my family, they did have the tendency, at the first sign of sadness, to insist "Don't cry, don't cry. You are strong, you are fine." And sure, I was fine, and I was strong, but I also wanted to be allowed to feel sad sometimes. It would always make me mad. By discouraging these emotions, I think it also gives the message that we have no faith that the person can handle the sadness, that they are incredibly fragile and will not be able to recover.

So now my message is totally different. I communicate that I am here, I am present. "I got you if you need me. Go through whatever you have to go through, you are allowed. Stay in the moment and feel what you have to feel. If you want to fall out even, go for it. I am here to help you up. Not only that, but I also trust that you are capable of going through it and coming up on the other side. Like dipping into the blues, you have to go through it to resurface on the other side. I will be waiting, and if you get stuck, you can call on me to assist." Again, I understand the urge to immediately want to console because you feel someone else's pain. I purposely don't take that pain in anymore. I will witness and have compassion, but their pain is their pain. It is an element of their journey that they are allowed to go through. And it is because I care that I respect that journey.

Some of us have a hard time extending compassion towards others. If one has dwelled in the realm of *the dominant* for too long and was never forced to be concerned with the story of *the other*, extending compassion might not feel natural. If one has dwelled in the realm of *the other* for too long, one might have become numb and insensitive due to repeated slights and experiences of marginalization. Why should I care if they, my environment, the world continuously lets me know that people don't care about me? Caring might be hard on either side because of the nature of our stories, and yet we do. We do because it is something deep inside us that we all long for, and because we are connected. And thus, on some level we are always inclined to go there, or to have access to it, even if we struggle with it.

As we learn to extend compassion to others, we need to extend compassion to ourselves because, as a member of the community, we are equally deserving of care, respect, and validation. Some of us are willing to extend care or compassion to another but find it difficult to extend that compassion to ourselves. Religious teachings that glorify self-sacrifice, suffering, and humility also do not help matters much. I am not a religious scholar by any means, but I would offer that by diminishing oneself at the expense of another is also a slight to God, as you are not honoring God's work. Key is that extending care, whether to another or to oneself, requires extra effort, it requires love-work. Arthur made a decision to treat his sister a certain way despite his annoyance. He demonstrated love-work in action.

Dealing with the outcome of *the dominant and the other* divide means dealing with annoyance, frustration, disappointment, disillusion, or anger on many occasions. What does it take to start using care as a means to start chipping away at that dynamic? In my work in the Netherlands, I deal with young people in education, especially those of immigrant heritage, who are confronted with a world that treats them as *the other*. From an education system that systematically gives them advice to aim lower than their Dutch heritage counterparts, to a job market that makes it harder to gain access or advance once entered, to a nightclub scene whose standard procedure is to refuse them access, to an entertainment world that hardly includes or represents them, and so on, their positionality provides them with constant challenges and messages of not belonging. These challenges are not insurmountable but are worthy to be addressed. In my field of education, knowing that these children are confronted with an environment that systematically underestimates their abilities, I always make it a point to acknowledge their brilliance. I make it simple, matter-of-fact, and will always treat them with a given that they are brilliant. How they choose to live up to that potential is up to them. It is a small thing, but something that will hopefully cause a shift, even if it is in how they view themselves.

There is a group of former colleagues and members of my research team—Hester Brauer, Ruben Boers, and Daniel Rambaran—who took this element of care and translated it into an approach to work with students. They developed a program to help delayed students cross the finish line of their academic journey and called the program "The Powerhouse." They created a program in which they purposely created a culture of success. They used symbols, including a theme song "You've got the Power" when gathering. The fact that these students were going to be successful was consistently communicated. Success, given hard work and commitment, was presented as an achievable outcome. More importantly, they communicated that they were going to be successful because they were capable of doing so.

After studying the systematic obstacles these students faced in the pursuit of their education, they came up with the concept of "educational vulnerability". From the numerous elements that played a role, one that stood out was the element of stigma. These students were stigmatized both within the educational system and outside of the educational system, but worse, they had internalized that stigma. Aware of this phenomenon, these staff members developed an approach that specifically overcame this hurdle. They opted to create a culture of care that reinforced the students' strengths, challenged their commitment, demanded communal responsibility, and set high expectations. They also started with this concept of brilliance, but they refer to it as *symbolic mastery*. Their starting point is that these young people are young professionals and that they have something to offer. Rather than looking at where they are lacking or behind, they start with looking at what they are capable of. They demonstrated to these students that they cared about them and that they were worth the effort to be supported. For many of these students, that message was the difference between being jolted into action or remaining stuck in self-stigmatized limitations.

A program with these principles should not have been unique, but unfortunately it was. Care in education is often communicated through the restrictions that rigorous standards and beautifully carved out trajectories bring. We care about your education, that's why we have designed these beautiful high-level programs, that unfortunately you have to have a certain profile to fit into. And if you don't, oh well. It is not that the people that design these programs don't care. They obviously care about offering high quality education, but something is missing. Care generally is not translated into "you're worth the effort", and more specifically "your story is worth the effort". That is the secret to the love-work and the difference in whether we stay stuck on the *Crazy Bus* or if we are able to get off.

Gran tangi. Thank you for the lesson about the reminder that we ought to care and be treated with compassion because we are worth the effort.

COURAGE

End — Ch. 4

One of the most important and necessary skills in holding space is the act of courage. As overcoming *the dominant and the other* divide is one of the key essential tasks of holding space, it requires serious courage. Going up against this system that is deeply conditioned and set in all kinds of mechanisms is not an easy task. Because of the conditioned normality, disrupting that normality might be met with resistance, ridicule, alienation, or worse. Being committed to implementing change not only requires skill, it requires an internal fortitude, and an ability to handle one's vulnerability. One must be courageous.

Courage is treated here as underscoring an individual endeavor. As an individual, there is a certain level of risk and vulnerability which is cushioned when acting in a group. Even when one steps forward to act as a group, however, one first has to make an individual shift or first step to participate. Courage is treated here as that individual skill, but always within a communal context and aimed at the relational outcome.

Having courage is not just about being brave enough to kick in the door and spoiling the party; courageous work needs to be done wisely and strategically. A momentary courageous action can have long-lasting effects. Hopefully, those effects will be for the betterment of our collective story, but there is no guarantee. It is this lack of positive outcome guarantee that often withholds the person from taking courageous actions. And the inaction maintains the status quo. That is how the system is designed.

That momentary courageous action might be fueled by anger and discontent, but must be driven by compassion. If not, there is the possibility to overshoot the target. Things will be disrupted, which is the goal, but they must be disrupted so there is room for repair and rebirth, not just destruction beyond repair. One must be able to transform oneself in a split second from outrage and anger to draw from a sense of compassion and connectedness, because the ultimate goal is to work through and on the cracks of our connectedness.

Courage can be big, and courage can be small. If one has been conditioned and grown used to being silent, it takes courage to speak up. Just opening one's mouth and speaking can be a courageous act. Sometimes it takes a lot of work to come to that first effort to break the silence. For those who are always quiet even a whisper can make a statement. Perhaps we should start by understanding courage as making a statement.

One of my favorite readings that I would discuss in my introductory anthropology class was one about adaptive ritual. In it, the author discussed how, as a child, he first saw how ultraorthodox Jews dressed in warm clothes would stand in the hot sun in the middle of the day, praying in front of a wall in Jerusalem. Given the climate, their behavior made no sense. The author explored several anthropological theories and eventually, inspired by behavior ecology, came to a plausible explanation. He calls it the *costly signaling theory*. What it means is that the cost of the behavior is so high that it communicates a strong message. Freely translated, the ultraorthodox Jewish ritual is basically saying, "I know this is extreme. Look what I am willing to do at what cost. This must show how seriously committed I am to my faith".

He then illustrates that theory by looking at the springbok, a type of antelope found in southern and southwestern

Africa. When a springbok spots a predator, rather than running away it starts to *stot*, meaning it starts to make high jumps, with its legs stiffly facing down. It also pulls down its tail and makes its white tail hyper-visible. So, from a survival perspective, not the best move. However, from a *costly signaling theory* what the springbok is communicating is: "Look at me, you know I must be crazy, and my legs must be incredibly strong. You know I will outrun you if I am crazy enough to do this, right here, knowing you are watching me, so you don't need to even bother". Or something like that, I am imagining. The crazy thing is, it works. Predators mostly leave them alone unless they are breeding, and their numbers are not endangered, which shows they are surviving if not thriving.

These examples highlight certain behaviors as ritual or ecological survival behaviors linked to cost. I like these examples not only because they are interesting, but because I believe they can be used to underscore the concept of courage as making a noticeable statement. Sure, with ultraorthodox Jews their behavior is linked to a display of their faith and commitment to the community, but the extreme statement does something else as well. Similarly, with the springbok, the extreme behavior makes a statement that forces the onlooker to question themselves.

When Holding Space, we need to be courageous not just for its own sake, but because we want to create a crack in what is established. We want to cause a disruption in the status quo. We can do that by making a statement to make people stop and question what they think they know. That is a primary goal of our courageous acts. Being courageous, then, can involve stepping out and making a statement either so bold or so different that it catches people's attention and makes them question what they are attached to knowing.

Being bold and catching attention for the cause is key, but

being strategic and wise about that step is just as important. When one is bold and visible, one is also vulnerable. In the Netherlands, there are those who have committed to changing the well-loved children's tradition of Saint Nicholas by demanding the end of Zwarte Piet, the Moorish character who is the servant of Saint Nicholas. Every year they go to public places with signs and shirts displaying their message. Every year they are exposed to escalating abuse and violence.

They are aware of the risks but face them because they are so committed to the cause. They are also strategic, however. Their protests are well thought out, planned and prepared. They demonstrate at the end of the year at the time of the holiday, but they are active throughout the year as well. They visit and talk to people, schools, and organizations. They use multiple avenues to try to force cracks in Dutch consciousness around the appropriateness of the black character as part of this holiday and they are steadily making progress. What contributes to their courage is not only their conviction, but their numbers, as well. They have groups who support each other throughout the country, hence stepping out – even in the face of violence – is made easier because of the support.

Any courageous act implies taking risks and it is important to consider and weigh those risks. One time, when I was teaching a seminar to a gathering of European education students, one shared that they knew of somebody in Poland who had painted a Madonna with a rainbow-colored halo. They had wanted to make a pro-LGBTQ+ statement. The artist was thrown in prison for their action. The student sincerely asked me whether I thought they should or should not engage in these types of actions to try to implement change.

I told them I could not decide that for them. I continued stating that if the person in question was a single parent for instance, they might rethink such an action, meaning there are a context and acceptable risk factors to each person's situation. However, it is actions like these that have started revolutions or caused significant cracks. There are people who have risked their lives for what they believe in, from Buddhist monks who have set themselves on fire to protest religious persecution to Chinese college students that faced armored tanks for the sake of democracy in Tiananmen Square in 1989. So, courage can be about taking compassionate, bold action, but with a willingness to accept whatever the outcome of that action may be.

Last but not least, there is another form of courage that is needed for Holding Space. Simply put, one has to be creative on the spot. One has to be willing to step out, in that moment when that crack presents itself, while not knowing what to do. In the philosophy of the Blues Aesthetic, this is referred to as the solo or riffing on the break. A good blues or jazz musician must be able to improvise. There will come a break in the music, a crack, when one has to step forward and deliver something, anything. Jazz musicians call this "The Moment to Shine". This moment of grace under pressure is an opportunity to shine, make one's mark, and is seen as a chance to bring out the best in a person. The Blues Aesthetic purports that improvisation is a basic skill to navigate the hardships and setbacks in life.

From a psychological perspective, the pressure of the moment will jump-start some creative process. Instinctually, there is the will to survive. This instinct has been suppressed by a lifetime of conditioning and social norms, but when given a chance, is available to be of assistance in a moment of need. From a spiritual perspective, even when one steps out in the unknown for the solo performance, one is never alone. One is connected to forces seen and unseen that one can tap into at any given time. Stepping forward and acting in the unknown is then a matter of trust and faith in those relationships. Regardless of the perspective one holds, the moment on the spot can indeed be "The Moment to Shine".

Gran tangi. Thank you for the lesson on the need to be courageous and the understanding that we have the inner resources at our disposal to do so, always.

HUMILITY

Holding space requires humility. It requires a sensitivity to the fact that people make mistakes and that we make mistakes ourselves. The challenge is to extend grace to others and ourselves, to see people as human beings no matter how atrocious their behavior. This might be one of the hardest things to do. It is easy to value the stories of those we like, but those we don't... wow.

Valuing the story of the other does not mean that we should accept or tolerate any kind of story that violates us. It does challenge us to leave that person in their humanity, no matter how flawed the way they may choose to express it. They can remain in their humanity but at the same time one can set boundaries as to what one can accept as acceptable in one's space. We are talking about the complexity of applying the "F" word, *forgiveness*. How do you do forgiveness? How do you forgive but not excuse? Is that even possible? People always say that forgiveness is for yourself and not the other person, ultimately. That sounds very nice, but what does that mean and how do you do that, really?

I have had the honor to work with refugees and being involved in their lives to some extent. They taught me some of the most powerful lessons about humility. I met people who had experienced some of the most horrible forms of violence one could imagine. Yet at every gathering they always started by giving thanks for how far they had come. Their gratitude and appreciation for life was relentless. It fueled them to take steps to move forward, often from point 0. People who had been professionals were now reduced to cleaning hotel rooms or working in factories. I don't want to romanticize their lives because Post Traumatic Stress Syndrome and other forms of violence also followed them into their new lives. Their outlook on life was very much fueled by their religious beliefs, however. Their sense of gratitude and choice to focus on the present and possibility, instead of solely focusing on the past, was remarkable if not inspiring. Whether they had forgiven their perpetrators I could not tell you, but I did see that they put most of their energy on cultivating the positive and investing in moving forward.

People do dumb things. People do horrendous things. They do hurtful things on purpose. They also do hurtful things not on purpose. Does it really matter whether they do things on purpose or not? For the person on the receiving end, it might not necessarily matter. Hurt is hurt, regardless of the source. It might seem that it would make it easier to forgive those who did not mean to do harm. "They did not mean to, so oh well." But what about those who don't mean to do harm but keep hurting somebody over and over again? What then? Forgiveness seems to signal that "oh well, but you are still okay." That consequently means that those who we deem unforgiveable are not okay. So, the world would seem to be divided between those who are okay and those who are not. Those who are nice at heart and those who are not. If only it were that simple. I once asked a Sufi Muslim friend of mine if they could explain what the meaning of extending mercy or grace was. They explained that mercy or grace meant that God held a hand over your head and said you were still okay as a human being in spite of what you might have done. I thought it was simple yet powerful, and I have drawn upon that wisdom many times. Because there is nothing that I would rather do sometimes than wield that machete of Ma Po and cut people loose and dismiss them from the human race, but they are still human, according to this philosophy.

In my search toward understanding forgiveness, grace, and mercy, I have studied literature and reflections on Truth and Reconciliation committees in Africa and South America to look for answers. The Reconciliation approach was an alternative to the Retribution model that was used in the aftermath of World War II. The Retribution approach to justice stipulates that in order for justice to prevail there needs to be some form of payback, restitution, equivalent suffering, and so on. It underscores a principle that there are certain acts that are unforgivable, a premise that is questioned in the Reconciliation model. Now mind you there has been plenty of opposition to the Reconciliation approach in South Africa, Rwanda, Sierra Leone, and other countries where these courts have taken place. And the execution of these approaches has not all been the same, but there are certain lessons that can be drawn for our use.

The Retribution model is based on an approach where the focus is on individuals as victims or as perpetrators. The Reconciliation model introduces social restoration and communality in the justice process. The Truth and Reconciliation Committees show how forgiveness, even for the most atrocious offenses, can contribute to some form of restoration. These gatherings are not meant to be merely symbolic or ceremonial but are meant to set some things in motion that can lead to individual restoration, communal reconciliation and, ultimately, to healing of the community as a whole. Certain elements are considered key, such as giving public account and acknowledgment of wrongdoing; having to listen to the impact on the victims; getting a full picture of the horrendous past events; and having to ask for amnesty or forgiveness – depending on the country. It is believed that writing people off as monsters is too easy and absolves the perpetrators from having to do atonement work. It is also believed that no matter how horrendous the behavior, these people are still members of the community, in spite of all their flaws. Thus, the community also has the responsibility to do work to negotiate how to relate to these people.

Again, there were those who believed forgiveness was not possible. It is argued, however, that the Truth and Reconciliation process could at least contribute towards creating conditions in which forgiveness became a possibility. And in instances where the perpetrators initially showed no remorse, when they had to face their victims' families personally, in public court, and had to humble themselves and physically engage through either kneeling or prostrating, something shifted for all involved. Forgiveness is not about letting people go scot free, but to create the conditions where they can be held accountable and take responsibility for beginning to do the work, the hard work, the love-work, to fall back in the graces of the community. Thinking back, then, to my friend's explanation about holding a hand over the perpetrator's head, I think this idea can be extended to say: "It is okay, you are still a human being,... now prove it." Forgiveness, then, is about creating a shift and a space for the perpetrator to redeem themselves and to work on their healing, if they so choose. That space we grant contains compassion for the perpetrator, but also for the victim, as it allows the victim to stop carrying the emotional burden, which is often what they tend to do. When somebody has been injured or violated they tend to hold on to the resentment and pain, while the perpetrator goes on their merry way. Forgiveness, then, helps the victim to create a space to let go of the disappointment about how things were not as they should have been. Ridding the space of disappointment, resentment and pain creates fertile ground to receive positive input and grow.

Why did I go so deep, so far to explore forgiveness? Why did I go to people who have experienced genocide and other horrible wrongdoings, when looking for answers to help people hold space? The wrongdoings we encounter consist of dismissals, neglect, devaluation, excluding language, and so on. These activities are harmful, but not even close to genocide or other war brutalities. This is exactly why I went to people who had these kinds of stories. If people who have gone through the worst of the worst are able to extend grace, who are we not to? Our grievances are far smaller, yet we need help. Other than the level of grievance, one major difference is that in the Reconciliation cases the perpetrators confess, are contrite or appear to be, and aim for forgiveness. In our grievances, our perpetrators are unaware and/or do not necessarily come forward to confess or ask for forgiveness. The Reconciliation process identifies the public sharing of truths and coming forward as essential to the restoration process. What if that phase is not present? What if somebody violates us, does not acknowledge it, knowingly or not, how should we forgive them? Why would we forgive them?

As a person dedicated to promoting inclusive environments, while fighting for my students and staff, I unfortunately have had to navigate my own experiences of marginalization at the same time. It has been normal, par for the course, but is still trying at times. When I worked as an adjunct instructor at a community college in Kentucky, one of the black professors there had taken me aside. At the time, the college was contemplating offering me a permanent contract. He told me that I could take it but that I needed to be aware that I was going to be treated differently. There were going to be those among the staff as well as the students who would not treat me with respect, no matter how hard I worked. That conversation happened about 20 years ago, but I would be reminded of it every now and then. At one job assignment, I had a colleague who kept undermining me, not on everything, just on some big issues. Each time, I would take the time to confront the person and tell them what had happened, the impact it had had on me and that I would prefer that it not to happen again. The person listened sympathetically and agreed. It may seem like an easy thing to do, but it wasn't. It took courage to have these conversations each time. I had to be sensitive, speak in a certain way to get my point across, but preserve the relationship. Each time, I gave this person the benefit of the doubt and gave them another chance, suppressing my Ma Po machete instinct to cut them loose, because I was invested in making this work. I would rather have walked away, but a commitment to my work demanded that I address it and address it properly. It was emotionally tiresome.

After doing this for a few years, another incident happened. This was the one that broke the camel's back. I was livid, angry, and ready to put my fist through the wall, actually wanted to put my fist through this person's throat. It wasn't just about the person, but about this conglomeration of insults and slights and disrespect. The fact that this kept happening specifically to me and not to my white colleagues was the ultimate salt in the wound. I was done. I walked it off. I had to walk it off for a day or two, because if I had responded in the moment, Ma Po's machete would have been vicious and merciless. After I calmed down, I made arrangements to make sure that this would not happen again. I had to protect myself. It was obvious that the talks throughout the years had not made a difference. Once I put the arrangements in place so this person could no longer hurt me came the hard part, I had to forgive them. I had to forgive them because each time I would think about them, choice curse words would come to mind, my jaws would lock and my muscles would tighten. I had to set them free so that I could set myself free. Sufi Islam teachings instructed me to look at the lesson. What was the lesson they were here to bring me? They taught me that I deserved better and that I had the right to demand better. I had acted on that. They taught me that they were a human being who made horrible choices about how to treat people. This was about them, about where they were in their story. All I had to do was to untangle myself from that story, and respectfully let them go, without any hard feelings. They had done the best they could, given where they were in their story. Once I understood that, not just intellectually, but fully, I could let them go. They were free to work that trait out in their story, but that was their story. It would be nice if one day they learned how to treat people better, but it was not my job to be involved in that in any way. They were welcome to be a flawed human being, but they were going to live that out in their space and time, not mine. And with that understanding, I became free. I was no longer attached.

Doing that for another is work, but still, it is usually easier to do than when we have to do it for ourselves. Sometimes we need something, some jolt, to shift out of the attachments we have to the expectations we hold for ourselves. I myself experienced such a jolt, which I refer to as "Elmo". Sometimes our lessons come from the most unexpected places.

When my marriage ended, it was painful. Even though it was a contentious separation, I was quickly able to forgive my soon-to-be-ex. As disappointed as I was, I had to be honest and admit that he, in fact, had not changed a whole lot since we had gotten together. It was Mama Walks on Water who asked me "Yes, he told you all those wonderful things he had to offer, but did you take the time to find out if he could deliver on those promises?" I had to admit to myself that I had not. Forgiving him for not living up to my expectations, which turned out to be mostly fictionalized, was actually not that hard. What I was left with was an incredible sense of grief, not about the past, but about the future that was never going to happen. Secondly, I was overcome with self-loathing. How did I get myself into this situation? If I was supposedly so smart, how come I had been so stupid? And so on and so on. The grief combined with the self-loathing got me in a very low place.

One morning I lay in the bed just awash in my depressed, self-chastising state. I lay staring up at the ceiling, caught up in self-loathing. I remember listening to my heartbeat, wondering why it was still beating when I so clearly just wanted it to stop. I listened to my breath, thinking it made no sense that my body kept functioning. I was such a failure, I just wanted it all to stop, I just.... As I was indulging my condemnation I was all of a sudden disrupted by a little voice. "Momma, get up, I want to watch Elmo!" As much as I wanted to stay in my dark place, reality in the form of Elmo beckoned me back into the real world. Instantly, that hand of God was over my head and let me know that in spite of my horrible shortcomings, I was still... human... and I had better get up and find that Elmo video. I can laugh about it to this day. I got up out of the bed that day and got back to the business of life. I never drifted that low again. Every day, with grace, things became more bearable until I could fully embrace that, indeed, I was okay.

Holding Space requires offering a space of validation and non-judgment. It is important, then, to learn to let go of the trespasses that settle and dampen our spirits. Forgiveness requires work, some sensible mental gymnastics that help us look at things the way they are and then absorb that knowledge with every fiber of our being. People are flawed, they make mistakes, and do dumb things. They say stupid things. And yet they are human. We ourselves are one of those people, are related to those people, and as we learn to extend compassion, grace and forgiveness to them, we had better learn to apply that to ourselves.

There is a Sufi Islam teaching that says that there are no bad people, only people who bring us life lessons to help us get to our higher selves. We might need some more mental gymnastics before we can fully embrace that lesson, but until then, let's start accepting that we all need that hand over our head from time to time and the reminder that we are human beings and, in spite of our shortcomings, okay human beings with the potential of becoming good ones.

Gran tangi. Thank you for the lesson that humility involves extending grace and that doing so requires serious love-work that might be difficult but is oh-so-necessary.

LISTENING AND CONNECTING

End — Ch. 6

There are some high notes and low notes in motherhood. One of the definite low notes is when I found out that, at age four, my youngest was hard of hearing. All those times when he was with his back turned to me and I yelled at him "Don't you hear me? Why aren't you listening to me!". Turns out he was not actually always hearing me. Aahh... that stung, and the self-loathing was brutal.

It didn't help matters much that he kept passing the hearing tests. He was so smart that he had figured out that the nurse gave small behavioral cues as to which side the noise was coming through in the headphone. So, he would not pay attention to the noise that he could barely hear, instead he would intently watch her. When we figured it out and made him redo the test with his back towards the nurse, we were able to confirm that he indeed had some hearing issues. He was good at faking it.

Sometimes we are good at faking it. Well, we might not be as intentional as my child, but we might give the appearance of listening when, in fact, we are not. One of the core skills in Holding Space is being able to listen. It seems so obvious and yet is hard to do. People often appear to listen, when in reality they are not.

I personally see a difference between hearing versus listening. In hearing there is an exchange of a communication stimulus between a sender and a receiver. The receiver receives the stimulus and consequently is focused on the reception and how the stimulus impacts the receiver. Listening requires the same process but adds an extra step. The communicated stimulus is received, but rather than sticking with the focus on the reception, the receiver shifts their attention back to the sender. They take the source into consideration and particularly the state of the sender. The message never consists just of the stimulus itself, there is the stuff not said, implied, the intent of the sender, the state of the sender, etc.

Why is it so important to take that extra step? Because hearing leads to quick and superficial reactions, often based on incomplete information. These reactions in turn can make the sender feel misunderstood, not "heard" or cared for and they will get turned off. Consequently, a true connection will not be made, and, at its worst, the sender will decide not to engage again. Often, then, what is perceived as listening is really just hearing.

What is wrong with hearing? Why isn't it enough? Hearing taps into the fragility of one's person. It feeds the misconception that the individual self is so important, when in fact one is always in connection with others. Hearing implies one-dimensional questioning along the lines of "How does it affect me? What does that say about me? What does it do to me?" Whereas listening carries deeper questions: "What does it say about us? What does it say about how we relate to each other?"

Like a good American football player, one can have all the right skills to catch the ball midair. But the good player is not just technically skilled at embracing that ball, they are also aware of the person that throws the ball. They know their moves, their style, their strategy, and hence can make preparatory choices to best ensure that reception. The exceptional player takes not just the thrower but the context of the whole field into consideration.

The work of true listening, then, is to extend outside of one-self, to be in tune with the interconnectedness within which the exchange takes place. One time I attended a conference and participated in a small session. The German speakers informed us about a concept they called *sticky stairs*. Apparently, as engineering is a big and successful part of German culture, many immigrants encourage their offspring to pursue engineering to achieve upward mobility. Those who do, find out that even with their degrees, achieving upward mobility is far harder and slower for them than for their German counterparts. This is what they called the *sticky stairs* syndrome. Unfortunately, disillusion and depression are part of this experience.

The few of us in this small conference session engaged in good conversation about the role of the educational field, in particular our responsibility to prevent people from falling into disillusion. The discussion was thoughtful and engaging and, in spite of the sad subject, I left energized and inspired. As I left, I ran into a colleague and shared my enthusiasm about what I had just learned. I went into detail about the *sticky stairs* concept and how we discussed our role in it. As I finished, without catching their breath, the person immediately countered "Well, white people have it hard too, you know." I sighed politely, but the conversation was basically over after that.

The person, who was white themselves, in hearing a story about the plight of immigrant people had inadvertently heard an attack on white people. At least, that is what they communicated. By not missing a beat and immediately countering with their response, they communicated one of the following messages: "Hearing stories about the unequal plight of immigrants is *ongezellig*; hearing stories about the unequal plight of immigrants says something negative about me as a white person/white people in general; hearing stories about the unequal plight of immigrants should not stand on its own but must always be linked to the un-equal plight of white people; I must defend the cause of white people, etc...".

It is all speculation of course. I do not know what went on in-side their head. I could have just asked why they responded that way. But I was already turned off, had written them off, and didn't feel them worthy of pursuing a relationship any further. And so, I walked away determined to never engage with this person again in any type of conversation where the story of *the other* was central. Ma Po's machete had made a clear break.

This is what happens a lot. Failing to hold the space for each other's stories and immediately asking clarifying questions or making defensive statements because of hearing, results in the sending party cutting off and checking out. They might be so skilled you don't even notice it. A polite smile does wonders in covering up the action of the machete.

For those used to dwelling in *the dominant* realm, truly listen-ing to the story of *the other* can be extremely challenging, giv-en that *the dominant* story has always been treated as valid, first, most important, and normal. Having to take a backseat by truly listening and possibly being confronted with the in-validation of their own normal story is *ongezellig*, to say the least. For those in *the other* position, so used to being over-looked and silenced, having to listen to a sincere story from *the dominant* realm can be difficult, as well. There might be no patience or compassion left, or there is the assumption that *the dominant* story will automatically trample their own. However, listening is a skill that can be cultivated.

Listening starts with the commitment that one engages in the practice because one wants to connect with and honor someone's story. There are plenty of people who are merely engaged in hearing to pick up on pieces of information that they can use to construct a counterstatement or argument. They are engaged in battle and are aiming to win. They are not interested in connecting to the other party's story or to be transformed by that story. They are only engaged to seek affirmation of their own story.

This commitment to connecting and honoring others' stories is a primary step and, to be honest, is not an easy step. In order to commit to honoring the story of the other, one has to be comfortable and confident in one's own story. One has to understand that holding the space for the story of the other does not take away from one's own story. Our stories can co-exist. They do co-exist, whether we see or hear them or not. Ultimately, every story is an opportunity to be reminded that we are connected by our stories. Not everybody is that far yet, however. Committing to honoring the other is probably the biggest hurdle to overcome. If I listen to these stories what will happen to mine?

Second, one has to be able to respectfully tune in when the story is told. One of the most powerful and supporting ways of listening is *witnessing* as seen in the African American church. The African American church has been a major vehicle in the psychological survival of black people in the United States. In the sanctity of the church, people share their stories of woe and struggle. A congregation listens attentively and nods at points of recognition. They may rock in their seats and hum, adding to the rhythm and cadence in the atmosphere. They make utterances like *Yes...; Well...; Preach chil'...; Go on and tell it...*, and more. They don't judge but are present. They hold the space. Their comments give affirmation to the storyteller that their story has a right to be there, that their story is valid. Inspired by African American *witnessing*, the challenge is to be merely present, attentive and non-judgmental when somebody shares their story.

Next, one has to be willing to receive the story and give it room to sink in and settle-- despite our tendency, especially among those of us in academia, to immediately analyze and seek a response. One does not have to do anything, including coming to conclusions or analyses, but just witness and hold the space. One does that by simply taking a moment to breathe and calm the mind.

The next step is to regard the received information and reflect on the sender. One has to extend outside of oneself. Take a second, if not more, to consider with compassion where the story is coming from and respond accordingly. What that response will be one does not know in advance, but if one responds out of sincerity and an obvious willingness to connect, chances are the communication will continue.

In my particular encounter with my colleague around the topic of *the sticky stairs*, the speed with which I received a response sent a strong message. They didn't bother to let my story sink in. My story was too *ongezellig* to be fully digested. If they had simply taken a breath and said something like "Wow, you seem really excited about your experience", or "It sounds like you learned a lot", I would have continued talking. Instead, the machete with a smile did its work. Mind you, the intention of the listener was not an issue here, but the inadvertent message they sent was. I could have extended grace and forgiveness, another important skill, but I didn't. On that day, at that time, it was just too much. It was just not something I could muster. For the person who is used to not being listened to, that's an important factor. That particular day, I was just done and let the machete fly. Intent does not absolve impact.

How we listen, and how we communicate that we are listening, shapes our interaction. It is not necessarily about the content. We can disagree or agree, but how do we communicate the validation of the story of the other? Through actively cultivating our listening skills, we can become better at holding spaces where our stories are acknowledged as valid. Like my child, sometimes you need an intervention or reminder that faking it is not enough.

Gran tangi. Thank you for the lesson of how important and how labor intensive it is to be a good listener.

SPEAKING

My mother is known in the family for her quick and sometimes sharp tongue. I have seen her eviscerate people with her words while smiling at the same time. She can be very direct, and her sense of justice and fairness are strong. She can also be wrong, however, and I have seen her do some unnecessary damage. Luckily, she is also very kind and devoted to building relationships, so she will also do the work to repair the damage, but it is still work.

Some people have told me that I look like her. I disagree. My sons have told me "Ma, you know you intimidate people." I think my "intimidation factor" – if there is such a thing – has to do with a multitude of factors. The fact that I don't cower when I speak, the size of my body, that I have a deep voice, etc. I believe it is these things more so than what I say that make an impact. If anything, I am quite deliberate about my speech. I try to mean what I say and say what I mean. I don't like to have to back-track and have to recover from unfortunate things I said in the spur of the moment. I also don't mind not speaking. I don't have the strong urge to correct people, especially if I am not invested in a personal relationship with them. We don't always fix things by speaking, sometimes all we do is stir the pot.

Speaking is an essential skill in being able to hold space, however. I come from a culture with a rich oral tradition. Knowing when to speak, how to speak, to whom and in which way, are all part of a rich Surinamese culture. *Lobi singi*, love songs, proverbs, jokes, stories, riddles, crafty veiled insults even, but also ritual and ceremonial incantations, are part of an extensive Surinamese oral repertoire. This tradition hails back to its African roots, a continent where the power of the Word is embedded in a rich oral tradition. From griots who sing and narrate ancestral lineages, to talking drums that charge the air with tones that mimic the spoken language, there is an understanding that words are vibrations and, as such, have the power to transform.

That rhyme from my childhood "Sticks and stones may break my bones, but words will never hurt me", was cute, but entirely untrue. Words not only can hurt, they can hurt deeply and their damage can last for years, even generations. Our African ancestors teach us that words charge the air. What we say and how we say things then, matter. Our words when added to the atmosphere can change that atmosphere for better or worse. My friend and mentor during my anthropology graduate school days, Thom Ball from the Klamath Nation in Oregon, told me about the importance of having to sing my prayers. "That's how your intentions rise up and reach the heavens." Words have the power to heal, but they also have the power to wound or destroy. We have to be careful with our words if we want to create nurturing environments. The Blues Aesthetic calls for brutal honesty, something my godmother Walks on Water also instilled in me. But it is not as simple as it seems. Brutal honesty is not just about blurting things out. Mama Walks on Water taught me you can be tough and honest, but still need to come from compassion. One has to keep in mind, then, what the goal is when speaking. There are some who speak to make a point, to be heard, to contribute to the relationship or the atmosphere. But there are those who speak just to fill the empty space, to get attention, or to hurt others. When we are brutally honest, that honesty can come from pain, but can it still come with compassion towards the listener? Are we willing to take the other into consideration?

If we choose to speak with consideration, we need to choose

our words carefully and strategically. Again, the easiest thing to do is to blurt things out, but the risk is that words get lost and don't reach their intended target or reach it ineffectively. When we make a commitment to speak with consideration, we are also willing to be accountable for the effect of our words, and hence might even choose to hold back some words.

The question "Where are you from?" is an innocuous but loaded question for Dutch people with non-Western, immigrant heritages. It seems a simple question, but for many people the impact is quite unpleasant. In the broader context of the story of the Netherlands, the Netherlands has always prided itself on being tolerant of immigrants. Note that "tolerant" does not equal "accepting". Dutch people are tolerant if one is willing to totally conform to their norms. Consequently, Dutch immigration policies since the 1980s have emphasized terms such as *delay, failure to adapt* and *failure to integrate* in their deliberations. This framing of immigrants through the lens of not quite fitting in has seeped into all aspects of Dutch society, from the healthcare, to the education, to the entertainments systems. The question "Where are you from?" and the follow up "No, where are you really from?", as innocent as they may seem, imply that you are from elsewhere. The Dutch even created a word to highlight that one is from elsewhere, "*allochtoon*". The Dutch citizen with an immigrant heritage is always reminded that one is never fully Dutch. That is quite uncomfortable for those second, third and even fourth generation immigrants who were born in the Netherlands but are continuously reminded that they never fully belong. These innocent phrases also imply that there is some question or hope as to when one will return to their fictional homeland. It's like that children's singing and tag-out game "One – Of – These – Does – Not – Belong". The last one tagged is out. And the tag always falls on you.

I have heard Dutch people say, "But I am genuinely interested in where they are from!" That might be so, but the question is experienced as hurtful, plain and simple. Therefore, I choose not to ask that question. Instead, I invest in the relationship and if it is meant to come up, it will come up. How do we want to use our words to contribute to a space that validates everybody? There is a range of ways that speaking can be used to hold the space: giving testimony, witnessing, atoning, signifying even. What matters is the intention with which we speak and the purpose of the utterance. If we want to be effective, we have to be wise and considerate in the choices that we make when speaking.

Using speech wisely also requires not speaking at times and withdrawing into silence. Self-silencing does not necessarily have to represent censorship or repression. Silence can be the necessary space for contemplation and reflection. Silence is powerful when it comes to communication. It is important. Silence is also the work of editing our speech. Not everything needs to be said. There is a time and a place to use certain words to have impact. An overflow of words also risks having the message miss its target. This is why poetry can be so profound. One of the people I admire in his ability to succinctly say a lot is my friend, the former Kentucky Poet Laureate and founder of the Affrilachian poets, Frank X Walker. Frank and his fellow Affrilachians have created a space for an overlooked population, those of African descent in the Appalachian region. More specifically, he embodies the concept of love-work not only in his writing, but in all his other arts endeavors, as well. He purposely and unapologetically creates spaces of validation for black people in his work, from the unsung York and Isaac Murphy, to the phenomenal Medgar Evers, to the anonymous black boy in elementary school and his woodcarvings of slave ships. In his poem "Monarchy" from 2017, he describes his experience and role as a black role model when he enters an elementary school.

The last two paragraphs read:

> I am the disciplinarian
> promising consequences
> for their unacceptable behavior,
> pushback for their initial disrespect,
> Hell to pay for their indifference,
> remedies, directions, and road maps,
> for their short attention spans,
> for their yet unrealized dreams
> but only because I love them.
> I love their potential.
> I love their wide-eyed promise.
> I love their well-masked fears.
>
> I say all of this
> without ever opening my mouth,
> with a gentle but firm hand
> on every shoulder
> with serious eyes
> and a don't test me smile
> every time I arrive any place
> with a room full of cubs
> where I am the only lion.

So much is said in these two paragraphs. Learning how to edit and use our speech for validation is a highly valuable skill. Strategically constructed speech can be used to hold the space or to force people to pay attention and rearrange the space. This takes practice. There are times when an honest, impulsive reaction can be just as effective, like my experience when I called out the teacher for using a slave auction as a fundraising activity. I spoke up out of pure incredulity, expecting others to be abhorred by this as well. Like the child pointing out the Emperor's nakedness in the fairytale, an innocent outburst can shake things up. But there is always a risk. In retrospect, I wonder if I had thought about it and I had brought it up differently, might I have been able to engage my fellow students in the deliberation, rather than shock them into silence?

I can recall one incident where I did speak very deliberately on an incongruity and where I was able to force people to take a stand and make a shift. When I lived in Maryland, I worked for a number of years in specialized foster care. It was called specialized foster care because most of these children had special circumstances, and required more than standard care. I was the family recruiter and trainer and would prepare families to become foster families. I worked alongside the social workers who were the case managers and at times I would be called into team meetings to discuss their charges, especially in times of crisis. This was such a case.

There was a teenage boy who had been in specialized care for a number of years. The crisis I was called in for was that this boy kept running away from his foster families, but he kept running to either his mother or his grandmother. His mother was on drugs and lived in a bad part of town. His grandmother was elderly and could not really care for him. When he would be brought back, his behavior would be out of sorts for a while. This was all a major problem. I could see it was a problem, but I also felt sympathy for the boy that longed to be with his family.

The social workers and the psychiatrist saw it differently, however. They started to discuss how problematic his running away behavior was. His running away was the cause of the problem. As they continued, I felt like I was getting lost in an Alice in Wonderland nightmare. Were these people for real? When I heard the social worker ask the psychiatrist if there was not a medication that could curb his running away behavior, I nearly screamed and jumped out of my seat.

This was like that *drapetomania* madness from slavery days, where they actually labeled the running away behavior of slaves as a mental illness! I was the youngest person in the room and the lowest on the totem pole. But I was also the only one who was going to speak up for this boy. I needed to address the highest person in the room, which was the psychiatrist. So, I waited until he started to speak. He was fully on board with this being addressed as a mental illness issue. So, I interrupted him. "I am sorry for interrupting, but can you help me understand something? Are all of you saying that the problem is that this boy longs to be with his family? And is there an actual medicine that can make you stop wanting to be with your family?"... The answer was silence. Then I looked at the others around the room. "No, please, I want to understand. Are you all saying that you want this boy to stop loving and wanting to be with his family and you want to find medication to help him do that?"... Then I withdrew into silence. I sat back and gave them the space and room to come up with an answer. I don't remember exactly what was said. There were some uhs" and "aahs", some stuttering and red faces. All I know is that medicine was off the table after that. I think we came up with a schedule of supervised visits. It doesn't matter. I had forced them to shift. I had held them accountable as a fellow professional, even though I was the youngest in the room. Courage was a big part of this effort, but I could not *not* say anything. I owed it to that boy and to myself. I know that if I had not said anything, I would have had to answer to myself, and my ancestors would have made me pay for it.

Did I mention that I was the only black person in the room and that the boy was black? I don't know if that made a difference. It did not matter to me. If he had been green, purple or a peg leg pirate, I would have spoken up for him. This is the work, the love-work, that once committed to you can no longer deny in yourself. Your voice can be a mighty sword for justice, but like any sword you have to handle it carefully.

Gran tangi. Thank you for the lesson about the power of the Word, and the importance of investing in using it wisely and with compassion.

SEEING

End — Ch. 8

I grew up in my household as the only person that did not wear glasses. I never knew my parents without glasses, and I remember when my brother got his. He was four years old I believe. I was two years older and in the first grade. I remember him going to school with his coat over his head, not wanting people to see his glasses. But he got used to them. It became normal.

I was thirty when I walked in the supermarket and all of a sudden noticed that the signs that hung over the aisles were blurry. I went from one aisle to the next, hoping that something would change, but unfortunately it didn't. From there I went to a random optician in the mall and had my eyes checked. There the horror was confirmed. My eyesight had changed and I, in fact, needed glasses. I was in shock.

I had to come back and get fitted for the glasses. I remember trying the contact lenses and fighting with putting my finger in my eye for 30 minutes before giving up. When I walked out of the shop with the glasses on my nose I was depressed. I also saw for the first time how many people walked around with glasses and felt instantly an eerie kinship with them, we the eyesight-compromised. But I got over it and it became normal.

It becomes normal to see a certain way. Apparently, for some it becomes normal not to see. Those in the realm of *the dominant* don't see the full story of *the other*. *The other* does see and knows of the story of *the dominant* intimately. It is the story they are fed from the moment they enter the arena. Every aspect of the story of *the dominant* is told again and again. They cannot not know. Given that the story of *the other* is hardly ever told, or when told, only in superficial or consumable portions, *the dominant* is mostly oblivious to *the other's* story. They have, what is appropriately referred to as, "blind spots".

They even refer to them as blind spots. "That is one of my blind spots. Can you help me figure out what my blind spots are?" For some reason, I always cringe at the mention of the term blind spots. It is usually mentioned when an oversight has been made in regard to an interaction with *the other*. But it is an "oops" reaction. One refers to blind spots matter-of-factly, like it is understandable, like a natural deformation in the eye. They usually shrug it off with a sheepish smile. It is an oversight that is forgivable, or at least should be. But is it? It softens the real underlying message that they are so conditioned to disregard the story of the other as insignificant. Afterall, it is normal.

I was once asked to give feedback on a lesson a teacher had prepared for social studies. They had chosen to focus on several forms of civil disobedience and even started the lesson with the announcement that the students were going to learn about breaking the rules. The teacher worked their lesson plan for the students as if they were a homogenous group that could freely experiment with civil disobedience. The lesson was creative and even encouraged on-the-street, real-life exercises, but reading it as a mother of a black son, I was horrified.

When I pointed out their lack of attention to safety and risk involved for the children of color in this particular lesson, they admitted their oversight. When they responded with a smile stating that it had indeed been a blind spot, I wanted to scream. I wanted to scream because that statement so diminished the gravity of the situation. In their "oops" moment, they had communicated that the value of the stories of their students of color mattered less. The safety of our children, that we worry about every day when they leave our houses, did not even cross their mind. Safety from the risks we regularly warn our children about was somehow optional.

As parents of these children, we worry about what they might encounter every day when they leave our houses and enter a world that does not value them. We instill in them the lessons of abiding by the rules because the margin of error for them is so small and the repercussions can be so detrimental. I thought about the anxiety, worry and the prayers we send up to keep our children safe in a world that does not want them, does not value them and does not see them, unless they do something wrong. And I thought about not only my children, but the many students who have come to me and have cried about their experiences of not being seen or being valued.

But I didn't scream, because my parental anguish had no room here. As a colleague then, I just stressed the need to include safety and risk measures the next time the lesson was to be taught. As one who is dedicated to Holding Space I was left with the question: How do I force someone to see? How do I force someone to care enough about the other to include their story? I first had to remind myself that not seeing is not necessarily a reflection of not caring. I needed that reminder to lessen my anguish. Not seeing, then, is a reflection of being conditioned not to see, a conditioning that has been hundreds of years in the making. How do we break through that? How can we break through that? How do we make seeing not an optional endeavor, but a standard, normalized pursuit?

To move from the optional to the normalized there needs to be a sense of urgency. But urgency is hard to use as a guide when it is not felt. Rather than urgency, we can use the concept of blind spots as a starting point. Let's take it as a given that we are conditioned to have blind spots in a world dominated by a *dominant and other* divide. All of us dwell in the realm of *the dominant* at any given time, hence all of us have blind spots. Therefore, when we develop some type of programming or action, no matter how perfect we think it is, we should start with the premise that there is something we have overlooked. Rather than aiming to finish and deliver, we should include an extra step if not two before delivery. It should be finish, review, adjust if necessary, and then deliver.

By practicing this every time, we organize our activities, programs, lessons, or even research projects, we chip away at our conditioning until seeing fully becomes normal. Another step to reach an inclusive vision is to engage and connect with the story of *the other*. It is when I became familiar and started working with a young woman in a wheelchair that my vision broadened. Of course, I was sympathetic to the plight of people in wheelchairs and their access. I was aware that sidewalks in different countries varied in terms of being wheelchair accessible, but, truthfully, I might have become aware of it when I had to push my children in strollers. But that's where my awareness stopped. My vision was still limited.

When I learned more about her story, about the amount of energy she had to expend in finding out to what extent buildings were accessible, public transport delivered on its accessibility promise, and so on, I was floored. One would think that for a country as progressive as the Netherlands this would be a done deal. It was not. She changed my view and thereby changed my life. I cannot walk into any building without noticing how handicap accessible or inaccessible it is. Are there only stairs? If there is a ramp where is it located and how steep is it? If there is an automatic door is it working? If there is an elevator and it is out of service what kinds of alternatives are available? It is because I carry her with me, as part of my story now that I see differently. And her story of a mobile disability has transferred to other limitations on disability. As 2020 has imposed face masks as part of our normal landscape, I immediately wondered what it would mean to those hard of hearing and others who rely on facial cues for communication. What part of the story are we not seeing?

We have to create and function with the mindset, then, that being disconnected from the story of the other is no longer an option, but in fact an act of incompletion. We are inherently connected to the other, any other, all others, but we have to make an effort to recognize that and stop giving ourselves permission to yell "oops" and sheepishly shrug it off. Instead, we have to take the coats from over our heads, like my brother had to do way back when, and normalize and accept that, indeed, we are seeing impaired and need help to see better.

Gran tangi. Thank you for the lesson that not seeing does not necessarily mean not caring, but that we must not excuse our not seeing either, and put forth our greatest effort to fight our conditioned blindness.

EMBODIMENT

Put your back into it. Putting your best foot forward. Hop right to it. Put your shoulder to the wheel. Our language is full of references of using the physical body as an essential catalyst for action. Yet when it comes to the traditional approach to holding space, we tend to prioritize the intellect. "Once I have enough information, I will know what to do." There are plenty of people who will tell you what to do, but not necessarily how. Interventions are well thought out but remain stuck in the brain and refuse to seep through to the rest of the body. We have mastered the act of thinking and planning, but continuously fall short of doing. We value highly the art of understanding but are still ill-equipped at fully being.

Interestingly, it is our body that is our biggest obstruction when it comes to implementing all these wonderful things we are inventing for Holding Space. Because of our disconnection between mind and body, we freak out or freeze the moment feelings of *ongezelligheid* appear in our bodies. It feels uncomfortable, hence there must be something wrong, therefore I will withdraw into a mode where that feeling of *ongezelligheid* is gone or at least manageable. One can have it all figured out in their head, know exactly what to do, but taking that first step into action is the biggest hurdle.

Yvonne Daniel, in her study of African Diaspora dance, has explored in-depth the phenomenon of embodied knowledge. She refers to intellectual knowledge as "disembodied knowledge", as knowledge that is compartmentalized and limited in perspective. In order for it to be complete, it needs to be infused with physical, intuitive and spiritual information. She states that because this type of knowledge does not easily lend itself to empirical analysis and rejects the European and American mind/body duality it is not accepted as valid by *the dominant* realm. She purports that practitioners of African Diaspora traditions have embraced both forms of knowledge and therefore have a more holistic frame of reference with which they engage the world.

I believe the mind/body split is not as valued as it once was. There are many health, sport and therapy practices that have promoted the importance of the body as an essential part of our culture. Yet, in general and in *the dominant* realm especially, the body remains secondary to the intellectual domain. The fortress of information has become such a staple of the culture that the intellect receives preference over bodily sensing or intuition.

This separation of the body from the mind does not just go back to the elevation of the mind and the duality as promoted by Descartes. This development went hand in hand with religion, which regarded bodily urges and expressions as sinful, or where bodily functions such as giving birth or breastfeeding were seen as natural, hence closer to nature, hence less intellectually inclined. The closer to nature, the more primitive. Embracing the body as an essential part of knowledge keeping or knowledge production is quite a challenge then, where this disdain of the body is such a longstanding and engrained part of the general story.

We don't just tend to favor our mind over the body, we have learned to distrust and ignore our body's capacity as an ingrained and valuable messenger. Yet, we know the significance when somebody shows up and brings all of themselves. We know the difference between somebody who expresses care and concern and the person who, without being asked, shows up to assist and is fully present. There is an urgency to holding space. There is an urgency to show up fully committed, body, mind, and spirit. People have been talking and writing with all kinds of beautiful insights for decades without any significant change. The subsequent level of disappointment and distrust is so high that we need to see the commitment in our embodied actions. In addition, there is a need for all this intellectual knowledge to become more united with an active body. Great intentions do not get you across mountains, walking does.

Showing up and using our bodies fully is not necessarily about being large and visible. It can be about being subtle. Are we using all our senses? Do we listen to our senses? We have been taught to distrust our senses for the sake of the intellect. And we have been tricked into thinking that the first physical sign of *ongezelligheid* confirms that a certain situation is unbearable and thus is to be avoided. We have to relearn the potential of our body as a source of information and communication. We have to relearn how to reconnect and align our bodies with our intellect and our extended sense of self. We have to unlearn to judge certain feelings of unpleasantness as signals of something being wrong, and instead appreciate them for signals as means to inform us. If we build up that "muscle" through practice and combine it with a sound mind and trusting an element of non-knowing, we can reach that embodied knowledge that Yvonne Daniel was talking about. It will enable us to move and act with full confidence and trust in creating alternate spaces.

I had such a profound experience myself. In the days when I was still working in The Hague as a lector, I would ride my bike to the station every day, about four to six minutes, where I would take the train. This particular day I had a flat tire. I could walk for about 12 minutes, or if I timed it correctly, take the bus. I opted for the bus. As I got on the bus, there was a young man of African descent, probably Surinamese heritage, around age 20 or so, sitting on the first chair opposite the bus driver. I sat down one or two seats behind him on the seat that was perpendicular to his position. I could see him to my right and could see the rest of the bus. There were quite a few people in the bus at this time of the morning, all on their way to work, no doubt.

He was wearing earbuds, but the music was still loud. The bus driver asked him in a friendly manner if he could turn the music down. The young man immediately responded very aggressively and loudly and told the bus driver in no uncertain terms to mind his own business. An exchange started to take place that quickly became louder and more aggressive. A Surinamese lady to my left joins in. "You are wrong! You are disrespectful! The bus driver asked you nicely! All you have to do is listen!" I recognized the sentiment immediately. A Surinamese momma who does not tolerate public misbehavior. It is oh- so-familiar. However, her tone only adds fuel to the fire.

The young man then turns towards her and immediately starts yelling at her to stay out of his business. Profanities are hurled. He alternates between yelling at her and the bus driver. The rest of the people are tense. I take a deep breath and listen and watch. A white lady gets up and goes and sits beside the Surinamese lady. Good, so she is protected. But the young man does not let up. The bus is stopped by now and the bus driver is threatening to call the police.

As I am sitting there, I feel the familiar burn in my belly. My ancestors are signaling me and I know I will have to do something. Between Ma Po and my father and who knows how many others, I tune into that presence and know the time to act is near. I am just waiting for that moment. I am purely listening and sensing and ready to respond. Now for clarification, one has to understand that I bring a particular story to this moment. First, I am a mother of three black sons, so I am not afraid of young black men. If anything, I have a special affinity for them. Secondly, I come from the United States, where behavior like this will get a young black man killed. I have a very strong feeling about standing by versus getting involved with young black men prior to things escalating with the police. I had rather have them interact with me than with the police. It can be the difference between life or death. From me, they can get some compassion, from the police more than likely they will not.

When the young man stood up and started walking towards the bus driver while yelling and threatening "What are you going to do about it!.", I stood up. It was as if my body moved by itself. I took a deep breath, called upon my people *Un yepi mi*, "Y'all better help me out", and slowly started to walk towards the young man, all the while making eye contact. I didn't charge him but moved and talked slowly in my most soothing voice. "Hey man, I see that you are angry. I am so sorry you are having a hard time this morning. But I know you are not going to hit this man, so what are you going to do?" I stopped where I stood, gave him his space. He looked me dead in the eye, angrily. Silence. I waited. He took a deep breath, lowered his eyes, bent his head and walked towards me. He passed me and kept walking to the end of the bus. I moved forward to the bus driver and asked if he was okay. The situation was de-escalated.

I don't recommend for people to start jumping into potential fights. That is not what this story is about. This experience was about surrendering and being fully present and connected. There were a lot of factors that came together in this moment. When I got up and moved it wasn't a conscious decision, it was a driven decision. It was a fully embodied informed action. It was the result of years of fine tuning and learning and trusting in all that I am connected to. He could have physically attacked me, which is why I was as non-threatening as possible and why I gave him his space. But even that chance I was willing to take. I had rather he attack me than get into it with the police. No young black man will die on my watch if I can help it. My body, mind, and spirit are committed to that reality.

When I engage people with singing, dancing, or theater activities, we are doing it to have fun and to lower inhibitions, but also to build on that muscle of embodied knowledge. People don't always get that, and that's okay. They don't understand the urgency of being able to show up fully committed. That's why I shared this story.

Gran tangi. Thank you for the lesson that in order to show up fully we have to reconnect and reinvest in our embodied knowledge.

ENVIRONMENT

In Suriname, when you state your name people generally know which part of the country you hail from. With a population of less than half a million and a history of plantation slavery, last names of those of African descent are easily traceable to the plantations one's ancestors hailed from. As such, your being is linked to a particular place, a distinct physical location. The highways that connected the plantations were the riverways, thus one's identity is often also connected to a certain river.

A visit to family ground usually begins with the encouragement to go say hello to the ancestors and nature spirits. Little cousins, used to the ritual, jump out of the car and run around yelling *Famiri un doro!* Family we have arrived, we are here! From very young they are taught that they are connected to their ancestors, but also to the natural, physical environment.

As societies evolved from reliance on hunter gatherers to food production, the role of community and connection to the environment was maintained. As we have come through the industrial age, however, and are now in the information age, the rise of individuality and disconnection from our natural environment has taken over. The argument can be made that, in our current information age-oriented society, the need for connection is still being expressed but via digital channels. Indeed, the COVID-19 pandemic has also shown that underneath it all we are still social human beings and that we need connection for our mental survival.

Still, our connection to nature has often been reduced to recreational or other enjoyable practice, unless you are a farmer, but not necessarily as a core part of our being and relating to each other. When we say *Aho Metakuye Oyasin* and we say "Me and all my relations", we mean we are connected to all and include the natural world in that. In Suriname as well, the sense of self is extended. In times of disharmony, one is easily encouraged to go and engage with those extended forces one is connected to. Take water and pour it into the earth while talking to ancestors or spiritual forces.

When I moved to Suriname in 2003 to do research for my anthropology dissertation, and stayed at a particular house, I couldn't find rest. My mind kept racing at night and I always felt on edge. When I shared with my aunties my problem they came to my house and sat me down. They explained to me that every place has a spirit. They told me I needed to introduce myself to the environment and make my intentions clear. I needed to pour sweet drinks to show my good intentions as I did so. Under their tutelage I did what they told me to do. Something shifted and I slept like a baby from that point onward.

Now, was it my direct actions that made a spiritual shift? I don't know, it is possible. Was it because my intention and focus shifted? It is possible. Was it because these two women when they heard about my state immediately came to me, sat with me, talked with me, and guided me through a ritual? Was it because they demonstrated "you are one of us and we got your back"? It is possible. Frankly, I think it was a combination of all of those things.

Connecting to the environment can mean many things. What and who is part of our environment, seen and unseen? Is our environment constructed in a way that it is nurturing or harmful to us? Are we honoring or ignoring what is part of our environment? Do we pay attention to how we are navigating that environment? Connecting to our environment means that we look outside of ourselves and understand that we are part of something bigger. It means giving up some illusionary control and tapping into that environment, even if it is just for inspiration.

If one has a spiritual practice, it can be as in depth as my aunties demonstrated. But if one does not have that conviction, there is still room to tune into the environment. How is the space organized in which we gather? What is the temperature, air quality, smell, soundscape like? Are there physical obstructions that prevent people from connecting? Is the environment conducive to surrendering?

This is not a skill one acquires overnight. It is a skill based in sensing. It is not to be confused with intuition, which can be translated into feeling and then knowing. Tuning into the environment does not need to be linked to knowing. Instead, it is about paying attention and then to open up to the connection that was already there. One has to trust, then, and surrender and be willing to give up control.

I once learned this lesson in a powerful way. At age 26, I had moved with my three-year-old son from Kentucky to Maryland and worked in Washington, DC. People had warned me about DC and indeed it was different. DC is an ambitious town. People will smile in your face while going behind your back, trying to steal your job. It happened to me more than once, with black women I trusted, no less. In addition, I worked in a place that I loved and where I had a lot of responsibility, but where there were all kinds of irregularities. I noticed the irregularities but didn't know what to do with them. I put them aside. But the pile kept getting higher and higher. It became clear that this wonderful job was more than likely a front for some illegal activities.

My boss, who had initially treated me as his little sister, also started to act differently as he got more involved in what he was doing. In the meantime, my finances were being compromised while the excuses kept coming. I called my ex and told him I needed him to take our son. He said sure, and that weekend I made a 12-hour drive to Kentucky, dropped off my son, spent the night and made the 12 hour drive back. What to do?

Every day I drove to work incredibly tense, gnawing my teeth. My hands were gripping the steering wheel and I kept beating myself up for being so naïve and getting involved in this situation. And the tension did not let up when I was at work. When I drove back home from work it was the same. Interestingly, my drive back and forth to work was across the most beautiful parkway, lined with the most beautiful trees, for a stretch of at least 20 to 25 minutes. Here was my natural medicine but I didn't see it. I was just staring ahead with gritted teeth, cursing to myself in a state of frustration. Until one day... I looked up. I saw those beautiful trees waving at me in the most fantastic fall colors. I looked up and saw them, really saw them, and for the whole ride I just let their stillness and relentless waving and beauty wash over me. I relaxed my hands, unlocked my jaw, and slowly peace washed over me.

When I got to work, I resigned that day, packed up and left. I called the IRS to make sure that the irregularities on my paycheck were reported. I went to five different temporary employment agencies and signed up for work. I knew I would be fine and went home. Within a week, I was working at a law firm with wonderful supportive employers. Within the month I was able to go and get my son back.

Did the trees literally heal me? My aunties might say the spirit of them did. It is possible. The way I look at it, is that I chose to connect with their message of peacefulness and beauty. The waving back and forth, that rhythm, was like a well-needed massage and forced the crack that I needed to shift from focusing on the darkness towards all the beauty that was still out there. I shifted from being in a state of tension into being in a state of calmness and being able to breathe. That in turn allowed me to move forward to create a new story for myself, not a story where I was stuck, but one where I was free.

The lesson is that these sources of inspiration and nourishment are in our environment all the time and always at our disposal. What are we honoring and what are we ignoring? Tuning in and surrendering to that connection is a skill that we can develop and use to Hold Space for each other.

Gran tangi. Thank you for the gift of abundance and nourishment in our environment and teaching us that we can partake in it for Holding Space at any time.

PATIENCE

End — Ch. 11

One of the most fun lessons I would give when teaching introduction to anthropology would be about the concept of time. I would always give an elaborate explanation about the *West vs. the Rest* in order to explain different worldviews and how these different worldviews shape our experience of culture. I now use *the dominant* and *the other* to frame these discussions, but at the time I used the *West vs. the Rest* framework. One of the things I would highlight would be the difference between a circular versus a linear concept of time. In the West, people tend to think of time as a linear phenomenon. History is taught and memorized according to timelines, when things start and end, for instance. With circular or spiral time perception, people tend to regard things in terms of cycles, and one is connected to the past as well as the future.

I would explain to my students by using the Dutch as an example, how the public transportation system is very keen on time. When the train is scheduled to leave at 10:11 it is not expected to leave at 10:10 or 10:12, but 10:11. Hence, you will see people running for the bus, train, or whatever. They now have visual devices at many bus and tram stops where they post the number of minutes until the bus or tram is expected to arrive. And thus, people get upset when there are delays. Bus and tram conductors get fined for veering too much off schedule. Timeliness is important. Timeliness means something. The further south you go towards the Mediterranean, the less that is the case. When I was in Southern Spain, the train was scheduled to come at 4pm, but if it would actually get there by that time nobody could tell me. Nobody was particularly upset about that fact, either. In Suriname, similarly, the bus leaves the bus station when it is full, not at a particularly scheduled time.

In visiting Western and non-Western countries, I learned that this different approach to time is not due to not caring or not being time aware, but to different values and priorities based on the storied context. In well-resourced countries where electricity, water, or fuel, are always at one's disposal, there are different expectations about when things get done or when things should take place. If you live on an island and there is one boat and one boatsman to bring the supplies, you change your expectations. The boatsman might be sick, the engine might be out of fuel, etc. So, the material will come when it comes, not necessarily when it is scheduled.

There is this concept of "good time". Things will happen when all the conditions are in alignment for it to be so. In India, they refer to this as "auspicious time". In my Native American teachings, this is considered the time of not knowing, that dark time when things work on getting into alignment. Think of it as an incubation period. Either way, in the 21st century where time constantly seems to speed up and we have more and more information at our disposal in less time, this concept of "in good time", "auspicious time", or space of not knowing, is a challenge, to say the least. In the world in which I have resided most extensively—i.e., academia—time linked to information falls into this difficult category. We prefer to have the right answers and would like to have them yesterday. Teachers are forced to get more and more done in less time. Efficiency and expediency are the grand pursuits, leaving burned out people in their wake. "Hello, how are you, nice to meet you" are replaced by "What are we going to do and what am I going to get out of this?" This approach is shaped by having limited time but is also shaped by a conditioned sense of entitlement and status.

This approach of "I want; therefore I shall have... now" is an explicit representation of entitlement, often associated with false conditioning of dwelling in *the dominant* realm. Having one's story so comfortably placed in a position of prominence gives one a sense of superior value. This sense of superior value might be elevated to a believed superior status through engaging with the fortress of information. I am well informed, and have superior knowledge, so my superior status should be unquestioned. This sense of superior status in turn leads to a way of engaging the world without restrictions. "Of course, I can have. Of course, I should have...", and so on. The fact that some information might be inaccessible, even temporarily, can be totally foreign. The fact that the information given might not be immediately understandable might also be a total anomaly, because not only should things be logistically accessible, they should be intellectually accessible, too. When one's way of seeing and engaging the world is established as a given, that is a natural outcome. Now, those in the *other* category can have issues with entitlement, as well. People who are hungry will take what they can get, especially when one sees that others do get fed. Those who have been deprived will grab any chance, because one might not know when the chance will appear again. It is the comparative factor that does them in. Seeing that others get, while some don't, for no apparent fair reason, contributes to that urge of having one's wants fulfilled. "I want; therefore I shall have.... now."

Those of us of immigrant backgrounds with relatives in countries with far lesser means might have been surprised by the seemingly outrageous requests for certain luxury goods. I remember as a teenager getting requests for designer tennis shoes, I couldn't even afford for myself, let alone to buy for somebody else and ship halfway across the world. The fact that I would have access, and therefore they would indirectly as well, was assumed. There were a number of steps that were left out of the equation, because there was no awareness of those steps. In a world now filled with an internet vastness and social media where wealth and access are constantly displayed, often falsely, this phenomenon is not getting any better. We want to achieve certain things, instantly, but certain steps are missing.

The transition to go from "I want; therefore I shall have... now" to "I would like, and it will come to me.... when the time is right" is the lesson of learning patience and requires challenging our sense of entitlement. There are things that have to happen, steps that have to take place, steps we might not understand or be aware of. We might have to enter that place of not knowing, incubation, before we have access. The challenge in being able to sit in patience is often not in the intellectual understanding, but in one's personal state. It can be perceived as an affront, strengthened by a false sense of superiority. "What do you mean I have to wait?!"

After working as a foster parent recruiter and trainer in specialized foster care, I transitioned into working as a therapist at a community mental health center in Baltimore. I enjoyed it, but I was still quite young. In foster care, I dealt with the parents. I supported them and guided them, but they had to do the work. I was one step removed from the children in care. Unless there was a crisis, I did not really get to deal with their struggles, and only then for a very short amount of time until the crisis had subsided. As a therapist, I dealt with people with a range of issues, with a range of life experiences. I had done my therapy internship at the University counseling center, so my clients there had all been in the 18 to 25-year-old range, with a rare exception. At the community mental health center, I dealt with adults of all ages, and with people with dual diagnoses who had mental health as well as addiction issues. It was a new adventure and a challenge, but I was up for it.

There was one client that I had some difficulty with. It was not that the client was that challenging, it was her age. I was thirty years old and she was in her mid- to late 70s. When I looked at her, I could only see my grandmother and I had to suppress my urge to have an approach of total deference. How was I going to relate to this woman? I had had a similar feeling when I was in college. At Berea College, they had a program called Body Recall, where senior citizens would visit the town and take all kinds of classes, including fitness, on campus. Often, they would eat in the cafeteria with us. These were well traveled, worldly, active seniors, yet I was terrified of talking to them. These were elders with all kinds of life experience, how could I talk to them? I, who barely knew anything about life. I was horrified and at the same time in awe of how my best friend with her open Kentucky charm would connect with our guests at the dinner table. "Hey, how y'all doing? What cha been up to?" No fear, just boldness and pure interest as if they were equals. Smiles would be the result and a nice conversation would always be the result. I would mostly be quiet, marvel at her gift of gab, nod at appropriate times and convinced myself I could never do that.

Well, here I was. I was quite a bit older now, but that initial terror was still there. This was a revered elder. How was I going to connect with her as a regular person? It turned out that it was not that hard. She just needed support. That, I could offer. After I listened to her daughter and her about her sense of isolation, we decided on a plan. I knew there was a community center for senior citizens close by. It might be the perfect solution, but I did not want to send her there until I had checked it out for myself.

A day or so later I left work a little bit early and just went by. I was greeted by two ladies who sat behind a desk. One was dressed in leopard spandex, the other in tiger spandex. One had a fluorescent headband and bow, the other also complemented her outfit with something bright and neon. The make-up was bright, and wrinkles were galore. They looked like some characters from Saturday Night Life, but they were real, very real. "Hi hun', what can we do for you?" When I explained that I would like to see what the place was like because I was considering letting my client come there, they laughed at me. "How old are you? You are nothing but a baby! Our young ones are 55, you are not even close to being 55! There is nobody your age in here!" I took a deep breath and again explained calmly that I did not need the tour for myself but for my client who did have the right age. They looked at each other and thought about it. They might have made a phone call or went to consult with somebody, I don't recall exactly. I waited patiently for the verdict and tried not to think about what I would do if the answer was no. The answer was yes, and I was told I could come back the next day at a certain time.

I rearranged and went back. The dynamic duo was waiting for me. They were a sight for sore eyes once again and had obviously spent a lot of time on their appearance. They were sure to tell me that this was an exception, because people my age were usually not granted access. I was way too young, you see. The young ones were in their mid-50s and I was really just a baby. Yes mam, I understood. They gave me the grand tour. With grand authority, they explained everything into detail. They became nicer as the tour went along. By the time they finished they hugged me and told me I could come back any time and they hoped my client would come. Mission accomplished.

I was relieved and had to admit I had a ball. This had been a true cultural experience. When I had my next supervision session, I shared my experience with my supervisor, also an elder, and a rather authoritative one at that. She was not pleased with the way how I had handled things. "They said what to you?! You should have demanded access! You should have told them that you have a master's degree and you should have made them give you that tour!" I listened attentively to her wisdom and smiled and nodded, but there was no way in the world I would ever do that or regretted the way I had handled things. She had wanted me to draw from that fortress of information to assert my authority, because that authority entitled me to having my needs fulfilled, on the spot no less.

At the senior center, however, there was a whole other reality at play. There, I was a mere baby, as they reminded me more than once, and all the credentials in the world would not have changed that. My supervisor was incensed that they put me down and disrespected my credentials. I did not mind in the least. They could call me whatever they wanted, after all I wasn't anywhere near 55 yet, and they were Fab Fabulous grannies. Given my cultural background, I could never assert my authority like that with my elders. I am pretty sure it would have backfired, too. I was a baby in their eyes and had to be respectful and become worthy of being granted access, so I was patient. Because I was not attached to my academic status in this situation, I could easily do so. My academic status was totally irrelevant, but that I acted as a respectful child was.

There is a proverb that says *All roads lead to Rome*, meaning there are multiple ways to achieve one's goal. If we can rid ourselves of our obsession with time expediency, our sense of entitlement, and our false sense of status, we may cultivate patience and come to appreciate incubation. Things will happen when they are meant to happen, when all steps are taken, or not. Even with that outcome, we have to be okay.

Gran tangi. Thank you for reminding us that we have to be more patient and trust that we will get to where we need to go when the time is exactly right.

NEUTRAL

End — Ch. 12

When you learn how to drive a stick shift, neutral is the home base. It is the place of rest from which all driving starts. It is therefore also nerve-racking as it is from here that you have to go into that first gear. Do you do too much, or too little in those first moments to move out of neutral? Will the car stall out? And there is nothing worse than being stuck in neutral at a stoplight with eager drivers behind you threatening to take off and overrun you and you can't get out of neutral.

Neutral, that ambiguous place, is seen as boring, lackluster. It is also seen as a space of indecision, a space of inaction and weakness. And yet we need it, desperately. I believe it is a space of saving grace. It is a space of being rather than doing, a virtue much frowned upon in our 21st century go get 'em global society.

When I lived in Lexington, Kentucky in the 1990s I was very much involved with the numerous artists that lived in the city. One of those artists also wrote a column in the paper. I didn't know her that well, but I liked her as a person, and I liked her work. She was one of those people who was always smiling and pleasant. I am intrigued by people who have that disposition. One day, she wrote a column about struggling with her child. He might have been about five years old at the time. From the moment he got up he was obstinate and did not want to comply with anything she wanted him to do. She described how she stayed calm and stated to herself "I don't deserve this".

My first reaction was to roll my eyes and say to myself "Oh, a typical white momma." It was judgmental, I admit, but it was also testimony to a major ethnic schism when it comes to child rearing and how we look at each other's child rearing practices. In black families—whether that be American, Caribbean, or African—disrespecting your parents, acting out, and worse, embarrassing your parents is simply unacceptable and generally corrected with swift and effective corporal punishment. This is about learning codes of the community, but also about survival. We want our children to behave and fall in line because the margin of error for their behavior outside our community is very small.

When we look upon white children acting out in public—and worse, yelling or cursing their parents—we watch in amazement, horror or disbelief, and are quick to judge the lack of home training. What we fail to see in that moment is that these children are raised with a sense of freedom. They have a right to be in the world as they are. Their parents know that, and no matter how uncomfortable in the moment, they grant their children that room so they can learn about that freedom.

Black parents don't have that luxury. What initially can be judged as hostile and harsh is really an expression of fear. For black mothers especially, the fear of what will happen to their children, and to a larger extent the community, is something that has become part of a black momma's DNA. And so, in spite of my skepticism, I was intrigued and read on.

Step by step, she described how things did not get better with her son. Things kept escalating. She described how she had lifted him up and how he kept fighting her. I could see him flailing, a swinging arm hitting her in the face, intentional or not. A black momma would have beaten his a** by now, I thought. I kept reading on. Throughout the ordeal she kept repeating "I don't deserve this". As I kept reading, I kept hearing her mantra "I don't deserve this" ring inside my head. In the end he did calm down, I think. But what stuck with me was how she used her mantra to create a space of serenity for herself. She claimed her worth no matter what was hurled against her. It was not about him. It was about her.

As a woman, a black woman who was raised in a culture where you are expected to put everyone else first, this claiming of sanctuary was mind blowing. It made a great impact on me. It has stayed with me all these years. From time to time, I am reminded of it and use that mantra. More importantly, I used it as the impetus to start my own mantra and to develop the concept of a neutral zone.

Neutral zone is the space that is carved out in front of me. Imagine a capoeira circle or a wrestling circle that is in front of you. You stand at the edge of the circle. People have to traverse through the circle before they can get to you. Once in the circle people can become afflicted with whatever ails them. You remain on the edge and do not step in. You can observe, wait, or walk away. Key is that, from the edge, one has to be non-judgmental. This may seem or sound easy but is in fact the hardest thing to do.

In general, especially in vulnerable situations where the inequality of *the dominant* and *the other* is addressed, a person might want to bring their frustration, pain or fragility to you and lay it at your feet. There is not only the expectation of acknowledgement, but the inherent anticipation that the receiver will fix, or appease, the aggrieved situation. The neutral zone takes all that away. Borrowing from the Buddhist concept of detachment, the neutral zone is an area a person steps into with their frustration, grief or fragility. They are the owner of that issue because it is part of their journey. Within the neutral zone, they are allowed to work out their relationship with that issue in whichever way they need to at that time, without being judged. It took me a long time to properly understand the Buddhist concept of detachment. I had a hard time separating detachment from not caring. To be detached does not mean that one does not have compassion. On the contrary, you grant somebody the room to do their journey their way because you honor that they are entitled to do so, which, in fact, demonstrates compassion.

So, there can be kicking and screaming and whatever form the discomfort needs to be expressed, and you recognize that that is part of their journey. You honor that journey by stepping back, giving them room and not judging. However, one also does not have the right to lay these issues at the feet of someone else. That also doesn't mean that one should never receive help. It does mean that one has responsibility to fully engage one's own journey and should not bypass the steps that are "*not gezellig*". Like the little boy in the column's story, one is allowed to throw temper tantrums, but not in a way that violates others.

The neutral zone does four things. It allows space for people to enter before they get to you and grants them the freedom to explore their journey in a judgment free space. It implies a trust in the person that they are capable of working things out in their own way and in their own time without needing immediate rescue. Secondly, it allows space and room for serenity on the receiver's end. It absolves the receiver of having to take immediate responsibility for others' suffering. Coincidentally, it is for the receiver a measure of self-care to not take on others' burdens unnecessarily and to consider oneself as valuable in one's own right and not subservient to the needs of others. Thirdly, by standing as a non-judgmental witness at the edge of the neutral zone, the receiver has room to wait, respond or walk away without guilt. Lastly, treating both parties as equally valuable in a non-judgmental way allows one to shift the dynamic, as there is room for growth and transformation. For in a space free of fear, judgment and guilt, one can truly fly.

The mantra I have chosen to create my space of serenity is "Isn't that interesting". In combination with a grounding breath, it allows me to create that neutral zone. I don't jump in to assure people that "oh, it's okay" or that "it doesn't matter" when they have made some type of insensitive violation. Instead, I stay neutral, take a step back and wait. I give them room to explore and do whatever it is they have to do. It is not for me to fix and make better. If they are seriously contrite, they will make an effort to process and act accordingly. If not, maybe they are not yet ready at that time. I don't even need to wait on the outcome, because it is their journey after all, not mine. The neutral zone gifts them the room and the honor of the journey. The neutral zone gifts me by relieving me and preventing me from walking around in bitterness and resentment.

Neutral might be seen as boring, but it grants us a space of being rather than doing, where multiple parties are allowed to be without judgment. In a world where so much is shaped by validation, judgment, and likes, that is a powerful space to offer. That is a gift. More than anything, it is a space from where transformation and flight can take place. The gift of being is in fact the gift of becoming.

Gran tangi. Thank you for the lesson about the neutral zone and teaching us that spaces of being have to be created as stepping stones into our transformation.

CRACKING

Have you ever as a child walked the sidewalks and skipped and hopped to either avoid the cracks or explicitly jump on the cracks? Wasn't there a rhyme: *Step on a crack and break your momma's back!* Was it just me?

I use *the dominant and the other* in an effort to have a theory that is truly inclusive. I use it to stress the relational aspect of how we function in a context of inequality. I prefer it over a model that uses the concepts of oppressor versus oppressed because that approach implies separation. When I think of an oppressor and an oppressed, I envision someone who has their foot on the neck of someone else.

But to me it is not about an individual, nor is oppression a permanent status. That person who oppresses at the office can be the oppressed when they go home. It is not the person who has his foot on someone else. It is a system that temporarily empowers somebody to embody and enact the force of oppression over another.

That system, which developed over hundreds of years, consists of a set of rules in which we all participate, even those in *the other* position. How is that possible?, I hear you think. As human beings, whether in *the dominant* or *other* position, we learned our role. After a while, those roles became normalized, as uncomfortable as they may be. We became conditioned. There are plenty of learning theories that explain how we are conditioned. I recall Pavlov and his dogs from my early psychology classes.

The systems we have inherited might have been designed and put in place hundreds of years ago, but they were ultimately put in place by human beings, and so human beings can dismantle them.

Rather than focusing on the conditioning, we need to look at the fissures, the disruptions, the cracks where we can chip away at that conditioning, so that change can take place. From the dance world, we learn that monotone repetition leads to automation, which serves a purpose such as protective technique or reaching states of trance. However, it can also become quite boring. When we look at ritual dancing, we see the purpose of repetition as creating a certain energy. The monotony and repetition facilitate a numbness that cannot be maintained. All of a sudden there will be a crack, an opening, an opportunity. Something will shift.

In Haitian ceremonial dance, they call this *casser*, which means "breaking". There will be a break in the rhythm and the movement as the spirits enter the circle. The person is chosen as a vehicle, their body contorts, jerks, and falls out of line from the others. The ancestor or spiritual energy comes through with noticeable disruption. The community who has been expecting and preparing for this moment, rather than withdrawing in fear, holds the space. They will welcome, if not question the entity that has come to partake, for there is a reason why they are present at that particular moment in time. The hope is that the supernatural presence will contribute to some sort of transformation for the group.

A similar physical transition is pursued in hazing, whether it is in the army barracks or on the college grounds of fraternities and sororities. People are stripped of their individuality. They are forced to live, act, and move as a unit. It becomes their normal, temporarily. They are brought to the point of cracking, breaking, losing it, because it is at this point that they are most susceptible to receive the new information

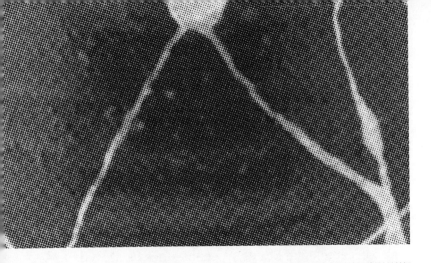

that will allow them to embody their new identity and become part of the new story of the group.

The cracks, then, are places of opportunity, places of growth. I have heard someone poetically state that the cracks are where the light shines through. The Japanese art of kintsugi embodies that same principle. Rather than discarding broken pottery, the pieces of ceramic are repaired with gold, silver, or platinum, thereby highlighting the cracks. It underscores the belief that the repaired product is in fact more beautiful than the original, because of the cracks and because it shows that the piece has history.

However, like an organism responding to the site of an anomaly, rather than embracing, defense and rejection may occur. On a cellular level, we have been designed to maintain and protect an equilibrium and send white blood cells, the first line of defense to restore the organism to normal. Introduction of something new, out of order, puts white blood cells on alert. In our real lives, not everybody is happy with the cracks, either.

We are living in a time when people, and particularly our young people, are highlighting the cracks and are throwing them in our face. Like kintsugi, they not only highlight but force us to see what we do not necessarily want to see. They highlight the history that connects us. From colonial memories displayed in statues, to educational curricula set in European perspectives, they are forcing the cracks down our throats, and the automatic defense mechanisms are swift and forceful. From circumvention to ignoring, from denial to attack, all forms of resistance are unleashed to fight the *ongezelligheid* this brings to the fore. Yet we purport that it is at the cracks where opportunity lies. It is the cracks that we claim we need in order to grow.

I find affirmation for this claim in the art and philosophy of Holy Hip Hop, the branch of hip hop that is religion based and pushes hip hop as a means for religious conversion. Practitioners refer to their own art form as *earthquake music*. Dedicated to spiritual conversion, it is born out of the social, financial, communal, and environmental upheavals that shape the lives of its adherents. Rather than using their art to connect with their roots, they use their art to reconvene the shattered pieces into new stories, better stories.

Holy Hip Hop is not just a lyrical, musical, or spiritual endeavor, it is a profoundly spatial endeavor, as well. Hip hop has always had a strong spatial and locational element. Hip hop is about territorial representation, and crossing boundaries musically, culturally, and commercially. But hip hop is also about claiming space, marking space in a world that prefers to ignore, if not actively erase, its practitioners.

For Holy Hip Hop, a genre that does not neatly fit in traditional hip hop, nor in religious music genres, not being recognized in the space is an important part of the context. Not fitting in and not being welcome are some of the essential broken pieces that have to be included in the rebirthing of the new story.

Functioning in *the dominant* paradigm, *the other* is always confronted with not quite fitting in the space, unless they are willing to conform and able to relinquish that which makes them unique. In Holy Hip Hop, artists state that their stories have been made invisible in the landscape, but they are there. They might not be part of the visual landscape, but they are part of the soundscape. In order to connect with their stories, one has to listen closely.

Holy Hip Hop, then, aims to cause fissures, cracks, and seismic shifts on purpose. They see it as the only way to create new, better stories. For some, the cracks might instill feelings of *ongezelligheid* and automatic responses, but for those who crave change those cracks are surmountable. The cracks may seem to reveal our brokenness and confirm separation. That could not be further from the truth. The cracks reveal our connectedness. Like kintsugi, they highlight the glue that connects us. They highlight that we have a history.

The cracks are needed to break through the conditioning, so we can be reminded of who we are collectively. The cracks give us opportunity to restructure our story in a new way. According to Holy Hip Hop artists, conversion to a new story is not a momentary event, but a process, a process that requires the support of a community, crew, or posse. It is not meant to be done alone. *Aho Metakuye Oyasin.*

Step on a crack and break your momma's back. Whatever the origin of the rhyme was, it implied an ominous foreboding that something might happen. Indeed, it might. Not only are we meant to welcome the cracks, we might cause them on purpose and might Hold the Space as a posse for those who need to use the cracks for their conversion.

Gran tangi. Thank you for the lesson about the need to not only welcome, but to cause, honor and facilitate the cracks as a community if we want to chip away at our conditioning and create better stories.

TRANSFORMING

I have raised three sons. The oldest son, an animator and well-versed in anything comic book related, from early on introduced the world of superheroes in my household. When he became an older brother, he would entertain his younger brothers by creating stories about them with super-powers. I would hear them in his room after school. What kind of superpower do you want to have? Stories, drawings, and adventures would quickly ensue, in which I had no part. They would always leave his room smiling. There is some-thing to be said for having powers bestowed upon you and consequently being able to change the universe, even if it is within the confines of one's big brother's bedroom.

Transforming is the power to transform the energy in the room by using all the key ingredients of awareness, care, courage, humility, trust, listening, seeing, speaking, si-lence, neutrality, embodiment, and surrender to do so. The need to transform generally comes from a state of dishar-mony in the space that is palpable, if not potentially dam-aging to those involved. Hence, it is a vulnerable situation. The transformative goal is to function as a catalyst and to commit to everybody in the space, even the ones one might personally disagree with. The job, then, is to connect with the humanity of the people present in the space and to help them connect with the humanity of each other, regard-less of their position. Ultimately, the transforming agent is to transform the space so that some type of crack can be caused to create a potential growth opportunity.

The key to transformative action is threefold. First, it starts with awareness or the pre-action phase. Second, one commits to transforming something within oneself. Third, one has to surrender and commit to transforming the energy in the room (where people are present) by using all those means available. The goal is to shake things loose and use the cracks to break through the grid lock that has developed and create room for moving to a next step.

The pre-action phase is the phase of awareness. It is a combination of careful listening, connecting with the story of the others, paying attention to what and how things are said, paying attention to the silences and what is not being said, and being in tune with the environment and the physical responses one has to what is going on. It is not about knowing necessarily, or even understanding, but one can train oneself to become aware that something is happening or is about to happen. It forces you to not be self-centered, or you will miss what is going on. It forces you to pay attention to everything, not just the obvious, visible, or loud action that might be in plain sight, but even the behavior and response of the quiet person in the corner. Sometimes all you notice is a shift. Sometimes that is all you need.

The second phase is the self-transformation. One has to put oneself in a state that one is open to participate in whatever is about to happen, even when one is not sure what is about to happen. It is therefore important to be grounded and take a deep breath and draw strength. Stepping forward requires some courage and some trust. One has to be committed to transforming the energy out of a position of care and compassion and not out of self-righteous anger. This is hard to do because sometimes things simply seem either good or bad, or right or wrong and one feels the need to take a stance on a particular side. Taking a few seconds to ground oneself and taking a breath can make the difference between being emotionally drawn in and being able to create some neutral space from which to enter. You are human and your own emotions might be raging. It is important to be able to calm those emotions so you can be most effective.

The third phase is the transformation of the group or the space. Once you step forward, you make a commitment to joining and transforming the collective. It is not about you as a person, or the people individually, it is about us. Transforming is not necessarily about *doing for* or *doing to*, but about *being with* and using one's whole being to shift something in the collective and perhaps cause some necessary cracks to highlight and remind us that we are connected and that we have history. *Aho Metakuye Oyasin.*

A beautiful story was shared with me by a South African colleague who gave me her permission to pass it on. This colleague, who is my age mate, was raised during the Apartheid era in South Africa. Like *"gezelligheid"*, *"apartheid"* is a Dutch word with powerful meaning. It is, unfortunately, one of the most well-known Dutch words all over the world. She was raised as a colored person and explained to me that there was a caste system in South Africa. At the top were the whites, those of European descent. They were followed by Indians, then colored people, and then black people. She explained that she was raised in a bubble. Everybody in her community, school, environment, belonged to the colored category. Similarly, in the Netherlands, which up to the early 1970s was a pillarized society, society was structured in a way that people mostly associated with people in their own religious or ideology groups.

In her twenties, she had the opportunity to visit America. Here, she was introduced to a whole new world and a whole new way of connecting and being with others. For the first time she felt free. On her way back, she had a layover in Amsterdam. As she went to the connecting gate for her flight to South Africa, she said she felt a heaviness as she got closer. She walked up to the gate five times, each time returning.

People were seated according to caste. Here in Amsterdam, she was confronted with what she was about to go back to, and she just couldn't. Each time she tried to walk to the front, the heavy sense of dread overwhelmed her, and she would walk back to the edge of the waiting area.

She knew she had to go back, but she also knew she couldn't, not as the same person. She looked around and made a decision. She found an old white lady and purposely sat down next to her and started a conversation, something she would never do in South Africa. Something happened, something shifted. They engaged in pleasant conversation and when she looked up, she saw that other people had started to engage in conversation across color lines. It is hard to say if people were able to hold on to this new, free behavior once they entered the plane or once they landed in South Africa. They might have ventured into this behavior because they were inspired by her, because they were in a place other than South Africa, or both. We just know that her action set something in motion. She also shared that she was never the same after that.

After returning to South Africa, she no longer limited herself to only socializing with people from her own caste. She made a point of bringing people of different ethnicities to her family house, something initially not appreciated. But her family adjusted and adapted and thus she was able to contribute to transformation there, as well.

The act of transforming involves a conglomeration of many skills. It may seem that it relies purely on feeling and intuition and therefore cannot be taught or learned. However, it involves a lot of skills that can be learned and improved upon with practice. It involves getting out of one's intellectual head and embracing one's embodiment. It involves understanding that we are working from and on our core connection with each other. It requires becoming in tune and connecting with what is going on and surrendering into the first action. Transforming is not necessarily about knowing what to do, but is knowing with all of your body that not doing is not an option. As such, we have the ability to conjure up our own superpowers.

Gran tangi. Thank you for the lesson that drawing strength from everything at our disposal can make us superheroes of transformation.

ALLYSHIP

When I think about an ally, I automatically think about who stands with you, besides you, behind you, or sometimes in front of you. Who has your back? Who stands in solidarity with you? Allyship can be that simple, yet is often one of the most misunderstood roles to play in *the dominant and the other* realm. I am reminded of walking into a rural classroom in Northern Ghana. First graders are diligently copying what the teacher is dictating to them and writing on the board. "Mother stands besides, in front, behind the child." When I greet one of the children and ask their name they smile and say "yes". Come to find out they have no idea what they are writing down. They are merely copying what is written on the board. Sometimes it can seem so simple, but it is yet so complicated.

Allyship is indeed complicated, as it is not just about one group or person wanting to join and support others, it involves the stories that the persons bring to this union. There have been stories of appropriation or *the dominant* group coming in and centering themselves and their way of doing things in supposed spaces of solidarity. That only has to happen once for trust to be broken. As potential allies join solidarity initiatives, people have to be sensitive to the conditioned behaviors that people bring along with them. For those from *the dominant* category, that means humbling oneself and perhaps waiting on the sideline until one gets permission to act and fighting that urge to be in the lead. For those in *the other* category, it may mean setting the agenda and being open and clear about the ways in which allies can function, and fighting that urge to reject people before they have proven themselves.

Traditional allyship has generally focused on a specific cause, yet stories and relationships are interrelated and complicated. In addition, there is always part of the story we don't even see, that takes on a life of its own. This is the space of not-knowing Indigenous knowledge talks about. So, allyship and spaces of solidarity are not just about a cause and the people that are involved, but about something else. Our stories, even our stories of protest and noble causes, are part of a bigger story, a story of how we live together, or can live together. It is quite possible then that even the most ardent warriors don't necessarily see the big picture or the end goal. Hence, one should be careful in quickly rejecting potential allies. One does not know what gifts they come to bring to the larger story.

Ideal allyship would consist of a focus on crossing boundaries and forging reciprocal relationships while forming a united front. It is out of the relationships that things start to shift and change, if the relationships are built with trust. Ideally, relationship-based allyship and the love-work involved would become "our work" instead of "that group's work". There are many examples of true collaborative and reciprocal alliances, such as the black and indigenous community in Canada, Palestinians who supported the Black Lives Matter Movement in Ferguson, or Argentinian women prisoners who were encouraged by their counterparts in Vietnam, China, Algeria, and Palestine, and more.

Ferguson, in particular, showed us a unique and effective form of allyship. Many black queer activists were on the front lines and had leading roles during the protests. Their visibility and leadership contributed to a shift in thinking among the protesting population, some of whom were known to be LGBT-phobic. Queer activists were purposeful in engaging in dialogue and discussing their presence. Queer activists asserted their presence as normal, and it worked. There are reports of people shutting down homophobic remarks publicly, and there being an emphasis on a sense of being in the struggle together. This model of allyship as normal and a given, based on relationships, is a preferred form of allyship for Holding Space. Stepping forward in solidarity because it is the right and obvious thing to do, rather than out of pity, has a better chance of preserving somebody's dignity. That was my personal experience with my allies during my tenure as lector in the Netherlands.

When I started in my role as lector, I was taken aside by two of my white male colleagues on separate occasions. They each told me that my options of displaying my work on the official website was rather limited and that I should consider creating my own. They told me of others who had done so and who simply charged it to the university. One actually sat me down and took the time to show me his website. He also explained that the university did not mind as long as you did not use their logo. They would prefer that it be kept separate. I appreciated their kindness and considered myself informed.

When I designed my research team, I had purposely created the Student Branch. I believed that you could not work on creating inclusive environments for students without their input. We needed students to be part of the movement on their own terms. In this branch, students could also do research, support each other, etc. I didn't have it all worked out yet, but I figured the young people would help give it shape. I hired two young people to run the Student Branch and we started to develop its vision and a mission.

When I sent my request to the communication department to create an additional page for my Student Branch on the lectorate website, I received a message in return that it would not be possible. I was the only lectorate out of 26 that had such a construction, and it was important that there was uniformity in how the lectorates were presented, thus it could not be approved. No problem, my colleagues had prepared me for this.

When the departmental communication worker came for his regular visit, I sat him down and informed him that I was going to create my own website for the lectorate. "Absolutely not!" he exclaimed as he slammed his hand on the table. I took a deep breath, looked him dead in the eye and told him in my calmest voice: "Oh, you misunderstood me. You thought I was making a request. I am not asking. I am just informing you, out of respect". "Oh, oh", the response came. I continued: "You see, there is work I have to do that I have to be able to display that I cannot in the current format. So, I have to do what I have to do."

"Oh, well...", he countered. "Yes, you are right, and the communication department has been working on that. They are becoming more flexible. Would you be willing to hold off till I talk with them and see if they could be flexible?" "Sure, no problem", was my answer. "As a matter of fact, there are several other lectors who have their own website", he now offered. Now he was pulling up the website that my colleague had shown me. He even repeated that it could be done as long as I did not use the university's official logo. Apparently, he did know about the options, but for some reason he chose not to share that information until forced to do so. Eventually, the answer came back from the communication department and the answer was still no.

From that moment on, I started to work on the website that I wanted, with input from my research team, but especially from my Student Branch team members. Via a colleague, a professor in design, two students, young women, came and worked on creating a design template for the website. They created a color scheme, asked us about our core message, and created a visual style. Another student, this one a male from Information Technology, stopped by the office and said he saw what we were doing and wanted to volunteer his services and started the work of technically putting the website together. Another student and now graduate from design used the template from the two female students to create cohesive logos that pulled it all together. We ended up with a beautiful website, created with the help of students.

The lesson here is not about the unfairness or double standard involved in *the dominant and the other* divide. That is a given. What this story illustrates is how allyship can work. Allyship can be about commitment, in a matter-of-fact way, to those who might be classified as belonging to another group and to following through on that commitment, regardless of the obstacles. The impetus of this story was the creation of a space for students. That is what mattered. That was where the initial intent was focused on. There were hurdles in achieving that goal, but I had never any doubt that the goal would be achieved. When we start with purpose and intention some things are set in motion, including a part of the story that we are not privy to. My tradition teaches me that once something is set in motion, the right actors will show up at the right time to achieve that goal.

The men who took the time to take me aside and give me the inside scoop on how things really worked for them, and that it should work the same for their new colleague, were allies. The female professor who was inspired to offer her services and acted upon that inspiration was an ally. The young student who was inspired and decided to offer his services and ended up building the website was an ally. Each person entered the story at the right time. Each person helped propel the story forward and assisted in overcoming the obstacles. Something inspired them to act. In my culture, it would be said that their *yeye* was tuned in and responded to a signal from the universe, and they listened. Whether you believe in that explanation or not, many of us are all of a sudden inspired or moved to act in support of others. To follow through on that inspiration is another thing, especially in the face of obstacles. That is what true allies do. They step into the story when they are called to do so, no questions asked. Sometimes it is that simple.

Key to allyship is to listen to that inspiration, that inner radar to step in and stand up, just because. That radar is fed by a network of relations that we have. It requires some understanding of the sensitivity that might be involved in the story that one is stepping into, especially if that story involves a strong *dominant and the other* residue. Allyship is about offering what is needed, nothing more, nothing less. Allyship is about awareness of one's own place in either *the dominant* or *other* position, but not letting that be a limitation on the gifts one has to offer. It is about making a commitment to being in our common humanity and allowing that communal relationship to lead to what needs to be done.

Gran tangi. Thank you for the lesson that allyship is about being connected in spite of and allowing that relationship to lead to transformation.

THE ASSIST

End — Ch. 16

When I started my college education in the United States, I studied physical education and psychology. I learned quickly why the top three sports in the US were basketball, football, and baseball, and why the top global sport of soccer never made it into the top three. The top two sports are basketball and football, and – depending on the state – either might have the number one slot. In Kentucky, where I studied, basketball was the number one sport. Basketball was sacred.

I had been in some of the most isolated rural towns where children would come to school dressed in blue on game days for Kentucky college basketball, and where they could recite the names of the players as easily as they did their A, B, C's. Great would be their disappointment, when I as an alumna – a black alumna from the University of Kentucky, no less – did not know any basketball player personally, let alone could list their names. "Sports is about culture", my physical education professor told me. She told me that Americans like high scores, 88 vs 74 in the case of basketball, or 27 vs 18 in the case of football. Baseball's low scores received a pass because of the sport's social connotations, but soccer was way too slow and the scores way too low. Scores such as 3 vs 2 or 4 vs 1 were too low to hold an American's attention. The only sport where such low scores were tolerated was ice hockey and that was because of the speed of the game, but mostly because of the fighting.

I don't know if this notion was scientifically supported, but I believed her. This was the 1980s and since then Americans have become a more prominent presence in the world of soccer, so I do not know if this premise still holds. Regardless of the cultural status of these team sports, there is something they have in common and that is the role of the 'assist.' In all of these sports, regardless if it is about the high or low scores, praise does not just go to the person who makes the score, but to the person or persons who help set up that score. In basketball, only one person can receive that credit, but in soccer and hockey, two people can be credited with an assist for a goal. It is a beautiful reminder that no matter how high the individual accomplishments, these are team sports, and the value lies in the collaborative achievement.

In order to transform the spaces we have to deal with, we might have to be sensitive as individuals, knowing when to speak or act, and being brave enough to follow through on our own conscience. There is a lot that one can do by being in the space, and bringing change through one's own presence. But sometimes it is not enough. Sometimes you need an assist.

Fast forward 30 years to my academic job in the Netherlands, and my eventual decision to leave that role. Once the news of my pending resignation from my professorship in inclusive education became known, I was approached by several recruitment agencies for high level positions. I wasn't really interested in looking for an institutional position, but there were a few I was willing to consider. There was one in particular, for a position on a supervisory board of one of my favorite institutions. It felt good that participating in this board would not impose on my impending freedom and that I could contribute something to an institution that I liked, so I agreed to be interviewed.

It was not long into the interview when I already got the impression that it was not going to work out. When asked about my vision for the role of the supervisory board, it was clear that it clashed with the view of the current head of the board. When I disagreed with the premise that the board of the institution was accountable to the supervisory board, but stated that they ought to work in unison and are in fact accountable to the whole institutional community, their face and tone of voice spoke volumes. It came to no surprise then when the recruiter afterwards informed me that I would not progress to the next round.

"I just want to give you feedback as to why you did not progress. There was some issue because you did not have a vision for the supervisory board." I countered them saying, "I did have a vision; in fact, I was very clear about my vision. But it was clear to me that my vision clashed with theirs. You see, some people say they want different voices on their board, but in fact they do not. Ultimately they want people who think and talk like them." "That is not true," the recruiter encountered, "because the two people that progressed to the next round were black." It was out before they could stop themselves.

I took a deep breath and finally said: "It is not my skin color that is an issue; the fact that I think differently from them, is." I would have at least one other such experience while interviewing for positions during this period – not with the recruiter being so blatantly oblivious, but with the experience that, after initial interest in me, people quickly were turned off by my different approach or way of thinking. And you know it instantly. People want diversity, but that diversity should not bring too much difference. I was appreciative of the experience, as it truly set me free to quickly say "no thanks", whenever subsequent requests from recruiters came my way.

I was reminded of this experience, however, when I was asked to sit on a nominating committee for a supervisory board. I was not asked to interview for the board, which was good, because I would have turned it down. Instead, I was asked to sit on the committee to ensure that a person was hired to bring diversity. I did not immediately say yes, but made them convince me that they were serious about what they wanted to accomplish. After several talks, I agreed to serve.

In the pool of four nominees, there was one Asian woman, one woman of African descent, and two white women. One of the white women was okay but clearly below the level of the other three. All remaining three were excellent candidates, but the woman of African descent brought something different. She brought a passion that the others did not display, but most of all she was an ardent advocate for the marginalized population that she worked with. Thinking about the current all-white elite board, she was exactly what they needed, at least from my perspective.

To my surprise, something happened when we started to discuss these four applicants. We all agreed that the choice was really between the three more qualified women and not the initial four. For each, we discussed their assets and how we thought they could contribute to the current board. But that is not what happened when we started to discuss the woman of African descent. Immediately, there was a comment about her passion and how it was inappropriate. When they continued on the subject, I interrupted and heard myself explaining why, for a black woman in her position, she might express certain things in certain ways. While explaining, I was wondering why I had to explain this in the first place, because it had nothing to do with her ability to serve on the board. I was answered with an "Oh, yes", then a pause, and then people would move on to discuss something else. To my surprise, I observed how points that were seen as surmountable for the other candidates, were focused on as problematic with this candidate. She was not judged in the same way. Whereas the others were discussed regarding how they could potentially contribute, with this candidate the focus seemed to be on how she did not fit. I watched how one person would make a statement and how the others would just join in. Nobody questioned what was happening; well, nobody but me. But each time I would open my mouth, I would receive an "Ah yes, you've got a point," then silence, and then they would move on. It was fascinating and horrifying at the same time. "So, this is how it works", I said to myself.

I had been where this candidate was, but this time I was on the other side of the table. This time, I got to see the mechanism in action. Needless to say, I was not able to get her through, which I saw as a loss to the supervisory board. I was somewhat okay, as the other applicants were indeed excellent candidates, but I had not contributed to truly diversifying that board as I had committed to do. I was grateful, nonetheless, as I was gifted with an incredible lesson. I believe I had this experience for a reason, like when the Wizard of Oz was discovered as a mere man behind a curtain pushing buttons. What could I do with what I had learned here?

I had heard about bias in hiring practices, in fact I had read extensive literature on it. But it all focused on either the mental or individual aspect of it. Here I had seen it in action. It was a team sport, a collective activity. One person starts and the others join in and follow along. I had listened to my belly and spoke up when necessary. I was even acknowledged for doing so, for a second, and then the game continued as if I had not been there. Sometimes, your bravery and speaking out are not enough. Sometimes you need an assist.

I discussed what I had learned with one of my elders, a woman in a senior position at a university. She told me that she served on a committee with all men and one other woman. "Whenever either one of us wants to get something addressed, we discuss it with each other and have each other's back in the meeting. We have to, because otherwise they just don't hear us and waltz over us. There needed to be a second one of you in that committee. Some things you cannot do by yourself."

Whereas allyship is about being moved to stand with, for, or beside a cause or a group different from one's own, the assist is more strategic and planned. The assist is a reminder that one is only as good as the set up. There are two lessons here. As an individual, you have to set yourself up to be best prepared before entering a certain arena. You have to be purposeful about the assist that you need. You have to walk as if you are never alone, as if you are always assisted. If you need a physical assist, you might need somebody to back you up. Your assist might be your proper preparation before entering the arena. For those of us with spiritual practices, your assist might be what you call upon or carry with you. Either way, you have to be purposeful about the assist you need.

Secondly, do not underestimate the power of the assist. When you enter arenas where people have been playing with each other for a while and are used to assisting each other, you might have to be strategic about breaking through that pattern. Your standard approach might not be enough. My failure was not that I did not speak up. My failure was that I was not familiar enough with the game and therefore never really fully joined in.

Gran tangi, Thank you for the lesson about needing to be purposeful to join the game.

HONORING
AND CELEBRATING

End — Ch. 17

Nanga wan hiep piep piep... Hoorray! Surinamese people are known as people who are *gezellig*. They know how to celebrate and have a party. At any given moment in a Surinamese crowd one can yell *Nanga wan hiep piep piep....* And a number of people will yell *hurray*. Now, they don't do it like the British – stiff upper lip – *Hip Hip Hurray*, or the equally straightforward Dutch version: *Hiep Hiep Hoera*. No, the Surinamese response requires syncopated rhythm, swaying of the arms, preferably with a handkerchief, and the involvement of the whole upper-body. It is a sight to be seen, but more so, a pleasant feeling to experience. It is truly *gezellig*.

This exuberance has contributed to Surinamese people sometimes being seen as frivolous or party people. Nothing could be further from the truth. Surinamese people indeed go through great lengths to celebrate birthdays and other special occasions, often with live music, dancing, and good food. But this tradition comes from an earlier tradition of dance that hails back to the days of slavery. Dancing was a form of affirmation and celebrating one's humanity in a world that denied their humanity on a daily basis. It was in the dance that people connected with each other, nature forces and their ancestors. I dance therefore I am. It was because of the dance that people were able to sustain the harshness of daily life. That tradition has persisted.

Now there is no need to break out into dance and exclamation at any given accomplishment, but there is something to be said about honoring and celebrating accomplishments, even small ones. Dutch people are known for their no non-sense attitude. "Just act normal then you act crazy enough." It is similar to the American "pull yourself up by your own bootstraps". However within this context of *dominant and the other* where we are constantly bombarded with messages about how we fall short, honoring and celebrating are not only desirable, they are necessary.

We live in a world driven by "doing" rather than being, and it is getting to us. It affects our health and well-being. Not only are we busy doing, we are driven to go from one thing to the next. Whereas grounding and breathing are the starting point for holding space, an important addition is that of appreciation. In a culture that is about being driven, we tend to look forward to what's next. There is nothing wrong with looking ahead and being prepared, but it becomes problematic when we bypass the appreciation of the current moment.

I was able to remind somebody to that effect in an exchange at a university conference. At the conclusion of my keynote, the audience was invited to ask questions. Several people raised their hands at the same time. One man had a huge picture of an elephant behind him. I told him I chose him because of the elephant. We both laughed.

He shared that he had worked with his students and had guided them on a project in which they engaged the local social services. Many of these students had had experiences with social services themselves. Being able to investigate these services now as a student, rather than a client invigorated them. In fact, they far outdid what was expected of them. They had delivered excellent work. They were so inspired and empowered that they had let their professor know that they wanted to organize a meeting with the higher ups of the social service administration because they had recommendations they wanted to share. He confirmed that they had indeed done a great job, but that he was worried. "They want to go and meet with these people, but I work for an institution with rules and regulations. I don't know how to combine the two. I cannot just go out there and do these things."

As he talked it was clear that he was worried about the possible obstacles and that they were probably getting larger and larger the more he talked. The more he talked, the more the anxiety was palpable. He finally stopped and asked me what he should do because he was at a loss.

I asked him if he had celebrated with his students. He admitted that he had not. I told him that there was so much to celebrate in his story. The fact that his students had done well; that they had been empowered; that they were taking initiative, that they had a clear vision and a goal, were all good things and worthy to be savored. The fact that he had the resources of the university to tap into was something to be savored. He only saw the obstacles and as he kept looking they kept getting bigger and bigger and paralyzed him. I told him to be more celebratory. There was so much to celebrate here, even the fact that he had done such a great job was worthy of celebration.

I encouraged him to look behind him at that image of the elephant. "If you look at the whole elephant and try to figure out how to eat it you become overwhelmed. But if you focus on the foot first or the trunk and start somewhere, you will make progress. You have a goal. You do not have to know all the steps to get there. But start with releasing some of the worry and doubt." I encouraged him to celebrate and savor all the accomplishments and then figure out one step. The obstacle was not about knowing, but it was about the self-induced fear that became a paralyzing factor.

Sometimes it is hard to give ourselves permission to breathe and just enjoy. We tend to come from cultures where humility and piety are seen as highly virtuous and where self-congratulatory behavior can be frowned upon as arrogant or blasphemous. We are constantly on a mission to prove our worth and are anxious to get called out, fail or be revealed as imposters. Communally we have not created spaces where we feel safe to fail and experiment. Although joy is something valued in our culture, so is suffering and martyrdom. It can get so bad that we feel guilty for feeling good.

We fail to understand that feeling good actually serves a purpose. It is the oil in our engine. It keeps things running smoothly. Fear, doubt, worry, anxiety, tend to lock things up and lead to paralysis. That's why we start with grounding and breathing. That's to get us ready for appreciation which will lube us into movement. Being celebratory about accomplishments, especially one's own can be hard for some. However, I do believe that the concept of honoring the moment, honoring life is something that is permissible, regardless of one's religious orientation or worldviews. In fact, I see it as part of our DNA. As we are connected to everything, we should savor it. The moment we stop, we feel disconnected and the negative feelings ensue. Many of us are so conditioned and afraid of doing something wrong that we lose our joy along the way. The best secret is that you can tap into that joy at any moment. We have to give ourselves permission to breath, stop, connect and enjoy the moment. Look at a tree, look at the sky, look at a piece of grass, breathe and enjoy.

We don't necessarily have to break out in a full celebratory dance with handkerchief, like my Surinamese folks, but a simple... *That was cool, that was great, nice one, thank you, breathe in - breathe out,* and so on can make a difference between being able to figure out a next step or getting stuck in a downward spiral. Honoring or celebrating the moment allows us to bring ourselves back into alignment with who we are meant to be and creates room and opportunity for the next thing to arrive.

Gran tangi. Thank you for the lesson that in spite of what we see in the world there is so much to be grateful for and joyous about, and we should.

CEREMONY

Human beings are social animals. We need contact and a sense of belonging. Even for those of us who are loners, we can do so within a context of community. Hence, we have used ceremony to affirm our membership in community and our appreciation of connectedness with our environment. There is evidence of ceremony being documented in cave paintings going back thousands of years. As we have moved into an information age where we can be informed through consulting our trusted phones and computers, many ceremonies have disappeared, but not all.

Ceremonies serve the purpose to bond in community, to slow things down and take stock of where we are in relationship to each other. It gives us opportunity to connect with nature or our direct environment, which in turn affirms our humanity in a very fast-moving world. Ceremony is central to holding space.

We called it *Fyo Fyo Light*, after the Surinamese *Fyo Fyo* traditional ritual. After several years of not teaching, I had the opportunity to teach a medical anthropology class for the summer school at a university in the Netherlands. Given that it was a summer school and I only had two weeks instead of the usual nine, I had some adjustments to make. The population was also special, international students from all over the world. The material had to be impactful, engaging and fun. I had accepted the challenge. One of the days was devoted to traditional healing methods.

I immediately called my cousin, the keeper of cultural traditions within our family. I asked her for a suggestion for some type of healing ceremony that would be suitable for students. We decided on *Fyo Fyo*. We discussed its purpose, how we could tailor it, but also how we could make it a secular ceremony as opposed to a spiritual one, as we didn't want to offend or scare anyone and we wanted to make it inclusive, regardless of anybody's religious background.

Hence, we came up with *Fyo Fyo Light*. *Fyo Fyo* is a ritual of atonement. In Suriname, we believe that when harsh words have fallen between people it contributes to disharmony within the spirit. And when afterwards we say "Oh, it's okay, I'm over it", when we are really not over it, it can do damage to one's psyche. Sometimes, the disharmony does not have to be the result of the exchange between two or more people but can be the result of a sole actor. When one has acted out of character towards others or towards oneself, disharmony can be the result. The idea behind it is that you have a higher self, a purer self, that is always present and listening. You can offend that higher self with your actions and words. The *Fyo Fyo* ritual is meant to atone for the offense to the higher self, to cleanse, and really let things go, while calling on the strength of spirit and the ancestors to do so.

This is a beautiful ceremony of self-care and that is how we decided to bring it to the students, without the reference to spiritual or ancestral assistance. We did start the ceremony by honoring and thanking each student's family for entrusting them to this journey and acknowledged that they stood on the shoulders of their ancestors, but that was the only reference to ancestors. For young people who are dealing with all kinds of pressures—school, social and world related—we invited them and encouraged them to take time for themselves to slow down. We guided them to atone for the negative messages they had ingested and were still carrying with them, and to release that burden.

We found a beautiful place in the park and made them take off their shoes so they could connect with the grass. We used certain elements, water and flowers. We used flowers to represent beauty and to encourage them to invite beauty into their lives. We used water, which represents life, nourishment and cleansing. We sang as a community to honor the moment and the gathering. We talked to them about being deserving of taking time out for themselves. They each received a cup of water and were instructed to get quiet and listen. We asked them to get in tune to some negativity that was said or done to them, that they were still holding on to. It might have been things they had done or said that were out of character and they still felt guilty about. Then they had to speak aloud and release whatever it was they had to release. They could walk, sit or stand as the urge dictated. When they were finished releasing, they could pour the water into the earth and then return to the group. Once everybody returned to the group, we closed it out with a few words of reflection and encouragement.

The ceremony was quite impactful, and they talked about it many days later. Since then, I have used this ceremony with young people, and each time have found it very effective. I have not only found it impactful for students who are enveloped with loads of work and affiliated pressures, but also with young people who are involved in social justice work. For them especially, learning how to let go and cleanse all the negativity they encounter is an essential skill. In this case, I drew from an existing and familiar ceremony from my family's tradition, but that is not necessary. We create ceremony out of a need. I am always amazed at how fast after an accidental or unfortunate death tributes arise. People bring flowers, stuffed animals, cards, candles, and other things to the site to create a memorial. They do so because their spirit has the need to connect and express itself in such a way.

Ceremony, then, starts by being still and listening to what is necessary. When we are committed to holding space, we are committed to being of service. Therefore, we have to be ever alert as to where people are. You have to tune in to where people are. There will be times when it is crucial to step in and facilitate some collective energetic shift. You do that through ceremony. You do that by grounding yourself, taking a deep breath, getting still, trusting, and taking a first step. For those of us with a spiritual practice, we call upon our ancestors or whatever forces we believe in when we take that first step. For those without a spiritual practice, the procedure is really the same. Key is that you step forward and trust. Trust in your abilities to contribute something. Trust that your presence can be meaningful. Trust that something will come.

And what will come does not need to be big. I have been in spaces where the whole room was in shock. I have been in spaces where the whole room was in deep pain. All I knew is that I had to do something, anything to support this particular group of people. I had to show that somebody had their back, that we could have each other's backs during this time of difficulty.

Ceremony is similar to transforming, but it is different. Ceremony is generally more purposeful and communal. Whereas an act of transformation can be an act of diffusing or changing course to create a breakthrough space, ceremony is generally used to bring people into connection with each other and bring some calm. Metaphorically, transforming is about breaking through, while ceremony is about healing the cracks. Sometimes after an intense situation has been diffused, people might need some room and time before they can participate in a ceremony that facilitates connection. Therefore, it is essential to be tuned in and flexible about offering a ceremony. The facilitator has to keep in mind that one is in service to the moment and the elements and not in charge of them. In ceremony, it is the collective action that shifts things, while transforming emphasizes the role of the individual as a catalyst to transfer the energy in a larger space. Both change the space, but each have a different goal and different means to do so, though both involve trust and surrendering.

Ceremony changes the space. Ceremony helps us to slow down, affirm and refocus. Ceremony brings us full circle and back to the beginning, the reminder that we are human. Again, it does not need to be big. It can be as simple as collectively taking three big breaths and quietly asking for strength from whomever we call upon. One of my favorites is a Japanese farewell greeting where people bow to each other and say, "I dare not say that I have finished". Having knowledge of some traditions is helpful, but the most important ingredients are still the trust in the community, the sensitivity as to where the people are, and surrendering into action.

Ceremony is the ultimate non-intellectual gift you can use to be of service. It is not about thinking or knowing what to do. It is purely about sensing, feeling, and trusting, which will translate into doing. And the only way to learn how to develop this skill is to try and practice surrendering.

Gran tangi. Thank you for the gift of ceremony as a pathway for us as a community to get back to who we are.

HOLDING SPACE

End — Ch. 19

In the documentary "Rize," which follows the development of clown and crump dancing in Los Angeles in the early 2000s, the audience is introduced to the street scene where a community of young people and old people hold the space for the dancers to enter and express themselves.

These dances are born out of the frustration with ever-present violence and struggle and allow for release and expression. The community surrounds the space selected in the street as their sacred space. As they enter the space, they receive affirmation. Here, they can be who they need to be, release all their burdens and if they are lucky... transcend. The scene cuts to a scene in an African village where wrestlers prepare themselves with drums and meditative movement before they enter the arena. Surrounded by a supportive community they get to show who they are. They are affirmed and with any luck... transcend. Our stories are interlinked, my mother taught me. Our stories are interlinked, the movie shows us[3].

As I watch, I am transported to the *winti prey* in Suriname, the communal spiritual ceremony where people dance collectively in a circle until either ancestors and/or spirits join the community and make themselves known. The community holds the circle and the person who is "ridden" enters and moves freely, supported by those who came to support and witness. This ceremony, dating back to the days of

 3   AFRICAN SPIRITUAL DANCE - IT'S IN OUR DNA (FROM BIRTH)
www.youtube.com/watch?v=2R1PKWNZofo

slavery, then done out of sight of the white dominant eye, served only one purpose: to affirm one's humanity and transcend an oppressive system that denied a people's humanity so fiercely. And from the back fields in Suriname to the streets in L.A., we see people Holding Space for each other. They offer alternative spaces where people can be just to be, just for who they are, just because they breathe.

Alternative spaces to the larger, dominant narrative give credence to one's value and humanity. These spaces where existence is resistance, are created out of a need, an answer to an inner calling to be affirmed in this world. When you know who you are in relation to the seven directions, you know who you are as a person and you are strengthened in your relationship with the world. Thus, the community surrounds you and holds the east, the south, the west and the north. You stomp your feet, touching the earth, connecting with the soil, allowing it to hold you up, reverberating from below that Mother Earth has got you. You raise your arms up to the sky, preferably out in the air at night, affirming that you are a star child, made up of the same stuff as all the nature that surrounds you, that you are connected to it all. Finally, you go in, inside and transcend.

This is our purpose, this is our task, to hold space for each other to use and acknowledge all of our humanity. There is a need for us, all of us and our relations, to do this love-work. The love-work requires us to shake off conditioned behaviors that had hundreds if not thousands of years to develop, become seasoned and settle in. It requires us to work on ourselves, to pick up on our conditioned habits and actively try to change them. It requires us to be honest and face our shortcomings, while using our gifts and sharing them with others. It requires us to no longer ignore the signals that alert us when things go off kilter in our space. It requires that we take the collective as a starting point, rather than the individual, and through understanding our connectedness, persevere to regard all people in their humanness and all of nature as our extended selves. It requires us to stay focused and committed to uplifting the community. It requires us to bring ourselves, all of ourselves, to do the work and to take care of each other, ourselves, and seek reprieve when needed. It requires us to stop, get centered, grounded, and reconnect when needed. Breathe in, breathe out.

Like Ma Po, we will clear the path unapologetically. We will put in the love-work as my godmother taught us. We will use our voices and bodies to transform and empower the space like my other godmother showed us. Like my father, we will acknowledge but persevere through the hard things we will encounter. We will affirm the humanity of all our relations according to the example of my auntie. We will draw strength from and commit to the interconnectedness of our stories, as my mother has demonstrated. And per example of my lovely brother we will appreciate, acknowledge, and enjoy the good things along the way.

When we are no longer afraid and can orient ourselves in relation to all our relations to the east, the south, the west, and the north...

When we are grounded in the earth and look up to the sky...

When we can go within and transcend our limitations...

Then, we will be home and know who we are. We will hold up the space where we all can function to the best of our abilities. Where we can just be and breathe. Breath in, breathe out.

That is my prayer for you, for all of us. *Gran tangi*. Thank you for joining me and honoring and holding my story.

INDEX

SOURCES
OF INSPIRATION

Abu-Lughod, Lila
1990   Can there be a Feminist Ethnography? *Women & Performance* 5 (1): 7-27.
1998   Contentious Theoretical Issues: Third World Feminisms and Identity Politics. *Women's Studies Quarterly* 26 (3/4):25-29.
2002   Do Muslim Women Really Need Saving? Anthropological Reflections on Cultural Relativism and its Others. *American Anthropologist* 104: 793-790.
2000   Locating Ethnography. *Ethnography* 1 (2): 261-267.
1999   Comment on "Writing for Culture" by Christoph Brumann, *Current Anthropology 40, Special Supplement on 'Culture - A Second Chance?'*, February: S13-S15.
1998   Contentious Theoretical Issues: Third World Feminisms and Identity Politics. *Women's Studies Quarterly* 26 (3/4): 25-29.
1991   Writing Against Culture, In *Recapturing Anthropology: Working in the Present*, edited by Richard Fox, 137-162. Santa Fe, NM: School of American Research Press.

Adelson, Naomi
2000   *Being Alive Well: Health and the Politics of Cree Well-being*. University of Toronto Press
2008   Discourses of Stress, Social Inequities, and the Everyday Worlds of First Nations Women in a Remote Northern Canadian Community. *Ethos* 25 (3): 316-333.
2005   The Embodiment of Inequity: Health Disparities in Aboriginal Canada. *Canadian Journal of Public Health* 92 (2): S45-S61.

Anzaldúa, Gloria
1995 -   Re-Thinking Margins and Borders: An Interview with Gloria Anzaldua
1996   *Discourse* 18 (1/2): 7-15. (with Ellie Hernandez)
1987   *Borderlands/La Frontera: The New Mestiza*. San Francisco: Aunt Lute Books.
1996   *Lloronas, Women Who Howl: Autohistorias-Torias and the Production of Writing, Knowledge, and Identity*. San Francisco: Aunt Lute Books.
1990   *Making Face, Making Soul: Haciendo Caras Creative and Critical Perspectives by Feminists of Color*. Editor. San Franciso: Aunt Lute Books.
1981   *This Bridge Called My Back: Writings by Radical Women of Color* (edited with Cherrie Moraga). Persephone Press.

Atshan, Saéd and Darnell L. Moore
2014   Reciprocal Solidarity: Where the Black and Palestinian Queer Struggles Meet. *Biography* 37 (2): 680-705.

Baer, Hans
1989   The American Dominative Medical System as a Reflection of Social Relations in the Larger Society. *Social Science & Medicine* 28 (11): 1103-1112.

Betasamosake Simpson, Leanne
2016   Indigenous Resurgence and Co-resistance. *Critical Ethnic Studies* 2 (2): 19-34.

Brants, Chrisje and Willem Pompe and Katrien Klep
2013   Transitional Justice: History-Telling, Collective Memory, and the Victim-Witness International. *Journal of Conflict and Violence* 7 (1): 36 – 49.

Brauer, Hester, Daniel Rambaran en Ruben Boers
2019   Powerhouse: Op Weg Naar Symbolisch Meesterschap *Powerhouse: On the Road to Symbolic Mastery.* The Hague: The Hague University of Applied Sciences.

Castillo-Garsow, Melissa
2012-   The Legacy of Gloria Anzaldúa: Finding a Place for Women of Color in
2013   Academia. *Bilingual Review* 31 (1): 3-11.

Daniel, Yvonne
2005   *Dancing Wisdom: Embodied Knowledge in Haitian Vodou, Cuban Yoruba, and Bahian Candomblé.* Chicago: University of Chicago.

Dossa, Parin
2003   The Body Remembers: A Migratory Tale of Social Suffering and Witnessing. *International Journal of Mental Health* 32: 50-73.
2004   *Politics and Poetics of Migration: Narratives of Iranian women in the Diaspora.* Toronto: Canadian Scholar's Press.

Gobodo-Madikizela, Pumla
2011   Intersubjectivity and Embodiment: Exploring the Role of the Maternal in the Language of Forgiveness and Reconciliation. *Signs* 36 (3): 541-551.

Goduka, Nomalungelo Ivy
2000   African or Indigenous Philosophies; Legitimizing Spiritually Centered Wisdoms Within the Academy. In *African Voices in Education,* edited by P.Higgs, N.C.G. Vakalisa, T.V. Mda and N.T. Assie-Lumumba, 63-83. Landsdowne: Juta.
2017   *Indigenous People's Wisdom and Power: Affirming Our Knowledge through Narratives (co-*edited with Julian E. Kunnie) New York: Routledge.

Godwin Phelps, Teresa
2014   Truth Delayed: Accounting for Human Rights Violations in Guatemala and Spain. *Human Rights Quarterly* 36 (4): 820-843.
2006   Narrative Capability: Telling Stories in a Search for Justice Transforming Unjust Structures: The Capability Approach. Springer DOI 10.1007/1-4020-4432-1_6.

Hill-Collins, Patricia
1991   *Black Feminist Thought: Knowledge, Consciousness, and the Politics of Empowerment.* New York, NY: Routledge.
1998   *Fighting Words: Black Women and the Search for Justice.* Minneapolis: University of Minnesota Press.
2016   *Intersectionality* (with Sirma Bilge). London: Polity Press.

2015   Intersectionality's Definitional Dilemmas. *Annual Review of Sociology* 41: 1-20.

1986   Learning from the Outsider Within: The Sociological Significance of Black Feminist Thought. *Social Problems* 33 (6): S14-S32.

2000   The Social Construction of Black Feminist Thought. In *Black Feminist Reader*, edited by J. James, and Sharpley-Whiting, T.C., P183-207. Malden, MA: Blackwell.

2013   Truth-Telling and Intellectual Activism (with Gloria González-López). *Contexts* 12 (1): 36-41.

Hunter, Margaret

2011   Buying Racial Capital: Skin Bleaching and Cosmetic Surgery in a Globalized World. *The Journal of Pan African Studies* 4 (4): 142-164.

Hunt, Sarah

2014   Ontologies of Indigeneity: The Politics of Embodying a Concept. *Cultural Geographies* 21(1): 27-32.

Hutak, Massih

2020   *Jij Hebt Ons Niet Ontdekt, Wij Waren Hier Altijd Al.* Amsterdam: Pluim.

Kelsall, Tim

2005   Truth, Lies, Ritual: Preliminary Reflections on the Truth and Reconciliation Commission in Sierra Leone. *Human Rights Quarterly* 27 (2): 361-391.

Kincheloe, Joe

2008   Afterward: Ten Short Years – Acting on Freire's Requests. *Journal of Thought* 43 (1-2): 163-171.

2012   Critical Pedagogy in the Twenty-First Century: Evolution for Survival. *Counterpoints* 422:147-183.

2008   *Knowledge and Critical Pedagogy: An Introduction.* Amsterdam: Springer.

Kovach, Margareth

2009   *Indigenous Methodologies: Characteristics, Conversations, and Contexts.* Toronto: University of Toronto Press.

Ladin, Joy

2009   The God Thing. *Prairie Schooner* 83(4): 55-73.

2018   *The Soul of the Stranger: Reading God and Torah from a Transgender Perspective* Waltham, MA: Brandeis University Press.

2014   Trans*formative Teaching (with H. Adam Ackley, and Cameron Partridge). *Transformations: The Journal of Inclusive Scholarship and Pedagogy* 25(1): 86-100.

Lang, Berel

2009   Reconciliation: Not Retribution, Not Justice, Perhaps Not Even Forgiveness. *The Monist* 92 (4): 604-619.

Lorde, Audrey

1984   *Sister Outsider: Essays and Speeches.* New York: Crossing Press.

1978   *The Black Unicorn.* New York: Norton.
1980   *The Cancer Journals.* San Francisco: Spinsters Ink.
2000   *The Collected Poems of Audre Lorde.* New York: Norton.

Mehl-Madrona, Lewis

2011   *Coyote Medicine: Lessons from Native American Healing.* New York:
        Simon & Schuster.
2010   *Healing the Mind through the Power of Story: The Promise of Narrative
        Psychiatry.* Rochester, VT: Bear & Company.
2007   *Narrative Medicine; The Use of History and Story in the Healing Process.*
        Rochester, VT: Bear & Company.
2015   *Remapping Your Mind: The Neuroscience of Self-Transformation through
        Story.* (with Barbara Mainguy). Rochester, VT: Bear & Company.
2007   The Nature of Narrative Medicine. *Permanente Journal* 11 (3):83.
Video   https://youtu.be/zQR_LDDQfB4

Mohammed, Patricia

2003   Like Sugar in Coffee: Third Wave Feminism and the Caribbean. *Social
        and Economic Studies* 52 (3): 5-30.
2000   The Future of Feminism in the Caribbean. *Feminist Review* 64 (Spring):
        116-119.
1998   Towards Indigenous Feminist Theorizing in the Caribbean. *Feminist
        Review* 59 (Summer): 6-33.

Mohanty, Chandra

1989   On Race and Voice: Challenges for Liberal Education in the 1990s.
        Cultural Critique 14: 179-208.
1988   Under Western Eyes: Feminist Scholarship and Colonial Discourses.
        Feminist Review (30): 61-88.
2003   *Feminism without Borders: Decolonizing Theory, Practicing Solidarity.*
        Durham, NC: Duke University Press.
        Under Western Eyes Revisited: Feminist Solidarity Through
        Anticapitalist Struggles. *Signs* 28 (2): 499-535.
2013   Transnational Feminist Crossings: On Neoliberalism and Radical
        Critique. *Signs* 38 (4): 967-991.

Morrison, Toni

2017   *The Origin of Others.* Boston, MA: Harvard University Press.

Motta, Sara

2016   Decolonizing Critique: From Prophetic Negation to Prefigurative
        Affirmation, In *Social Sciences for an Other Politics: Women Theorizing
        Without Parachutes,* edited by A.C. Dinerstein, 33-48, London/
        NewYork: Palgrave Macmillan.
2018   *Liminal Subjects: Weaving (Our) Liberation.* New York: Rowman &
        Littlefield.

Murray, Albert

1976   *Stomping the Blues* (with Paul Delvin) Minneapolis: University of
        Minnesota Press.
1996   *The Blue Devils of Nada: A Contemporary American Approach to Aesthetic
        Statement.* New York: Pantheon Books.
1973   *The Hero and the Blues.* New York: Vintage Books.

1970   *The Omni-Americans: New Perspectives on Black Experience and American Culture*. New York: Outerbridge & Dienstfrey; distributed by E.P. Dutton.

Video https://www.youtube.com/watch?time_continue=684&v=VIlB_R9eftk&feature=emb_logo
Hyphens, Heroes, & Dragons: Conversation with Albert Murray

Ong, Aiwa

1995   *Bewitching Women, Pious Men: Gender and Body Politics in Southeast Asia*. (co-editor Michael Peletz). Berkeley: University of California Press.

2011   *Worlding Cities, or the Art of being Global* (co-editor Ananya Roy). London: Routledge.

1999   Muslim Feminists: Citizenship in the Shelter of Corporatist Islam. *Citizenship Studies* 3: 355-377.

Ray, Benjamin

2010   "The Salem Witch Mania": Recent Scholarship and American History Textbooks. *Journal of the American Academy of Religion* 78 (1): 40-64.

Riggs, Reuben

2015   Meeting Queerness and Blackness in Ferguson. *QED: A Journal in GLBTQ Worldmaking* 2 (2): 184-192.

Sefa Dei, George

2017   A Call to a New Dance: [Re]Claiming and Implicating African Diasporic Indigeneity Through the Prism of Indigeneity as an International Category. In *Reframing Blackness and Black Solidarities through Anti-colonial and Decolonial Prisms*, 135-149, Springer.

1994   Afrocentricity: A Cornerstone of Pedagogy. *Anthropology and Education Quarterly* 25 (1): 3-28.

2018   "Black Like Me": Reframing Blackness for Decolonial Politics. *Educational Studies* 54: 1-26.

2004   CHAPTER THREE: Theorizing Power: Rupturing Dichotomies. (with Leeno Luke Karumanchery and Nisha Karumanchery-Luik). *Counterpoints* 244:59-80.

2016   Decolonizing the University: the Challenges and Possibilities of Inclusive Education. *Socialist Studies/Études Socialistes*. 11. 10.18740/S4WW31.

2017   *Knowledge and Decolonial Politics*. (with J. Mandeep Eds.) Leiden: Brill Sense. Reframing Blackness, Anti-Blackness, and Decoloniality. In *Reframing Blackness and Black Solidarities through Anti-colonial and Decolonial Prisms*, 65-80, Springer.

2013   CHAPTER ONE: Reframing Critical Anti-Racist Theory (CART) for Contemporary Times. *Counterpoints* 445: 1-14.

2000   Rethinking the Role of Indigenous knowledges in the Academy. *International Journal of Inclusive Education*. 4(2): 111-132.

2016   Revisiting the Question of the "Indigenous". *Counterpoints* 491:291-309.
2013   Unspeakable Things: Indigenous Research and Social Science. (with Elaine Coburn, Makere Stewart-Harawira, and Aileen Moreton-Robinson). *Socio* (2): 121-134.

Settee, Priscilla
2011   CHAPTER TWENTY EIGHT: Indigenous Knowledge: Multiple Approaches in *Counterpoints* 379: 434-450.

Shahjahan, Riyad A.
2009   Rekindling the Sacred: Toward a Decolonizing Pedagogy in Higher Education. *Journal of Thought* 44 (1-2): 59-75.
2011   CHAPTER TWENTY THREE: Revealing the Secular Fence of Knowledge: Towards Reimagining Spiritual Ways of Knowing and Being in the Academy (with Kimberly Haverkos). *Counterpoints* 379: 367-385.
2005   Spirituality in the Academy: Reclaiming from the Margins and Evoking a Transformative Way of Knowing the World. *International Journal of Qualitative Studies in Education* 18(6): 685-711.
2010   Toward a Spiritual Praxis: The Role of Spirituality Among Faculty of Color Teaching for Social Justice. *The Review of Higher Education* 33(4): 473-512.

Sosis, Richard
2004   The Adaptive Value of Religious Ritual. *American Scientist* 92: 166-172.

Spivak, Gayatri
1994   Can the Subaltern Speak? In *Colonial Discourse and Post-colonial Theory: A Reader*. edited by P. Williams, and L. Chrisman, 66-111. New York: Columbia University.

Tuhiwai-Smith, Linda
2005   Building a Research Agenda for Indigenous Epistemologies and Education. *Anthropology & Education Quarterly* 36 (1): 93-95.
1999   *Decolonizing Methodologies: Research and Indigenous Peoples*. London: Zed Books.
2012   *Handbook of Critical and Indigenous Methodologies*. (with Norman Denzin & Yvonna Lincoln, eds.) London: Zed Books.

Icaza, Rozalba and Rolando Vazquez
2013   Social Struggles as Epistemic Struggles. *Development and Change* 44 (3): 683-704.
2017   Intersectionality and Diversity Research in Higher Education. *Tijdschrift voor Orthopedagogiek* 7: 349-357.
2016   The Coloniality of Gender as a Radical Critique of Developmentalism. *The Palgrave Handbook of Gender and Development*: 62-73.
2016   *Let's do Diversity: Report of the University of Amsterdam Diversity Commission*. (with G.Wekker, M.S. Slootman, H.Jansen). Amsterdam: Universiteit van Amsterdam

Vazquez, Rolando

2020   *Vistas of Modernity: Decolonial Aesthesis and the End of the Contemporary. Essay 014.* Amsterdam: Mondriaan Fund.

Icaza, Rosalba

2018   Encountering (each)other: Decolonisation of Universities Across the Global North/South Divide at UVA Global Studies Conference "Global Kowledges & Local Universities". Charlottesville, VA

Video   https://www.youtube.com/watch?v=CW7PJauah5Q

Vazquez, Rolando

2017   The Museum, Decoloniality and the End of the Contemporary. Van Abbe Museum. https://www.youtube.com/watch?v=eIHCH--Ffto

Walker, Frank X

2000   Affrilachia. Lexington, KY: Old Cove Press.

2005   Black Box: Poems. Lexington, KY: Old Cove Press.

2003   Buffalo Dance: The Journey of York. Lexington, KY: University of Kentucky

2017   Ink stains & Watermarks: New and Uncollected Poems. Danville, KY: Duncan Hill Press

Video   https://www.youtube.com/watch?v=DcivE0771S4&t=13s

Wekker, Gloria

2009   "Afro-Surinamese Women's Sexual Culture and the Long Shadows of the Past". In *Sexuality, Social Exclusion & Human Rights: Vulnerability in the Caribbean Context of HIV.* edited by Barrow, C.; Bruin, Marjan de; Carr, Robert, 192-214. Kingston, Jamaica: Ian Randle Publishers.

1992   *"I am gold money": (I Pass through all Hands, but I do Not Lose My Value): The Construction of Selves, Gender and Sexualities in a Female Working Class, Afro-Surinamese Setting (Ph.D.).* University of California, Los Angeles.

2001   *Of Mimic Men and Unruly Women: Exploring Sexuality and Gender in Surinamese Family Systems.* Cave Hill, Barbados: University of the West Indies.

1997   "One Finger does not Drink Okra Soup: Afro-Surinamese Women and Critical Agency". Feminist Genealogies, Colonial Legacies, Democratic Futures. New York, NY: Routledge: 330-352.

2006   *The Politics of Passion: Women's Sexual Culture in the Afro-Surinamese Diaspora.* New York, NY: Columbia University Press.

2016   *White Innocence: Paradoxes of Colonialism and Race.* Durham, North Carolina: Duke University Press.

2016   Video — Never be Indifferent: 400 Years of Dutch Colonialism. TedXAmsterdamWomen. https://www.youtube.com/watch?v=aMwgzK9LGeM

2017   Video — Beyond White Innocence. BAK Basis voor Actuele Kunst. https://www.youtube.com/watch?v=GQbrVRVUnck

2017   Video —TALK met Gloria Wekker, Antoin Deul en Marco van Baalen o.l.v. Nancy Jouwe. Haags Historisch Museum. https://www.youtube.com/watch?v=-WMl_1hEcao

Willis, Paul. E.

1977   *Learning to Labour: How Working Class Kids Get Working Class Jobs.* Farnborough, UK: Saxon House.

Wilson, Shawn

2008   *Research is Ceremony: Indigenous Research Methods*, Black Point, Nova Scotia: Fernwood Publishing.

2013   Using Indigenist Research to Shape our Future', In *Decolonizing Social Work*, edited by M. Grey, J. Coates, M. Yellow Bird, T. Hetherington, 311-322. Burlington, VT: Ashgate Publishing.

2016   Video — Decolonizing methodologies: can relational research be a basis for renewed relationships? (with Monica E. Mulrennan). Living knowledge community of practice, Concordia University https:// www.youtube.com/watch?v=rqYiCrZKmoM&feature=youtu. be&list=PLo63BoDA555A2oCo6

Mama Wapajea (Walks on Water) and Maimouna Youssef

Video   https://www.youtube.com/watch?v=jXuc_Q9vYv4
Video   https://www.youtube.com/watch?v=oaIkLvsqGDs
Video   https://www.youtube.com/watch?v=ivR988qCPik
Video   https://www.youtube.com/watch?v=LdDTJ2lk-EE
Video   https://www.youtube.com/watch?v=DJ9qeDTVJ74
Video   https://www.youtube.com/watch?v=mReuFdzKxvY
Video   https://www.youtube.com/watch?v=C9-VTggwePA

Zanfagna, Christina

2017   *Holy Hip Hop and the City of Angels.* Los Angeles: University of California Press.

2011   Building "Zyon" in Babylon: Holy Hip Hop and Geographies of Conversion Black Music. *Research Journal* 31 (1): 145-162.

2007   Video — Flipping the Scripture: Holy Hip Hop, Religion, and Urban Youth. https://www.youtube.com/watch?v=asOpnUg82mk

Holding Space video playlist

www.youtube.com/playlist?list=PLcjgAdH8nFhqpU3i-rHF5u_jGkpjVlzbh

IMAGE CREDITS

Aminata Cairo, Ph.D.

Anthropologist, Psychologist,
Scholar, Storyteller, Love-worker

Aminata Cairo is an independent consultant
"who works with people". She is the former Lector
of Inclusive Education at The Hague University
of Applied Sciences (2017 – 2020),
the first and only research professor in
the Netherlands of African descent.

COLOPHON

**Holding Space
A Storytelling Approach to
Trampling Diversity and Inclusion**

Author: Aminata Cairo
Editor: Laura Rumbley
Artwork: Dafri Studios
Cover photograph: Gordon Cruden of Crudon Productions
Design and typeset: Since Today

© Aminata Cairo Consultancy
www.aminatacairo.com

ISBN Book: 9789083156101
ISBN Ebook: 9789083157924
IBN Audiobook : 9789083156118

Made in the USA
Columbia, SC
26 November 2021

49678919R00198